U.S. National Security Strategy
for the 1990s

U.S. National Security Strategy for the 1990s

Edited by DANIEL J. KAUFMAN,
DAVID S. CLARK,
and KEVIN P. SHEEHAN

The Johns Hopkins University Press
Baltimore and London

The Johns Hopkins University Press
701 West 40th Street
Baltimore, Maryland 21211
The Johns Hopkins Press Ltd., London

∞ The paper in this book meets the minimum requirements
of American National Standard for Information Sciences—
Permanence of Paper for Printed Library Materials,
ANSI Z39.48-1984.

Library of Congress Cataloging-in-Publication Data

U.S. national security strategy for the 1990s / Daniel J.
  Kaufman, David S. Clark, and Kevin P. Sheehan, editors.
      p.   cm.
  Includes bibliographical references and index.
  ISBN 0-8018-4163-1. — ISBN 0-8018-4164-X (pbk.)
  1. United States—National security. 2. United States—
Military policy. I. Kaufman, Daniel J. II. Clark, David S.
(David Sheridan), 1956– . III. Sheehan, Kevin P. IV. Title:
US national security strategy for the 1990s.
UA23.U237   1991
355′.033073—dc20   90-27634   CIP

To Kathryn, Tyler, and Donna

Contents

Foreword

A book about national security strategy is wonderfully appropriate at this moment in our nation's affairs. Any nation must have a strategy or plan, and surely the plan for the United States must take into account the dramatic changes in the world around us. U.S. national security strategy has been both implicit and explicit since the end of World War II. National policy has required our military both to assist our allies in defending Western Europe and to support the containment of communism elsewhere. Military strategy has been explicit for the former and implicit for the latter.

The difference has been due to the fact that requirements for the military defense of Western Europe have always appeared to exceed our resources. Strategy is only meaningful if it directs the application of resources. There has, then, been little room for strategy in support of containment, since there were no resources left over to be assigned to other missions.

For containment, and also for support of other national interests unrelated to the containment of communism, we have implicitly assumed that if we were ready for the most demanding task, we would be ready for smaller ones also. There has been little written that examines whether this supposition is so. Today that question surely needs to be asked, since the malaise of communism and the demise of the Warsaw Pact have markedly reduced the military threat to Western Europe.

Our record in combat in eleven countries, beginning with South Korea in 1950 and through Panama in 1989, should tell us something about the assumption that readiness for Europe is readiness for anywhere. We fought to a tie in Korea; we lost in Vietnam; we failed miserably on the desert of Iran; and we took an unconscionable amount of time and casualties to subdue a few hundred Cubans in Grenada. These less than desired results were often strongly influenced by poor political direction, and responsibility for military shortcomings in combat over the past forty years must be shared by both political and military leaderships. Nonetheless, it would be extremely self-serving of the U.S. military to contend that the military strategy was fully sound and only rendered less than effective by the political strategy.

In any event, over and above the changes in the communist world, there are other, equally important reasons to consider our national security strategy. One is the continuing advance of technology. The pendulum between the offense and the defense in warfare is today well over on the side of the offense. New technologies of reconnaissance are making it increasingly difficult to conceal the movement or the location of military forces. Remote targeting is making it possible to attack with accuracy whatever reconnaissance can locate. New forms of explosives, ranging from weapons of nuclear fusion to clusters of explosive pellets, increase the odds that an attacker can destroy whatever he locates and targets.

The collapse of communism is not the only political phenomenon we must take into account. Noncommunist countries are increasingly turning to democracy and independent expression of their interests. Much of that is good. It is just what the United States has espoused for the past two hundred years. But freedom of expression can also lead to conflict as nations strike out to assert their particular interests.

The Iraqi invasions of Iran in 1980 and Kuwait in 1990 are ample testimony to the possibilities for substantial and lethal conflict. If we consider the dangers of nuclear, chemical, and biological weaponry, the potential exists for conflict well beyond the confines of the neighborhoods of nations equipped with such sophisticated weaponry. We also are seeing subnational groups, ethnic or religious, take advantage of both new weaponry and the increasing vulnerability of a closely intertwined world society to wreak havoc through terrorism.

For forty-five years our military strategy has been built around the forward deployment of ground and air forces in Europe. This pretension to being a continental power has shaped, or perhaps misshaped, our military posture. We have indulged ourselves with equipments and tactics suited uniquely to continental warfare in temperate climes and in open, heavily populated terrain. Sixty-five-ton tanks are not readily transported to remote areas of the world nor ideal for jungle warfare, for instance.

We have also come to count heavily on having complex maintenance facilities in place next to the prospective battlefield, rather than seeking out ways to minimize maintenance requirements in forward areas, such as placing the sophistication in the weapons rather than in the aircraft.

Similarly, we have grown accustomed to having supply depots within arm's length and have neglected the airlift, sealift, and other mechanisms needed to stretch such support over thousands of miles.

There is increasing public concern today over our nuclear strategy. For most of the post–World War II period, nuclear strategy remained in the realm of specialists. Today the United States and the Soviets maintain over fifty-five thousand nuclear warheads between them, so it is easy for the man on the street to understand that something has gone wrong. Whatever the strategies each has held, they must be flawed to produce such a result. Perhaps the best acknowledgment of this failure is the degree to which both countries have been working to undo this result, that is, to reduce nuclear warheads substantially. But without a new strategy, it will be difficult to settle on some lower figure, to avoid the impulse that drove us to fifty-five thousand.

This concern with nuclear weaponry, our lessened concern with Europe, our growing interests as *the* global power in a shrinking and unifying world, and the unrelenting advances of technology are together forcing us to a major review of our national security strategy. National leadership can ignore this demand only at great risk. If the American people and their Congress are not persuaded that the national security establishment has a new vision or strategy, they will not support a robust security apparatus for very long.

There are immense competing needs for public funds today. Domestically, huge resources are needed for education, drug eradication, aid for the poor or homeless, ecological protection, transportation infrastructure, continued exploration of the frontiers of space, and the reduction of the national deficit. The U.S. response to the Iraqi invasion of Kuwait notwithstanding, the American public is likely to see the need for the military establishment to continue to decrease. No nation can be a significant military power without a sound economic base in anything but the short run, and it is clear that the Soviets have almost an intractable economic problem, compounded by an unsound political system that must carry out economic reform. If the military threat from the Soviet Union continues to diminish, the American public may well demand larger and larger peace dividends from the defense budget, rather than an increase in taxes, to meet nonmilitary needs.

The essence of the challenge today is to conceive a strategy that will enable the United States to project power wherever in the world we deem it necessary, still maintain sufficient capability to assist in the continued defense of our allies in Western Europe and northeast Asia, and preserve a nuclear deterrent, all within reduced budgets. Only a willingness to look problems straight in the face will bring us through the coming adjustments. This book does not solve the problem for us. It does not formulate a new strategy. What it does is lay out the kinds of considerations that must be taken into account. Toward that end, it is a key tool for those who will develop the strategy our country vitally needs in this exciting period of change.

STANSFIELD TURNER

Acknowledgments

The political, economic, military, and technological conditions that attended the formulation and implementation of U.S. national strategy in the post–World War II era changed dramatically as the last decade of the twentieth century opened. While no one can ignore the extent of the sweeping events in Eastern Europe, the Soviet Union, and elsewhere, what these changes mean for the nation's strategy is far less clear. Have the assumptions upon which U.S. strategy has been based since World War II been irreversibly altered, or are there persistent forces at work that require adherence to postwar notions of national security requirements? Whatever the long-term consequences of the enormous changes in the international political and economic environments, one fact seems clear: the United States will continue to need some vision of its role in the world and some appreciation for how best to conduct its affairs. It is toward a reasoned appraisal of these difficult affairs that this book is directed. That a book addressing these issues should be conceived at West Point is hardly surprising. The U.S. Army has devoted a considerable portion of its intellectual energy to the formulation and implementation of national strategy. The U.S. Military Academy has contributed to these efforts in a host of ways, from providing graduates to serve in positions of responsibility—from platoon leader to president—to hosting innumerable conferences assessing the requirements for national strategy at a particular time.

We owe a great deal of gratitude to our colleagues in the Department of Social Sciences at West Point. Donne Olvey and Jim Golden provided their usual endless supply of wisdom and support, and Ace Clark reviewed and made very helpful suggestions on a number of chapters. Donna Prewitt demonstrated not only technical wizardry in preparing the manuscript but infinite patience in dealing with fractious authors and editors. Finally, we must thank Henry Tom, Denise Dankert, and the rest of the fine staff at the Johns Hopkins University Press for their support and graciousness in seeing this project to completion.

The contents of this book in no way represent the official policy of the U.S. Military Academy, the U.S. Army, or any other agency of the U.S. government. All royalties from the sale of this book will be deposited in a fund for faculty research and development at West Point.

Introduction

As the 1980s ended, one could readily detect a new interest in national strategy among students and practitioners of national security affairs. Paul Kennedy's *Rise and Fall of the Great Powers* surged to the top of the bestseller lists; his carefully worded analysis of what he views as America's fundamental grand strategical problem engendered a debate that made its way from Sunday morning television news shows, to the op-ed pages of prestigious newspapers, to the presidential campaign.[1] Edward Luttwak's *Strategy: The Logic of War and Peace* and David Calleo's *Beyond American Hegemony* also attracted more popular attention than one might have expected for their efforts to encourage Americans to think in broad strategic terms.

One observed the same new emphasis on strategic thinking within government as well. Congressional interest in encouraging the executive branch to think strategically led to the requirement for the president to present an annual report on the *National Security Strategy of the United States.* A presidential Commission on Integrated and Long-Term Strategy (comprising a number of distinguished current and former government officials, military officers, and scholars) presented its principal report, entitled *Discriminate Deterrence,* in January 1988. When the Bush administration took office in January 1989, virtually its first act was to embark on a comprehensive review of U.S. national strategy. Thereafter, one of the most persistent concerns about the new administration was whether "Bush's team is capable of the kind of global vision the times seem to call for."[2]

What is most interesting about this renaissance in strategic thinking is that it came at a time when the world looked very much as it had for the preceding forty years. By the early 1990s the world was a very different place. Consider the epochal changes that have taken place since the summer of 1989.

1

In Nicaragua and Panama democratic governments have new hopes for success. Indeed, republicanism has become the dominant form of government in Latin and Central America. In Eastern Europe a host of countries have thrown off the shackles of statist oligarchy and begun their effort to institutionalize free markets and free political institutions. Indeed, the Soviet Union itself is wracked with internal turmoil stemming from nationalist crises, an inoperable economy, and the palpitations of democratic change. While it maintains a large army and a significant strategic capability, the Soviet Union is no longer feared militarily as it once was; the Warsaw Pact is effectively dead. These changes have been so dramatic that one analyst described them as constituting "the end of history"—a consensus that liberal democracy and free market economies are unchallenged as the superior form of social organization.[3]

The enormous changes in the Soviet Union, Eastern Europe, and elsewhere call into question the fundamental strategic orientation of the United States, an orientation that has remained essentially unchanged since the late 1940s. While most of these changes are gratifying for the people of the United States, the future is not necessarily benign. Associated with the recent changes has been the rapid reemergence of ethnic and cultural divisions, strident nationalism, and considerable economic hardship. While an increasing number of analysts argue that containment, the organizing principle of American foreign policy since the late 1940s, is an inadequate paradigm for America's action in world politics, there have been few substitutes offered. Even if recent events signal the end of the cold war and a U.S. "victory" in that competition, the need for a national strategy has not been eliminated. While the content of that strategy may differ significantly from that of the past four decades, the international political and economic systems are becoming more complex, not less. Thus, a major strategic reappraisal appears to be necessary to adjust American foreign policy to the requirements of a new and different decade. Fundamental to this undertaking is the development of a clearer understanding of what strategy is and an appreciation of how difficult it is to do well.

UNDERSTANDING STRATEGY

National strategy is traditionally defined as a state's effort to reconcile means (resources available) and ends (objectives). Stated more formally, national strategy is an effort to "coordinate and direct all the resources of a nation, or band of nations, toward the attainment of the political objective, . . . the goal defined by fundamental policy."[4] But this definition oversimplifies the concept. Stated more completely, national strategy is a state's effort to use available means to advance chosen objectives in a specific domestic and international environment that imposes constraints and threats. Yet even this more concrete formulation understates the difficulty of the reconciliation of ends and means, as we observe if we examine the components of strategy individually.

Objectives are the first element of national strategy. Objectives are drawn from interests and are of two types: those derived from a state's position in the world (external objectives) and those derived from a state's unique political and economic system (internal objectives). America's strategic advantage has always rested on the fact that geography has assured her physical security from external threats (with the exception of nuclear attack), and size and natural resources have made a semiautarchic approach to international economics more feasible. Of course, geopoliticists would argue that the United States retains vital external objectives, particularly the necessity to prevent any single power from gaining hegemony on the Eurasian landmass.[5] Apart from that objective, America's ends have been largely internal and consequently more subject to the continual debate that is endemic to the American public policy-making process.

Threats are the second element of national strategy. The problem is a familiar one: whether to rest a state's evaluation of the threat posed by another on the potential adversary's capabilities or on its intentions.

Means, or resources, are the third element of national strategy. Means are most commonly viewed functionally, consisting of military policy, diplomatic policy, economic policy, and intelligence policy. While there are, of course, a host of capabilities subsumed under each of these functional categories, this conceptualization of means is deemed useful because it corresponds roughly with the organization of most governments. The key to applying means well lies in ensuring that available means are adequate and appropriate for the task at hand.

But the difficulty of establishing clear causal links between the application of means and the advancement of ends is often vexing. The problem that states face is that their opponents have a clear incentive not to indicate the conditions under which they are coerced or deterred. The influenced state may hope that circumstances change; it may also fear that knowledge of what it holds dear will make it more subject to influence from competitor states in the future. It has very little incentive to make its unique calculation of costs and benefits known to an opponent.

The domestic and international environments make up the fourth element of national strategy. Domestically, a political culture, national values, and the organization of the political system make up the context within which strategy is made and impose real constraints on the choices available to decisionmakers. Internationally, decisions on strategy are affected by the context of the region within which a state operates as well as by the structure and process of the international political system.

Inevitably, the task of reconciling these disparate elements of national strategy is difficult. The task is only manageable at all when states make assumptions regarding what influences and interests others and rely upon prestige (or reputation for power) to "stretch" their perceived capabilities in the short term.

THE UTILITY OF STRATEGY

For all of the difficulty associated with its formulation, national strategy remains important to a state's national security posture. National strategy is important because history teaches that a state will be more capable of accomplishing its national objectives if those objectives are balanced against external threats and the type and quantity of available national resources. This conclusion appears to be valid over time and across cultures. States that failed to reconcile means and ends adequately ultimately had difficulty accomplishing their national objectives. Conversely, states that consciously attempted to match means and ends were generally more successful in the pursuit of national interests.

Ancient states were not immune to the requirements of strategy, as Thucydides describes in *The Peloponnesian War*. A prudent Athens had managed victories over Sparta and Persia by carefully marshaling available resources against specific external threats and never advancing too far from the city's walls. Yet, after consolidating their new-found power, the Athenians rejected the prudent strategy that had established their security. Ignoring advice from the Athenian commander Nicias that such a campaign to conquer Syracuse would overextend the empire, the Athenians embarked on just such an expedition. The results were ultimately disastrous for Athens.[6]

The problem of overextension is not confined to expansionist states such as Athens. As we suggested earlier, states inevitably rely on their prestige to narrow the gap between ends and means; such gaps are generally unavoidable. The problem is that a state presumed to be in decline will use up its reservoir of prestige quickly—and it may not be capable or willing to renew its supply.

In this regard, the history of the Roman Empire is instructive. As Edward Luttwak makes clear in *The Grand Strategy of the Roman Empire,* the Romans understood the need to integrate the components of national power, principally military and political, in order to accomplish their objectives. They understood that the dominant dimension of power was psychological, not physical, and knew to harness the military power of the empire to political purpose.[7]

One observes three sequential approaches to strategy throughout the history of the Roman Empire. During the period of "hegemonic expansion," Rome used client states and coercive diplomacy, backed up by flexible military power, to expand and maintain security. Luttwak notes that "the sphere of imperial control is limited only by the range at which others perceive Roman power as compelling obedience. The reach of Roman power and the costs of its military forces need not, therefore, be proportional" (192). The key point is that Rome was able to expand its empire without bearing the costs of empire directly.

In the second phase of the Roman Empire, ends and means were matched directly as military strength and effective power become proportional. Force was no longer used inexpensively, as an instrument of coercion; instead, lost prestige required that it be used as a tool of suasion.

In the final stage, of course, the Roman Empire dissolved, as the external and domestic environment created conditions under which resources were inadequate to deal with threats. In an environment of increased threat, with decreased power to coerce and marshal domestic resources, the Roman Empire simply could no longer cope with its security environment.

Finally, and perhaps most relevant today, is the example of British imperial decline. Great Britain's case is illuminating because not only does it point out the desirability of matching means to ends but it demonstrates the limitations in trying to do so. At the turn of the century, Great Britain was the preeminent economic power and a great military power. However, she was beset by rising economic rivals abroad, a declining manufacturing sector domestically, and increasing balance of trade problems.[8] At the same time, technological advances had put great strains on Britain's defense budgets while simultaneously giving her rivals the means to challenge Britain's naval supremacy.[9]

Although Britain's response was not part of a logical "master plan," it was a conscientious attempt to adjust to perceived changes in the strategic situation within the parameters established by the domestic environment. Economically, Great Britain maintained liberal trade policies and turned to her imperial system, allowing income from her service sector and primary exports from the colonies to offset excess imports.[10]

In the security realm, Britain attempted to create more resources internally and to allocate more of those resources to security.[11] These attempts were offset by perceived fiscal constraints and domestic politics.[12] In addition, Britain consolidated her military forces and abandoned the "two power standard." More radically, she abandoned some of her lesser defense commitments and entered into a number of alliances in order to protect other peripheral interests. Finally, Great Britain simply changed some of the assumptions about the environment to make means and ends meet. "Through a combination of treaties, appeasement, and wishful thinking, the threats to which the empire was exposed were deemed to have been miraculously reduced" (298). Ultimately, economic and political constraints were too great, and Great Britain was unable to maintain her dominant position. But it would be fair to say that British national strategy did help to delay and minimize British decline.

Many would argue that the United States today faces a situation similar to that faced by Great Britain in 1895. The world has become a much more complex place; neither the Soviet Union nor the United States is capable of imposing its will directly in most cases. Power has become a less tangible—and less fungible—quantity. The new salience of transnational relations and "people power" challenge traditional views of statecraft.

At the same time, threats to the United States have not disappeared. The Soviet Union retains an impressive nuclear arsenal and a very large army. European multipolarity creates the potential for ethnic and border clashes, as well as economic and political instability. The proliferation of biological and chemical weapons, as well as ballistic missiles, throughout many parts of the developing world is indicative of the sophisticated military equipment readily available to potential antagonists. Finally, environmental problems and international narcotics trafficking present threats that the United States can no longer ignore.

Traditional U.S. interests are likely to remain. The waning of ideological fervor in the Soviet Union does not eliminate the fact that Soviet (Russian?) interests in Europe, Asia, and the Middle East compete with those of the United States. In addition, a more unified Europe, a strengthened Japan, and a resurgent, unified Germany may all conflict to some extent with U.S. economic interests in the future.

Ultimately, the United States will need to craft a national strategy for dealing with these complexities. This strategy will have to be developed and implemented in a domestic political system in which power is shared and authority is fragmented, making both development and implementation all the more difficult.

ENCOURAGING STRATEGIC DEBATE

We do not argue that strategy, whatever its content, is a panacea for overcoming the challenges facing the United States in the next decade. Some problems may simply be irresolvable. However, the military and economic power of the United States make it unique among nations. Consequently, the nation will almost certainly be involved in an increasingly disparate environment of increasingly difficult issues. Like all states, the United States will be better able to accomplish its national objectives if its people have thought about, and debated, the components and alternative formulations of national strategy. The purpose of this book is to encourage that process.

The remainder of this book lays out the elements of U.S. national strategy. It is designed, not to offer definitive answers to difficult strategic questions, but rather to stimulate debate by defining the external strategic environments in which the nation is likely to find itself; describing the domestic political and economic environments in which the debate will take place; and presenting alternative formulations of national strategy for the United States in the 1990s.

Part I focuses on the external strategic environment and investigates the nature of the threats facing the United States in the 1990s. In chapter 1, Samuel Huntington assesses the evolution of U.S. national strategy. Notra Trulock examines the impact of technological and doctrinal changes on the Soviet military threat in chapter 2, while in chapter 3, A. R. Norton evaluates an emerging challenge, examining the forces of change in the Third World and their potential impact on U.S. interests.

Part II examines the nature of the domestic environment and the degree to which various factors enhance or constrain the ability of the United States to develop and implement national strategy. In chapter 4, Aaron Friedberg evaluates the effects of economic factors on strategy by examining the validity of the "United States in decline" school of thought. In the following chapter, George Edwards examines the impact of congressional-executive relations on U.S. strategy making in the next decade.

In Part III, we present four alternative formulations of U.S. national strategy for the 1990s: cold war internationalism, limited containment, strategic independence, and liberal internationalism. The continuation of traditional policies by new means, "discriminate deterrence," is delineated in the Report of the Committee on Long-Term Integrated Strategy in chapter 6. This view is followed by Steven Walt's strategy of "Finite Containment." In chapter 8, Chris Layne advocates a policy of strategic independence and limited disengagement in the next decade. Finally in chapter 9, Michael Doyle articulates a U.S. strategy based on liberal democratic principles.

The solutions to the problems posed by the strategic challenges facing the United States are not to be found in the pages of this book. If they exist at all, they will be found in the minds of the people who will confront those problems in the future: policymakers, scholars, and interested observers. This book is intended to stimulate their thoughts.

PART I

The Strategic Environment

1

The Evolution of U.S. National Strategy

A flurry of recent executive and legislative activity suggests that the U.S. government sees a need for "more" national strategy in dealing with security affairs.[1] Indeed, several authors in this volume suggest different directions that such a strategy might take. Before one rushes off optimistically to enact one's preferred strategy, however, it would be useful to examine how U.S. national strategy has evolved since the end of World War II. I will argue that such an examination suggests that efforts to enact a comprehensive U.S. national strategy are chimerical, because they are severely constrained by decentralization and diverging interests within the U.S. security policy-making apparatus. The U.S. government can, however, formulate a military strategy, and significant changes are needed in U.S. military strategy to adapt it to a rapidly changing security environment.

DEFINING NATIONAL STRATEGY

The first question, of course, is what is national strategy? This question is itself contentious, since scholars easily arrive at different definitions.[2] In the best academic manner, let me set forth my own definition of national strategy. In order to do so, let me first indicate what strategy is not—foreign policy. Foreign policy includes the goals that a government pursues and the means it employs in its external environment, whatever the nature of that environment. What is different about strategy in a meaningful sense is that it is conducted against an opponent.

People often use the term *strategy* in a much looser sense; for example, newspaper articles discuss the strategy for dealing with AIDS. Well, unless there is somebody around fighting for AIDS, it is hard in a precise sense to have a strategy against AIDS. One can think of a number of other contexts in which this term is misused. Strategy implies an opponent, a conflict, a competition, a situation where an individual or a group is trying to achieve a goal against somebody else.

National strategy involves the development and the use of the entire range of resources (political, economic, military, or some combination) by a government to achieve its objectives against the opposition of another government or group. National strategy is often confused or identified, for reasons that will become evident, with military strategy. But military strategy is, in theory, simply a subset of national strategy. Military strategy is the use of military resources by a government to achieve its objectives despite the opposition of some other group of people.[3] The term *national strategy* came into use after World War II. During World War II people talked about grand strategy.[4] The allies had a grand strategy for defeating the Axis, and this concept was carried over into the postwar period and came to be referred to as national strategy.

National strategy and *national security strategy* are not necessarily synonymous. A government quite conceivably could have national strategies devoted to the achievement of a variety of goals. The United States could have, and I am sure many governments do have, a national strategy for prevailing in the Olympics. That is a perfectly meaningful and respectable use of the term *national strategy*. Normally, however, when we talk about national strategy, we mean national security strategy, or the national policy of a government directed to promoting its security objectives.

THE EVOLUTION OF NATIONAL STRATEGY

If one goes back to the immediate post–World War II period and looks at the efforts to deal with strategy, one obviously has to focus on that classic document, NSC-68, which was indeed an effort to define national strategy.[5] Reading that document, one is impressed with the range of issues and topics it covers. There is some discussion of military matters in NSC-68, but that is subordinate. It is filled with discussions of economic questions and issues. The principal statistics in it, in fact almost all of the statistics in it, deal not with the military balance but with gross national product (GNP), coal production, electric power, oil, pig iron production, steel production, cement production, motor vehicle production. Those are only a few of the figures that are in there. NSC-68 also has extensive sections dealing with political and psychological warfare. In the section on U.S. intentions and capabilities, there are six pages on economic issues, four pages on political and psychological warfare issues, and only slightly over one page on military questions.

In the section on recommendations, there are three pages dealing with economics and politics and one and a half on military questions. This broad concept of national strategy involving economics, politics, military policy, and psychological warfare issues continued for the next decade or so. The New Look and the early strategy papers prepared in the Kennedy and Johnson administrations have a comparably broad approach.[6]

In terms of efforts to define strategy, a big change occurred in the late 1960s. Whether it is significant or not, it coincides with the arrival of Henry Kissinger in the White House. National Security Study Memorandum 3 (NSSM 3) and comparable documents from those years focus almost entirely on military issues. When the Carter administration came in and I was involved in the Presidential Review Memorandum 10 (PRM-10) exercise, we made a big effort (at least I made a big effort) to go back and take NSC-68 as the model. We were supposed to be developing a national strategy, and hence we did elaborate studies in that exercise on economic questions, technology, political institutions, intelligence capabilities, diplomatic support, and many other issues. The task forces that we created made very real contributions to understanding many of those issues. The output of the PRM-10 exercise, PD-18, however, was devoted almost entirely to military issues. The first two paragraphs made mention of economic questions and how the United States should exploit its economic advantages against the Soviets. But after that nod toward nonmilitary things, everything else was military.

My impression is that the same thing was true in the Reagan administration's effort, National Security Decision Memorandum 32 (NSDM 32). It was certainly true in the effort at strategy making produced by the Commission on Integrated Long-Term Strategy in January 1988. While the original mandate of the Commission was to look at things well beyond military issues (and I'm sure that was Fred Ikle's intention), the Commission's report is all about military policy. The national strategy review undertaken at the outset of the Bush administration was similarly focused on the military dimensions of national strategy.

Over the years there thus has been a redefinition of national strategy from something fairly broad involving political, economic, and other issues to something that seems to be almost purely military. This trend has been noticed, and people have attempted to correct it. In 1987, for example, Amos A. Jordan, director of the Center for Strategic and International Studies, published an article in which he said, among other things, that he "was focusing on national security strategy because the United States has given too little attention to nurturing and using nonmilitary instruments in advancing its interests."[7] In his article, however, he advances six major propositions, five of which deal almost entirely with military issues. Only one-sixth of the argument that he makes deals with nonmilitary issues. Although he rightly intended to restore national strategy to its broader meaning, he did not, I fear, succeed, at least not in that article. This example is not atypical.

THE NATIONAL STRATEGY PARADOX

The obvious question is, Why did national strategy in the broader sense whither away? There is one obvious answer: bureaucratic politics. It is rather interesting to look at the shift in the agencies that initiated these various efforts to draw broad-gauge national strategy. From the 1940s through the 1960s the initiative for these efforts was in the State Department. Paul Nitze was, after all, the head of the Policy Planning Staff in the State Department when he drew up NSC-68. The State Department also took the lead during the Eisenhower and Kennedy administrations. When the Nixon administration came to power, the action shifted to Kissinger's National Security Council (NSC) staff. In the Carter administration, PRM-10 was jointly sponsored by the NSC and the Department of Defense. My impression is that the same was true in the early years of the Reagan administration. The 1987–88 Strategy Commission was, in theory, a joint effort by the NSC and the Department of Defense, but in fact it was almost entirely a Defense Department initiative and action. Inclusion of the NSC was almost entirely a formality. So over a period of years the leadership shifted from Nitze and the State Department in 1950 to Ikle and the Defense Department in 1987.

One might conclude that this shift in initiating institution explains why national strategy has become defined in military terms. But this change is, I believe, more a consequence of other factors than a cause. The much more important factor is something else, something that Aaron Friedberg has elaborated on in his very interesting analysis and description of these efforts at national strategy making.[8] The tone and focus of these studies changed significantly in the 1960s—a change that reflects the receding of war as a real problem and as an experience. As World War II receded into the past and as, in a sense, World War III receded into the future, national security strategy came to be defined more narrowly in military terms. Certainly if one looks at NSC-68 or any of the other documents of the immediate postwar era, there is a sense of the imminence of war: we've got to gear up, there's a "year of maximum danger" two or three years away, the Soviets are a big threat, we must be prepared to fight them. In subsequent documents from the early 1960s on, this sense of the imminence of war and the need to prepare for war disappears.

The decline in the perceived imminence of war caused national strategy to shift in a more military direction. Only two communities in the U.S. government, the Defense Department and the intelligence agencies, remain really concerned with the competition with the Soviet Union. The other agencies that might at one point be involved in the drawing up of national security strategy and sometimes were (such as the State Department, the Commerce Department, the Treasury Department, the Office of Management and Budget [OMB], or the Agriculture Department) have other priorities in peacetime when war is not imminent. The U.S. government, with its great pluralism, with the dispersion of power, with the lack of institutional means of coercing bureaucratic agencies to do what higher authority (including the president) wants them to do, has no way to bring these other groups together to formulate a strategy for competition with the Soviet Union if they are uninterested in participating in such a process. This situation is at the heart of what can be called the national strategy paradox: the United States can only have a national strategy that is more than a military strategy either when the country is in war or when war is perceived as imminent. In peace, when war is not occurring or is not likely, the United States can only have a military strategy. The evanescence of a comprehensive national security strategy is a consequence of peacetime existence.

THE EVOLUTION OF MILITARY STRATEGY

That leaves us with military strategy. What can one say about the evolution of military strategy over this period of time when national strategy was undergoing this disappearing act? How has military strategy evolved since World War II? Here it might be useful to think of three aspects of military strategy: continuities, cycles, and trends.

Continuities

There have been many continuities in U.S. military strategy over the past thirty-five or forty years. They include: the emphasis on deterrence; reliance upon a mixture of both nuclear and conventional capabilities; since 1950 the forward deployment on the Eurasian rimland of American military forces both on shore and afloat; involvement in a whole series of complicated relationships with allies; and, of very great importance, use of our technological capability to maintain various forms of qualitative superiority over our opponent. All of these continuities in some respect reflect U.S. strengths: nuclear weapons (at least for a period of time), allies, maritime power to project forces abroad, superiority in technology. There may well be other continuities in American strategy, but these are some of the more important ones.

Cycles

There have been cycles in strategy with which we are all familiar. Strategic cycles tend to coincide with budget cycles, with the ups and downs in the defense budget. There have been three major expansion phases, during which most forms of military force tend to benefit.[9] A rising tide of defense expenditures does tend to lift all boats. This happened during the Korean War expansion, during the expansion in the Kennedy-Johnson years, and during the Reagan expansion. All three periods saw major modernization efforts with respect to our strategic nuclear forces, but conventional forces also benefited considerably. During the reduction phases, however, when the tide is falling, the falling tide grounds some boats before others. As we all know, things like readiness, training, operations and maintenance, and conventional forces are most likely to suffer when expenditures are going down. During these phases of the cycle, we tend to try to emphasize the contributions to achieving security objectives that can be made by cheaper forms of military force (such as reserve forces or nuclear weapons), and we emphasize the importance of our allies' increasing their contribution, as we are doing now.

Trends

Finally, there have been trends, some recent, some of longer standing, in the evolution of U.S. strategy. Perhaps the most obvious one is the declining reliance upon nuclear weapons to deter the Soviets as the Soviets increased their military forces. I do not think we are going to move into what Edward Luttwak refers to as a postnuclear world, but clearly belief in the credibility of nuclear weapons usage has declined quite considerably over the years. This has led to an increased emphasis upon problems of developing conventional forces and conventional deterrence.

Second, there has been a fairly consistent trend over the years in the direction of trying to achieve greater flexibility, precision, limitation, and selectivity in the use of nuclear forces. This trend dates back at least to Secretary of Defense James Schlesinger's limited nuclear options policies of the early 1970s but in some respects goes back to even before that, and it has been carried forward fairly consistently by administrations since.[10]

Third, and perhaps more recently, there has been an understandable reaction to our experiences in using conventional force, particularly in Vietnam. This reaction has produced a variety of developments, one of which is certainly the belief that if we are going to use conventional force in limited engagements abroad, we had better use it in circumstances where we can win quickly and avoid a slow bleed. It also has led the American military to become, as far as one can see, the principal proponent and certainly the most articulate and powerful opponent not only of the use of nuclear weapons but more generally of the use of military force at all.[11] This situation may well have some troubling consequences for our future.

Fourth, arms control considerations, postures, and negotiations have come to shape strategy in many important respects. Their impact reached its high mark to date in the Intermediate Nuclear Force (INF) negotiations and treaty. There considerations dictated by arms control conflicted with considerations dictated by a strategy of deterrence, and deterrence lost. The Strategic Arms Reductions Talks (START) and Conventional Forces in Europe (CFE) talks promise more of the same.

Fifth, at least during the Reagan administration, there was an effort to move away from the rather peculiar position we were in at the end of the 1970s. At that time our conventional forces and capabilities were largely, if not exclusively, defensive in character, and our strategic nuclear forces and capabilities were exclusively offensive in character. During the Reagan administration efforts were made to produce a more balanced offense-defense mix at both the strategic nuclear and conventional levels. These efforts included, at the strategic level, the Strategic Defense Initiative (SDI) and, at the conventional level, the Reagan Doctrine of support for anticommunist insurgencies, the Army's AirLand Battle doctrine, SHAPE's Follow-on-Forces Attack (FOFA) doctrine, and the Navy's Maritime Strategy.[12]

Finally, there has been a diversification of the threats we have to face, and some efforts have been made to diversify our responses to those threats.[13] We now have to have military strategy not only to deal with the Soviet Union but also to deal with a variety of Third World circumstances, including additional threats in Southwest Asia and Central America, terrorism, the drug mafia, and the like.

This diversification of threats is one factor that poses major challenges for the future. In the Strategy Commission report we attempted to deal with and carry forward some of the trends I have identified. We emphasized the desirability of preparing for contingencies other than strategic war and war in Europe, of achieving greater flexibility and precision in the use of our forces, and of developing a greater balance between offense and defense in our strategy.

CONCLUSIONS

Looking to the future, there are a variety of problems that our leaders will have to confront. In addition to the problem of the diversification of threats, there is also the fact that American power, military and economic, has declined relative to that of many other entities in the world. Many of the recent expressions of concern about this decline are exaggerated,[14] but obviously there has been some decline, and that fact will have to shape American strategy in the future. And that is the final point: U.S. strategy will become, and strategic thinking will necessarily have to become, more important in the future than it has been in the past.

General David Jones, former chairman of the Joint Chiefs of Staff, once commented that in the past we have won because we were bigger, not smarter.[15] In most cases we can count on winning in the future by being bigger but not smarter than our opponents. But this will not always be so—and it certainly will not be so in the most critical case. Hence, coming up with not only further emendations and changes in military strategy but also another effort at developing a national strategy should be a priority of the current administration. Given the past record, I don't think an effort to develop a national strategy in the broad sense of the term is probably going to succeed, but the process of trying to do so could, in both the short end and the longer term, be very beneficial.[16]

2

Military Threats to U.S. National Interests in the 1990s

NOTRA TRULOCK III

Predicting the evolution of military threats to U.S. national security over a substantial period of time is inherently fraught with uncertainty and ambiguity. Of course, it is always possible simply to make "straight line" projections of contemporary developments and trends. In fact, for most of the cold war era, such an approach has been at least adequate for forecasting major military threats to U.S. interests from its primary opponent, the Soviet Union. For most of the period after World War II, analysts have assumed that the competition between East and West would continue; more recently, the focus of this competition has shifted from the confrontation in Europe to other centers of instability, such as the Middle East and East Asia.

Reliance on this "straight line" methodology for the prediction of specific military threats is no longer acceptable, however. Few of the changes in the strategic environment for military planning in the mid-1990s could have been predicted from the vantage point of the mid-1980s. The recasting of the strategic situation in the Persian Gulf was hardly foreseen at the beginning of that decade. Although many would have acknowledged the Soviet objective of denuclearization of the NATO–Warsaw Pact balance at the beginning of the decade, few could have anticipated the major impetus for the achievement of this goal inherent in Soviet acceptance of the Reagan administration's proposal for total elimination of intermediate-range nuclear missile systems. The lack of a coherent response by the Alliance to the events in Eastern Europe after November 1989 is only one more indication of the failure to anticipate such shocks.

Similarly, although the cyclical nature of U.S. defense spending would have made the prediction that U.S. defense expenditures would level off or contract a safe bet, few would have believed that Soviet defense expenditures might also be subject to constraints by the end of the

19

1980s. Fewer still would have anticipated that Soviet political leaders and even some military authorities would advocate, at least publicly, the adoption of "defensive sufficiency" as the basis of future Soviet military planning. The announcement of Soviet unilateral force reductions in Europe and the pace of proposals from both sides in the Conventional Forces in Europe negotiations also appear to have caught military planners by surprise. Although the eventual shape and content of these proposals remain in doubt, the democratic revolutions that swept through Eastern Europe have significantly altered the security environment in Europe. However heartening these events may be in the West, the process appears to have contributed to one Soviet objective. The rationale for continued military modernization, not just of NATO's nuclear forces but also of its conventional systems, has been seriously undercut not only in Europe but also in the United States.

It is not simply a cliché, therefore, to say that the strategic environment for military planning for the mid-1990s is changing dramatically. Military thinkers in both East and West have concluded that the evolution of military affairs has accelerated rapidly in recent years under the impact of political, economic, and especially technological developments; consequently, the task of predicting threats to U.S. national security interests in the mid-1990s remains fraught with uncertainty.

The lack of clarity in certain critical U.S. national policies only compounds the difficulty of this task. The United States has yet to decide, for example, what exactly to think of General Secretary Gorbachev's effort to reform the Soviet economy. Is it in the U.S. national interest to see Mikhail Gorbachev succeed at his task? Or would continued Soviet economic stagnation pose less of a threat to U.S. interests?

The current phase of Soviet strategic withdrawal serves only to highlight the imprecision of U.S. objectives in other dimensions of national security policy. For example, the objectives underlying future relations with China, particularly in light of the political unrest and subsequent violent repression in mid-1989, and the role of the Asian-Pacific region in general in U.S. national security policy are less than clear. Is it in the U.S. interest to encourage Japan to increase its military efforts, or has the United States failed to consider the impact of this course of action on regional balances, as the Chinese (and others) have charged?

Of more immediate concern to U.S. national security planners has been the introduction of advanced-technology weapons systems, such as modern attack aircraft and ballistic missiles, into regions considered vital to the United States. The Soviet experience with the Stinger missile in Afghanistan, the U.S. experiences in the Persian Gulf, the use of ballistic missiles and possibly chemical weapons by both sides in the Iran-Iraq War, and the Iranian purchase and deployment of Chinese surface-to-surface missiles are only the latest examples of the lessons already learned by the British in the Falklands War. The proliferation of weapons of mass destruction, especially chemical but possibly also bacteriological weapons, and the mating of these weapons to missile systems only magnifies the scope of potential military threats to U.S. interests throughout the world.

The purpose of this chapter is to assess the range and scope of military threats that could confront U.S. national security interests through the decade of the 1990s. The chapter begins with a discussion of the trends that are likely to affect the strategic environment over the next decade and the threats that may emerge from those trends. Because it seems likely that our major military competitor over the next decade, and the only real threat to U.S. national survival, will come from the Soviet Union, the second section focuses on Soviet perceptions of the changing strategic environment and the challenges inherent in their forecast of an impending new stage in the development of military affairs. This analysis concludes with an assessment of the implications of the trends described in the preceding sections.

THE STRATEGIC ENVIRONMENT OF THE 1990S

The strategic environment of the 1990s will be shaped by a number of political, economic, and scientific-technical trends. While these trends are manifest in contemporary situations, the future direction and ultimate impact of such trends on U.S. security is uncertain. The decade of the 1990s is likely to be one of substantial change; security relationships and interactions throughout the world are likely to undergo considerable transformation during this period. While specific shocks and discontinuities may drastically alter the security environment, they cannot be predicted in advance. Consequently, the prudent analyst qua soothsayer must focus on the broader trends that can significantly alter the security environment over the next decade.

Political Trends

The last years of the 1980s marked a period of significant change in international relations. The establishment of more representative governments in Eastern Europe occurred not over Soviet objections but with explicit Soviet encouragement. The Soviet Union has, at least temporarily, seized the political initiative not only in Europe but also in East Asia. The extent to which the Soviets will succeed in constructing new security relationships in these regions will be determined by a number of factors, not the least of which is the success of the internal restructuring of the Soviet economy and society at large. In a similar fashion, the implications of the political upheaval in China on its foreign policy is primarily dependent upon the outcome of the domestic power struggle; the emergence of a hardline regime may stagnate China's economic, agricultural, and military modernization programs, perhaps retarding China's role in the future Asian security landscape. In a more immediate sense, the violent government response to domestic protest served to alienate Beijing, at least temporarily, from the West. The death of the Ayatollah Khomeini, and the possibility of the emergence of a more moderate clerical leader, could open the door for the return to a more stable security environment in the Persian Gulf region.

The decade of the 1980s also witnessed a remarkable surge in the spread of demands for democracy and freedom. The 1990s is likely to see this trend continue and spread into regions within the Soviet sphere of influence; the rebellious displays of sovereignty in the Baltic States and the landslide victories of noncommunist candidates in elections throughout Eastern Europe are indicative of the kinds of political uncertainty likely to confront Soviet leaders. It is entirely possible that political trends in Eastern Europe will determine the outcome of the Soviet restructuring program, yet U.S. planners have devoted little attention to U.S. objectives and influence in that region. Of course, a unified Germany presents new political and security questions for both East and West.

The power of democratic ideas can also be seen in the speed and magnitude of the reactions that accompanied the student protests in Beijing. While it is too soon to ascertain the outcome of this political unrest in China, Chinese political instability clearly will have a significant impact on the security environment in Asia in the next decade.

Political instability in critical regions will continue to pose threats to U.S. interests. In some cases, these threats could occur as the result of deliberate Soviet efforts and intentions; in other instances, they could arise from local causes without any direct Soviet involvement. While less threatening than any direct U.S.-Soviet conflict, outcomes adverse to U.S. objectives could seriously degrade future U.S. capability to defend political, economic, and security interests in regions vital to the United States and its allies. At a minimum, the potential embarrassment for the United States and the internal U.S. domestic complications that would arise from involvement in regional military contingencies lessen U.S. influence.

For example, political as well as historical and economic trends may leave the United States vulnerable on its southern flank. Political instability in Mexico could pose security dilemmas and potential constraints that have simply been absent from U.S. strategic considerations during the post–World War II period.[1] Moreover, the U.S. invasion of Panama in December 1989 may have only increased U.S. vulnerability in this region over the long run. The potential contribution of Soviet clients in the Western Hemisphere, such as Cuba, to political instability in the region or to the disruption and delay of reinforcement efforts in the event of a major war in Europe or elsewhere on the Soviet periphery cannot be overlooked. In addition, the Soviets are sure to seek opportunities to establish and expand political contacts (and subsequently perhaps additional military facilities) in the Western Hemisphere, Gorbachev's promises at the Washington summit in 1988 notwithstanding.

Economic Trends

Economically, the United States must contend not only with the rapidly growing economies of its East Asian competitors but also with the Europe of 1992. Little thought has been devoted to the security implications of the achievement of even a modest unification of Europe in the 1990s, let alone to the impact of a powerful, unified Germany. Salvaging the economies of the nations of Eastern Europe and incorporating them into the mainstream of European economic affairs will require considerable Western effort and resources. Furthermore, the proliferation of heavy and electronics industries in newly industrializing countries, such as Brazil, India, and South Korea, not only presents a challenge to the economic position of industrialized countries but also affects the ability of the United States to influence third powers that were previously dependent on it for heavy military equipment and support.

In the Asian-Pacific region, U.S. economic and security interests will demand that the United States devote more attention and more resources to protecting those regional interests. For several years, U.S. trade with the Pacific Rim has exceeded in value that with any other region, including Western Europe. U.S. interests in Asia are dependent on uninterrupted sea and air transportation routes, and a significant portion of strategic materials either originate in the region or transit the area en route to the United States.

Gorbachev has signaled no diminution in Soviet interests or attention to the region; on the contrary, he has launched a more diversified approach to achieving Soviet regional objectives. In his Vladivostok speech, for example, Gorbachev acknowledged U.S. interests in the region and included the United States in his proposal for an Asian-Pacific countries conference, a major shift from his earlier proposals for an All-Asian conference, with its obvious exclusion of the United States. The Soviet Union also has sought to improve relations with the

Chinese. The Soviets have acceded to Chinese demands to withdraw from Afghanistan and to reduce the level of troops stationed along the Chinese border. The portentous Sino-Soviet summit in Beijing in May 1989, while almost completely overshadowed in the West by the ongoing domestic unrest in China, is ample testimony to the importance the Soviets attach to improving their security position in the region. Continued deterioration of U.S.-Chinese relations in the aftermath of the suppression of the prodemocracy movement might make the People's Republic of China more receptive to the Soviet overtures.

More ominously, the Soviets have sought to expand their presence in the South Pacific. The Soviet Union has established diplomatic relations and economic ties with Kiribati, Vanuatu, and Fiji and, more significantly, have obtained berthing rights for Soviet "fishing boats" in the region. Continued Soviet access to forward basing facilities, such as the naval and air facilities at Cam Ranh Bay and Da Nang, will remain a significant military threat to U.S. access to sea lines of communication (SLOCs) in the region. Soviet military objectives in the region remain unchanged: to interdict sea lanes between the Pacific and Indian oceans; to threaten the maritime links between the United States and Japan; and to provide a strategic link between Soviet forces in the Pacific and Indian oceans.

The failure to resolve the exploding Third World debt crisis could threaten the stability of many of the governments in Central America, leading to calls for U.S. military assistance in maintaining domestic order and stability. Furthermore, such instability could lead to greater pressures to withdraw forces presently stationed overseas to perform border guard duties or protect vital interests in the region. Finally, increasing calls for military involvement in efforts to interdict drug traffic into the United States not only would divert forces from other operational requirements but also could contribute to greater regional tensions. The introduction of U.S. military forces into Panama in December 1989 to overthrow the regime of Manuel Noriega has reminded local populations of the long history of U.S. military intervention. Developments in Central and South America have the potential for creating the most significant new dimension for U.S. military planning in the 1990s.

Scientific-Technical Trends

Perhaps the greatest potential impact on the security environment in the 1990s is in the scientific-technical arena. By the beginning of the next century, probable revolutionary technological advances in several families of military systems could fundamentally change the nature of warfare. Several such new technologies are now under development, especially in long-range surveillance, target acquisition, and low-observable (stealth) delivery systems. These technologies will be integrated into the force structures of major powers in the coming decade. Other developments, such as directed energy weapons, autonomous smart weapons, and brilliant information-processing systems, are presently in the early stages of development and may begin deployment at the turn of the century. These emerging technologies will not merely make current forces marginally more lethal, they will revolutionize warfare.

Within the technological realm, several trends emerge. First, the number of countries that can successfully acquire, operate, and maintain high-technology weapons will increase. The point here is that the military threat the U.S. could face, even in the Third World, will be much more demanding.

In the Middle East, the military threat to the United States stems not only from continued political instability endemic to that region but also from the continued proliferation of high-technology weapons. Such systems will be more prevalent simply because the financial resources to attract suppliers are more readily available in this area. Oil revenues accumulated over the last two decades have created an enormous market for all types of the most modern military equipment. In this regard, the Soviet Union will continue to be a major supplier, if only because arms sales represent a key source of hard currency to support economic restructuring efforts. The need for hard currency is not unique to the Soviet Union. Chinese sales of the CSS-2 intermediate-range ballistic missile to Saudi Arabia, for example, provide the Saudis with extensive coverage of potential targets throughout the region and the Chinese with much needed hard currency.

These examples are only the most dramatic manifestation of the proliferation of high-technology weapons, especially ballistic missiles, into the Middle East. West European arms dealers have been very active in the region, both in exporting weapons and in providing the technical expertise to upgrade systems already deployed. Greater range and better accuracy have been achieved through the application of such expertise in the development of Iraqi military systems, for example.

Naval power traditionally has represented the most effective means of protecting U.S. interests and supporting U.S. clients in the Middle East. The U.S. Navy's role in the 1988 tanker war in the Persian Gulf served to reinforce the importance of a power projection capability in the region. Appreciation of the vulnerability of power projection, especially modern naval forces, to even one missile has been steadily growing since the Falklands/Malvinas War, however. Events in the Persian Gulf underscored this appreciation. While the concern for the vulnerability of surface ships has focused primarily on air-launched missiles, submarine-launched missiles will pose an equally severe problem in the future. Such attacks could be launched undetected from ranges as close as eighteen to twenty nautical miles at speeds up to Mach 2, leaving very little time for defensive reaction. Power projection forces also will encounter a more complex air operations environment in the 1990s, as more sophisticated air defense systems appear in the Middle East and elsewhere. The U.S. domestic intolerance of even limited losses could narrow U.S. options in the event of future situations similar to the Lebanon or Libyan air attacks.

A number of other suppliers of military systems, particularly ballistic missiles, have also found markets. Brazil, for example, has exported the Astros 2 rocket artillery suppression system to Iraq and is developing an anti-shipping missile to compete with the Exocet. It also has developed a battlefield missile with a range of three hundred kilometers, as well as ship-to-ship variants of its missile systems. More ominously, the Brazilians seem interested in exploiting their sounding and telemetry rocket technologies to develop longer-range systems. India is pursuing similar developmental efforts. The trend clearly points to greater diffusion of advanced technology systems and a more complex threat environment. The proliferation of these systems could have a dramatic impact on U.S. approaches to "low-intensity" conflict.

This emerging threat environment is compounded by the proliferation of chemical weapons capabilities in several states throughout the world. A number of states are known to have acquired such capabilities, and the relative absence of world indignation at reports of Iraqi use of chemical agents in the Iraq-Iran War may only serve to encourage others to develop and deploy such weapons. U.S. military planners must take seriously the threat of ballistic-missile-delivered chemical attacks on U.S. forces. Such capabilities not only would greatly complicate power projection tasks but also could undercut domestic support for such operations as a result of the potential shock and horror of unexpected chemical attacks on U.S. forces.

These political, economic, and technological trends have significant implications for U.S. security concerns throughout the globe. However, the principal geopolitical concerns for the United States in the next decade will remain first, and foremost, preventing an attack against the continental United States, and second, preventing any state, or coalition of states, from gaining hegemony over Eurasia. It appears likely that only the Soviet Union will possess the ability to threaten meaningfully either of those interests in the next decade.

SOVIET MILITARY THREATS IN THE 1990S

The domestic requirements associated with the restructuring of the Soviet economy and the Gorbachev foreign policy agenda would seem to portend a significantly reduced Soviet military threat to U.S. national survival and security interests in the 1990s. Whatever the outcome of these developments, however, Soviet military trends must remain the focus of Western analysis for at least two reasons. First, Gorbachev's restructuring may achieve sufficient results by the mid- to late 1990s to permit the Soviet Union to abandon its current "strategic withdrawal" phase and to reassume a more assertive role in international relations, backed by a fully modernized and high-technology military force structure. This time frame is clearly one envisioned by at least some Soviet military analysts in their consideration of the benefits of the restructuring. Alternatively, the restructuring program may prove a disastrous failure for the Soviet Union, leaving the Soviet Union few options beyond military force to retain its world prominence. The restructuring may, for example, have unleashed the forces of nationalism not only in Eastern Europe but also in the peripheral regions of the internal Soviet empire such as Central Asia and the Baltic States. While the central leadership could tolerate some loosening of control in Central Asia, such developments in the Ukraine, for example, would almost certainly be violently suppressed. Consequently, despite the outward appearance of stability and tranquility over the next few years, the situation in Eastern Europe and in the western regions of the Soviet Union could, in fact, become extremely volatile. The Soviet Union might seek to compensate for these internal difficulties through a more militarily aggressive posture in the world.

Similarly, it could be argued that the combination of the Soviet economic dilemma and the Gorbachev foreign policy agenda could also serve to make for a less threatening international environment. In fact, the Soviets have sought to portray their current approach to national security concerns in a nonprovocative, defensively oriented fashion since the Twenty-sixth Party Congress in February 1986. They have stressed the importance of political means to resolve these dilemmas and have emphasized that reliable security is unobtainable through reliance solely on military-technical considerations. "Reasonable sufficiency" and "nonoffensive defense" discussions, although of considerable relevance to internal political developments, have the added benefit of enhancing the image of a flexible, pragmatic political leadership interested only in reasonable security and occupied primarily with internal concerns.

The current Soviet political leadership understands full well both the economic dilemma and the implications of that dilemma for future Soviet power and world influence. They are currently in the process of devising both economic and especially political strategies to prevent slippage of the Soviet Union to the status of a second- or third-rate world power. These strategies are designed, in part, to exploit differences between the United States and its allies over threat perceptions, long-range Soviet objectives and intentions, and the benefits to the West of a revitalized and vigorous Soviet Union.

Gorbachev has said many times that the Soviet Union needs a stable and nonthreatening external environment in order to realize fully the goals of restructuring the Soviet economy. Soviet foreign policy has become more inextricably linked to domestic requirements since Gorbachev came to power. Soviet adoption of a nonprovocative military doctrine clearly serves to reinforce proclivities within Western elites and publics to perceive the Soviet Union as less of a military threat than in the past. Success in these endeavors could have a powerful effect upon future Western defense decision making. Denuclearization of Europe is only one of several Soviet objectives to be served by recent doctrinal developments, however. The overriding objective for Soviet foreign and defense policy is to continue to undercut the rationale for Western defense modernization programs and to slow the momentum of Western exploitation of the scientific-technical revolution for military purposes. The Soviets are clearly seeking to provide incentives to the West not to support defense expenditures at a level required to realize the potential of new military technologies. The emergence in the West of calls for an immediate moratorium on both nuclear and conventional modernization is indicative of early Soviet success in these endeavors. The Soviet military's reformulated assessment of the contribution of diplomacy is instructive in this regard. A nonprovocative approach is best suited to reducing the level of external tension and slowing the pace of Western defense modernization. Should conflict break out over the near term, military technologies that could offset traditional Soviet advantages would, as a consequence, simply be unavailable, at least in the quantities required to have much impact on Soviet operations.

Much is made in the West of the Soviet military's opposition to the Gorbachev agenda for restructuring. The military's influence in Soviet national security decision making is said to be waning, and many profess to see a major struggle underway for control over threat definition and the security agenda of the 1990s. Civilian national security experts have gone so far as to question the continued relevance of 1941 as an appropriate and valid case for contemporary and future military planning. Not surprisingly, this view has evoked a powerful and pointed response from the military.

Military opposition to the Gorbachev agenda seems to be concerned with marginal issues, however. Of course, the military was subject to harsh and severe criticisms in the aftermath of the Rust affairs. But these criticisms were leveled at problems already acknowledged by military leaders and may in fact have strengthened the hand of the General Staff reformers within the Soviet military. Moreover, the military continues to believe that it will be a primary beneficiary of the economic restructuring underway at this time. Military anticipation of the benefits it will derive from this program is based upon two considerations. First, Soviet forecasts of future military-technical trends indicate that the long-term competition with the West is likely to undergo a dramatic shift over the next ten to fifteen years. It is clear that the Soviet military has concluded that the Soviet economy was and will continue for some time to be incapable of producing the technologies required by the nature of the military competition in the mid- to late 1990s. The task of "strengthening the defensive capability" of the country remains one of the preeminent objectives in Soviet military analyses of the restructuring program. Despite potential economic constraints, military economists have argued that the fulfillment of the key objective of the restructuring of Soviet industry, the introduction of new technological processes and equipment, would shorten the production time of military equipment and reduce the material and labor costs associated with such production. Army General Lizichev, the chief of the Main Political Administration, set forth the military's view of the anticipated benefits from the "acceleration of the country's socioeconomic development and the fundamental restructuring of all aspects of our life and work." According to General Lizichev,

the country's success in the economic, social, and cultural spheres and in the development of science and technology have a decisive effect on the provision of the Army and Navy with the most modern combat equipment and weapons and on the supply of the necessary material resources, on their meeting with comprehensively trained military cadres and educated and spiritually and physically healthy personnel, and on the state of military science.[2]

Lizichev's assessment is in keeping with the military's anticipation that the restructuring is likely to produce a better-educated, more technologically receptive, and better-motivated recruit in the future. Soviet military concerns over the caliber of the manpower pool have been evident for some time. In short, the restructuring program, according to Soviet military analysts, not only would create new possibilities for resolving future defense tasks but, what is more important, would "strengthen the position of socialism in the competition with capitalism and the overall defensive capability of the country." Consequently, one wonders why the military would oppose, except on what must be considered marginal issues, the Gorbachev agenda. Whatever the outcome of internal political struggles and the fate of Gorbachev himself, the military rightly understands that the revitalization of the Soviet economy, and especially the vital machine-tool and metal-cutting sectors, cannot fail to improve the overall posture of the Soviet military.

The third and in some ways most critical factor shaping the strategic environment of the mid-1990s is the pace of military-technological change. Because of the critical role played by Soviet military power in shaping the strategic environment of the 1990s, it is instructive to examine Soviet views on the impact of military technologies on warfare over the next decade. Just as their Western counterparts have done, Soviet military theoreticians have traditionally devoted much of their energies to understanding the potential impact of new technologies on future warfare. The Soviets have long considered the "technical factor" to be the most decisive element influencing the nature of warfare. Soviet sources commonly justify this connection through reference to Engels' conclusion that "the successes of technology, as soon as they become applicable and put into practice in military affairs, immediately—almost violently and frequently against the will of the military command—cause changes and even revolutions in the methods of waging battle."

By way of analogy, contemporary Soviet analyses characterize the late 1920s and early 1930s as an era in which Soviet military art underwent a qualitatively new stage of development, with the formulation of deep battle and deep operations concepts. These analyses make clear, however, that even consideration of these concepts was predicated on the introduction of new technologies that substantially increased the firepower and especially the mobility of Soviet forces. Similarly, the revolution in military affairs in the early 1960s was realized only after the integration of nuclear-missile weapons in the armed forces of the major developed countries. In both instances, these changes were generated by what the Soviets refer to as a "qualitative leap in development of the means of armed conflict."

By the early 1980s, similar references to "qualitative leaps" and "revolutionary turns" in military technologies became frequent in Soviet military writings. In 1982 Marshall N. V. Ogarkov warned that a "deep, in the fullest sense, revolutionary turn in military affairs is taking place in our time."[3]

The transition to this new stage of development is already underway. In 1985, for example, Col. Gen. M. A. Gareyev, then chief of the General Staff's Military Science Directorate, declared, "We may now speak about a transitional stage in the development of military science and military art."[4] Soviet military sources generally agree, and few in the West would probably disagree, on four primary trends in the development of military technologies as providing the foundation for this "qualitative leap in the modernization of the means of armed conflict":

— the accumulation, further development, and qualitative modernization of nuclear weapons;

— the rapid development of military electronics;

— the significant qualitative modernization of conventional weapons;

— the development of weapons systems based on new physical principles.

The Soviets generally have divided their assessments of the development of these technologies and their implications for future war into two distinct periods. The first encompasses a midterm projection covering developments Soviet military planners anticipate to be fielded between the early 1990s and the year 2000. Soviet midterm forecasts generally incorporate projections of continuing modernization of the traditional types of conventional weapons—tanks, armored fighting vehicles (AFVs), aircraft—but seem to be focused more upon the first and early variants of the second generation of a new family of highly accurate, precision-guided delivery systems for nonnuclear munitions. These forecasts also encompass completion of the ongoing modernization of strategic offense and defense systems and perhaps the initial appearance of an early variant of weapons based on new physical principles (such as directed energy weapons rather than weapons based on kinetic or chemical energy). Also included in these forecasts are technologies that could dramatically increase the controllability of both weapons systems and operational forces.

Long-term forecasts, on the other hand, appear to concentrate on subsequent generations of conventional weaponry, the widespread application of low-observable technologies, and, in particular, increasing tactical applications for weapons based on new physical principles and other technologies under development in the U.S. Strategic Defense Initiative (SDI). Such forecasts would probably cover the years 2000 through possibly 2010–15 and are, consequently, of less interest to the purposes of this chapter. Nonetheless, these forecasts reflect the Soviet commitment to the continued development of such systems, the euphoria surrounding the Gorbachev political offensive notwithstanding.

The Impact of Change on the Soviet Threat

The crucial question for the United States is what impact these changes will have on the Soviet threat to the United States in the next decade. It might be argued that the announcement of Soviet unilateral force reductions and changes to Soviet military doctrine are indicators of a lessening of the Soviet military threat in the 1990s. However, none of these announced changes has resulted in a significant alteration of the trends in Soviet military production, force structure, or doctrine. While the apparent collapse of the Warsaw Pact in the aftermath of political developments in Eastern Europe ameliorates the immediacy of the Soviet military threat, it does not eliminate the requirement to continue to assess seriously the potential threat posed by the enormous Soviet military capability. In addition, the failure of domestic reform or the occurrence of an external "shock" might cause the Soviet Union to respond in a more militarily aggressive fashion. It continues to be critical, therefore, to understand the Soviet military's forecast of the nature of future warfare and the implications of these forecasts for U.S. national security requirements.

At present, it seems likely that nuclear weapons will continue to play an important but gradually diminishing role in future national security planning. At the same time, the existence of these weapons will continue to shape the operational context for military planning in the event of a future war. Col. Gen. V. A. Merimskiy, deputy commander-in-chief for combat training of the Soviet ground forces, has, for example, noted that the mere presence of nuclear weapons will continue to impose unique requirements on military planning.[5] For their part, Soviet commanders will continue to confront the dilemmas associated with the competing requirements to disperse in order to avoid the presentation of nuclear-suitable targets and at the same time to concentrate forces at decisive times and places in order to ensure success. Obviously, denuclearization of NATO and the Warsaw Pact force postures will alleviate these operational dilemmas, and, not surprisingly, Soviet Defense Minister Yazov has graciously declared Soviet willingness to restructure his forces along "nonnuclear principles."

From this and other Soviet statements, some in the West have concluded that the Soviet military and political leadership now sees little, if any, military utility for nuclear weapons. This judgment seems premature. First, as Merimskiy notes, the mere existence of nuclear weapons imposes certain constraints on the military planning of both sides. What is more important, however, the Soviets believe that in the event of a major war the possession of an effective and survivable nuclear force could potentially deter NATO from employing its own nuclear weapons to punish Soviet aggression through attacks on the Soviet homeland. The capability to deter such attacks by the threat of unacceptable retaliation represents a critically important function for Soviet strategic nuclear forces, a function that is unlikely to disappear in the 1990s. Equally important, the existence of secure and effective theater nuclear forces, and especially the threat to use such forces in an irrational manner, could deter an opponent from using his nuclear forces to deny achievement of the objectives of Soviet aggression. Consequently, the continued existence of such nuclear forces has a very real military utility in the sense that the intrawar deterrent inherent in such a capability could enable the Soviets to execute their concepts of a nonnuclear theater strategic operation unimpeded by NATO's nuclear attacks.

Soviet military planners are not content, however, simply to rely on threats of unacceptable retaliation to provide intrawar deterrence. Instead, they are likely to continue to focus upon provision of capabilities to support any of the various employment options open to Soviet decisionmakers: preemption; launch on tactical warning; or launch under attack, in addition to retaliation. In particular, Soviet attention to future strategic nuclear force developments centers upon improving the efficiency and effectiveness of these forces in scenarios of less than mass employment. Technological trends in the development of these forces would appear to support the achievement of these objectives. In particular, future nuclear systems should exhibit improved reaction times and greater accuracies in comparison with previous generations. The objective possibility of achieving dramatic improvements in accuracy should enable both sides to consider more discriminate use of these weapons. These trends are especially disconcerting in light of the fears of some Western observers that major cuts in strategic nuclear arsenals could leave the United States with a more destabilizing force posture than at anytime in the past. Consequently, at the nuclear level, it is not clear that the strategic environment will necessarily be less threatening in the 1990s.

The Soviets also anticipate that the combined effect of future technological developments will bring about fundamental changes in the character of combined-arms warfare. Generally, the Soviets believe that future warfare will continue to assume an increasing "land-air" character, as both sides expand capabilities and operations in the vertical dimension, not only to conduct deep-fire destruction but also to maneuver in depth. In this sense, it is unlikely that the Soviets would forgo their basic operational concept, which envisions the conduct of operations across the depth of enemy defenses. Acquisition of advanced capabilities enables the Soviets to execute this concept fully without the risk associated with reliance on nuclear systems either for deep targeting or to fulfill damage criteria. The Soviets seem to believe that this operational concept, which was validated in the Great Patriotic War and continued to retain its relevance through the revolution in military affairs, would continue to be the most appropriate concept for future war. What is likely to change and evolve is the character and complexity of future military operations, the methods by which the mission requirements of these operations would be fulfilled, and the structure and composition of military forces for the achievement of these missions.

A number of themes have surfaced with regularity in Soviet assessments of the impact of new technologies on future warfare. Soviet military theoreticians have come to believe that many of the analytic conclusions regarding the dynamism and tempo of nuclear warfare are increasingly applicable to conventional military operations. Consequently, Soviet analyses have focused increasingly on the potential impact of unprecedented attrition and disruption of control on the fulfillment of operational and strategic objectives, the increased "blurring" of the distinction between offensive and defensive means of combat, and the increasing scale of future military operations. The Soviets have reevaluated the factor of time and the role of surprise in modern warfare and are reconsidering many of their basic premises regarding the initial period of war. The two trends that appear particularly relevant to warfare in the 1990s are the increasing scale of military operations and the evolving offensive-defensive relationship.

By Soviet definition, the scale of military operations is determined not only by breadth and depth but also by the duration of such operations. By every indicator, Soviet military planners have concluded that the attributes of future nonnuclear systems might enable these forces to play an expanded role at not only tactical but also operational and even strategic depths. Few in the West have considered the global implications until recently; investigations at this level of warfare have continued to focus primarily on global nuclear conflict. Western specialists on Soviet military affairs have argued that Soviet interest in conventional warfare remains limited to peripheral theaters of military operation (TVDs) and have tended to discount any Soviet consideration of the strategic implications of new technologies.

On the latter point, it is evident that the primary Soviet strategic objectives would be sought in the theaters of military operation peripheral to the Soviet Union, since the central focus of any major East-West conflict is sure to be the Eurasian landmass. Consequently, the Soviets have long considered the potential strategic implications of prolonged conventional warfare. The trend clearly has been to develop forces and concepts to extend the conventional phase of a war as long as possible. It has become increasingly clear in recent years that Soviet military analysts have concluded that theater warfare could remain conventional throughout.

Beyond this conception, however, Soviet strategic planners have been considering the potential dimensions of conventional warfare conducted on a global scale for some time. Descriptions of future war in authoritative statements of Soviet military doctrine and military strategy have clearly indicated that while such a war would be global in scope and decisive in nature, it would not necessarily escalate to the use of nuclear weapons. By 1984 the Soviet General Staff had apparently concluded that the promise of these new technologies required a reevaluation of defense planning scenarios. In his 1984 interview, then Chief of the General Staff Ogarkov predicted that developments in conventional weaponry would permit "order of magnitude" increases in their destructive potential. What is more significant, however, as a result of the increasing range of these systems, the "zone of potential strategic military actions" would sharply increase as many of these systems become "global" in nature.

Ogarkov's prediction, which has been repeated in other sources, seems to be based on a set of planning assumptions that differs somewhat from those commonly employed in the West. Soviet spokesmen, such as Rear Services Chief of Staff Col. Gen. I. Golushko, have indicated particular concern over the potential vulnerability of logistics and resupply targets to precision-guided attacks, which could disrupt not only sustainability functions but also the overall capability to sustain Soviet operations and, consequently, the achievement of strategic objectives.[6] Although Soviet military scientists are probably doubtful of Soviet capability to fully execute this mode of warfare over the near term, a longer-term perspective that envisions widespread deployment of space-based reconnaissance and target location systems directly linked in real-time to long-range strike means might consider such a scenario more feasible. The Soviets apparently see no contradiction in the objective of extending the depth of conventional fire destruction throughout the theater and, eventually, into the strategic rear of the homelands.

Such a capability could also become especially important in the context of a prolonged war. With regard to this dimension of the scale of future military operations, the Soviets believe that they need to prepare for a prolonged conflict, whether this conflict is fought with nuclear or conventional weapons. They have explicitly stated their conclusion that a "future nuclear war will not be concluded rapidly," and Soviet preparations for this eventuality are generally recognized in the West. Although they hope to avoid protracted nuclear operations through a rapid and decisive nonnuclear victory, they also appreciate that the introduction of new conventional systems could reduce the likelihood of such an outcome. They believe that regardless of whether the war is fought with nuclear weapons or only conventional systems, such a war would be protracted because of the huge military and economic potentials of the opposing coalitions. The notion that the Soviets would only contemplate short-war, quick-victory scenarios also colors much of Western thinking on this subject. No one could deny that the Soviets would seek such an outcome, but the Soviets believe that it is naive to think that such an outcome would be easily achievable. Although the evidence is fragmentary, it appears that the Soviets are planning for a war of at least one year's duration.

Consequently, it would appear that the Soviet military is intent on proceeding with its plans to conduct nonnuclear strategic operations in the event of a future major East-West conflict. Soviet incentives to avoid global nuclear conflict seem sufficiently compelling to force Soviet military planners to consider prolonged conventional scenarios, despite the political risks associated with such scenarios, rather than rely on a quick victory achieved through the introduction of nuclear weapons. They have expanded their analytic attention to encompass worldwide non-nuclear operations extending over a period of possibly a year and beyond. The economic restructuring program would also seem to support the industrial and mobilizational requirements of such a prolonged-conflict scenario.

Closely related to the issue of increasing scale are evolving Soviet views on the future relationship between offense and defense. Soviet military theoreticians apparently have concluded that it has become necessary to reevaluate the mix of offensive and defensive activities in future operational planning. The trend was underway as early as 1960 but seems to have assumed increasing importance in the mid-1980s. Unfortunately, Soviet investigations of this issue have been obscured by the recent attempt to portray Soviet military strategy as nonprovoc-ative in order to fulfill the dictates of Soviet political strategy. This strategy has clearly been designed to reduce international tensions and provide sufficient breathing space for the Gorbachev restructuring pro-grams to take effect. Consequently, political leaders, civilian national security experts, and, to a lesser degree, military spokesmen have in-creasingly referred to a new Soviet military doctrine and military strategy that emphasizes the conduct of defensive-only military operations.

At the level of military theory, however, the introduction of high-accuracy systems, particularly given the depths to which these systems are capable of operating, has led Soviet and Warsaw Pact analysts to undertake "a complete reevaluation of the very essence of the defense on the future battlefield."[7] According to this analysis, defensive objec-tives were formerly achieved by actions conducted within the tactical zone designed to "pulverize" the enemy in a series of defensive battles. While enjoying the advantage of selecting the locale for the battle, the defender was forced to cede the more important advantage of the initiative to the attacker. The introduction of deep-strike, precision-guided weapons changes this calculation in several ways, however. First, the defender's strikes will not be limited simply to the tactical zone but may be conducted across the depth of the enemy's deployment. What is more significant, however, the opportunity would exist for the defender to seize the initiative himself rather than cede this all-important advantage to the attacker.

Attacks from the defense using high-technology weaponry could produce rapid and sharp changes in both the correlation of forces ("the weaker can suddenly become the stronger") and the overall situation. While the Soviets have long believed that such changes would characterize nuclear operations, they have come to realize that future deep-strike, precision-guided weapons would impart similar characteristics to nonnuclear operations. It may be this aspect, in particular, that underlies the Soviet view of the increasing similarity between nuclear and conventional operations and provides part of the foundation for Soviet forecasts of impending revolutionary transformations in the nature of future warfare.

This dimension of the Soviet forecast of the nature of future war has a number of potential implications for U.S. strategic planning. First, the Soviets obviously are fearful of the potential inherent in these systems to enable a defender to preempt an enemy's offensive preparations. For example, the Soviets have acknowledged the U.S. Army's AirLand Battle concept plans to achieve its defensive objectives through deep fire destruction not only against first-echelon forces but against the second echelon and reserves of the attacker, in addition to large-scale land and air maneuver. Over the longer term, the Soviets also anticipate air and missile attacks on Warsaw Pact airfields designed to disrupt sortie generation in support of the air operation. To the extent that the United States proceeds with the development and deployment of such systems, Soviet political leaders are likely to be deterred from consideration of military options to resolve East-West crises.

The second implication of Soviet conceptions of the nature of future war is a requirement to revisit the overall issue of defense within Soviet military planning. Soviet military scientists have become increasingly concerned that their military art was too preoccupied with offensive operations at the expense of a more balanced offensive-defensive mix. Reminders of the last such preoccupation with offense accompany many such Soviet analyses. The emergence of such a capability on the Western side has served to reinforce this trend in the Soviet Union. The military seems to believe that Soviet political decisionmakers might be far more cautious in the future and may not authorize the beginning of mobilization or the military preparations necessary to seize the initiative in the event of the outbreak of hostilities, in order not to trigger a defensive preemption by the United States and NATO. These conditions have led the Soviets to reconsider the potential advantages of a "premeditated strategic defense" similar to their Great Patriotic War experience at the battle of Kursk. In this event, Soviet forces deployed in Eastern Europe could play the role of covering forces to provide sufficient time for forces in the internal Soviet military districts to mobilize and begin strategic deployments. Given the potential impact of new high-technology nonnuclear systems, successful strategic defense operations could create more favorable conditions for a subsequent counteroffensive.

This concept may also be related to an additional dimension of the Soviet view of the changing strategic context. The Soviets, influenced by the above considerations, have also been rethinking many of their basic conclusions regarding the nature of the initial period of war and the role of surprise. Soviet military planners believe that they have been insufficiently sensitive to alternative contingencies for the outbreak of hostilities. Although there is little evidence that Soviet military scientists believe NATO would initiate offensive operations, the ongoing offense-defense reevaluation could force the Soviets to modify some longstanding principles. In particular, the preeminent Soviet objective during the threatening period and in the initial period would be to impose control over the course of events. Control is achieved by quick and decisive efforts to gain and hold the initiative over the enemy. As can be seen from the above, however, the Soviets may suspect that their ability to fulfill this objective may be in jeopardy. Moreover, officials such as General Gareyev have alluded to the impact of the imposition of political constraints on mobilization in crises and in the threatening period. Better integration of offensive and defensive efforts and the introduction of long-range systems with an effective doctrine for their deployment in defensive operations might offset the potentially disastrous effects anticipated in such scenarios.

CONCLUSIONS AND IMPLICATIONS

While there is a significant degree of continuity in the geopolitical and ideological interests that the United States will likely pursue in the 1990s, the nature of the strategic environment and thus the threats to the United States will be significantly different from those faced by policymakers in the 1980s. It may not be too bold to state that the early 1990s may eventually come to be regarded as a watershed period in the restructuring of the strategic environment in much the same way that we presently regard the period of the late 1940s.

Familiar issues will predominate the immediate future, with the principal military threat to vital U.S. interests emanating from the Soviet Union. However, political, economic, and scientific-technological trends seem to indicate that regional threats will emerge in importance. Political and economic instability are likely to result in regional conflicts detrimental to U.S. interests. The proliferation of sophisticated weapons systems in areas of vital importance to the United States could, at a minimum, impose drastically different operating procedures on U.S. forces charged with protecting national interests in those areas. In the event of a power projection requirement, U.S. military planners cannot automatically assume that American forces would encounter an unskilled, technologically unsophisticated opponent. Indeed, quite the opposite assumption will likely be more appropriate.

Finally, it is by no means clear that the Soviet Union will represent any less of a military threat to U.S. national security interests in the 1990s than it does today. First-order priority is being devoted to exactly those sectors of the Soviet economy critical to the support of modern military requirements. If the Soviet military is correct in its view of the benefits of economic restructuring, and those efforts succeed at some more than minimal level, the potential impact on the overall military correlation of forces could be enormous. If the Gorbachev political campaign succeeds at the same time in diminishing Western incentives to pursue admittedly costly technological initiatives, the effect of the Soviet modernization efforts will be compounded.

Moreover, the recent Soviet emphasis on defense could serve to reinforce the ambiguity associated with interpretation of Soviet intentions in the event of a major East-West conflict. A consistent emphasis on defensive restructuring and defensively oriented training and exercising could complicate Western intelligence assessments of Soviet military behavior in such situations. If the Soviets are correct in their conclusion that the distinctions between the means of offense and defense have been significantly diminished, it will become increasingly difficult to distinguish between offensive and defensive preparations. Such a determination would rest on a political assessment and judgment as to Soviet strategic intentions. It is exactly this process that will have been subjected to a Soviet diplomatic strategy intended to reduce and, if possible, erase the Western leadership's "enemy images" of the Soviet Union.

3

Nontraditional Challenges: Religion, Violence, and Change in the Third World

AUGUSTUS RICHARD NORTON

THE THROES OF CHANGE

Neither the United States nor its major rival has had great success in enforcing its will upon the independence-minded people of the Third World. The mere mention of Lebanon or Afghanistan underlines the fact that raw military power, though daunting to behold, may be only a symbol of impotence when it is intended to pummel Third World belligerents into submission. In both cases superpowers were thwarted by indigenous groups for whom Ibn Khaldun's *'assabiya,* or social solidarity, is a surer conceptual guide than the rationality of Max Weber. If these episodes are samples, the final decade of the twentieth century is likely to be a tough one for the United States, especially if policymakers continue to be ensnared by stereotypical and facile views of the Third World.

References to venerable Tunisian or German sociologists should not mislead the reader. The political forces that frustrated Soviet generals and American presidential advisers are by no means throwbacks to either the fourteenth or the twentieth century. Instead they are thoroughly up-to-date products of the global modernization syndrome, a process that put its stamp on the Third World even before it was called the Third World. One of the major features of this syndrome is the natural quest for self-determination and justice that finds expression in a number of forms, including the mobilization of political movements with religious symbolism and the employment of political violence and terrorism. In short, the United States now finds itself in contretemps with unfamiliar variants of modernity that policymakers failed to anticipate and are not attuned to cope with successfully.[1]

40

The Diffusion of Power

At the same time, the looming disappearance of the bipolar superpower-dominated security system will foster an increasingly unruly international regime in which Third World players may be prone to try to throw around their weight. As one scholar notes: "Accepting the fact of an international system fundamentally at sixes and sevens with itself—a division reinforced by the diffusion of organized violence—merely underlines the limits of military force and threats in promoting American values and interests."[2] In fact, the anarchic qualities of the international system have been exacerbated by the global dispersion of weapons (including nuclear and chemical weapons), the availability of sophisticated and lethal military technology through licensing arrangements, and the development of indigenous arms production capabilities, all of which serve to diffuse military power throughout the international system. As many as fifteen Third World armies possess ballistic missiles, and about ten more have active development programs. It cannot have passed unnoticed in military staffs around the world that the use of inaccurate SCUD missiles by Iraq against Iran's capital had a decisive effect upon Iran's willingness to accept U.N. Resolution 598, which shaped the successful cease-fire.

Persistent regional and internal conflicts, as well as the axiomatic dedication of military establishments to the protection of national sovereignty, will ensure that defense budgets will continue to consume a disproportionately large share of income in the Third World. Though the absolute military clout of the superpowers is unlikely to be seriously challenged in a full-scale war, many Third World countries now possess the means to thwart limited military operations, thereby rendering military solutions (i.e., intervention) less attractive and certainly more costly for the great powers.

The Third World Matters

Some policymakers and experts minimize the significance of the developing world for U.S. strategy, an odd thing to do considering that 100,000 American servicemen have died at the hands of Third World armies and irregular forces since 1945.[3] The Third World label is being used to subsume the developing countries of Africa, Asia, the Middle East, and Latin America, so many of the general observations offered here will be particularly inapplicable to the so-called newly industrializing countries of East Asia. Excluding these states, it is certainly true that even in combination the states of the Third World pale in economic significance next to Japan or Europe. However, this reductionist perspective fails on two levels: even putting aside compelling humanitarian arguments for an active strategy in the Third World, and economic comparisons notwithstanding, it begs common sense to presume that it is possible to ignore three-quarters of humanity. Third World problems will continue to intrude into the international system in the form of regional and internal conflicts and political violence. The United States will have to determine how it should respond to actions that may threaten the well-being of its citizens, as well as its economic and security interests. It may respond in a measured, carefully calculated way or spasmodically, but either way, it will have to respond.

Because conflict will not disappear in the waning years of the century, alliances with Third World partners will continue to be significant, and confronting inevitable violent challenges from the Third World will require some sensitivity among senior U.S. policymakers to the roots of discord. This requirement means that Washington is going to have to work harder to understand the social forces that give shape to politics. Of course, there is an alternative in the demonological perspectives so favored by terrorism "experts" and other entrepreneurs trading in unpopular variants of fanaticism, but these perspectives are likely to serve the United States as poorly in the 1990s as they did in the 1980s.

Change in the Third World: A Nontraditional Threat?

Third World political leaders confront rapidly increasing populations whose aggregate demands exceed or threaten to exceed governments' ability to deliver. The instability confronting the United States is an inevitable by-product of widespread social mobilization in the Third World. The United States will have to come to grips with the strategic implications of change and the increasing demands that will necessarily confront governments as a result of increasing access to education and the media of communications, as well as the impacts of sectorial economic changes and the increased mobility of people.

Demographic pressures exacerbate the impact of social and economic change. Throughout the world, but especially in the developing countries, the economically productive segment of the population is decreasing proportionately in comparison with the elderly as well as with the young. In the developed world the major trend has been toward a graying of society, in the sense that mean ages have increased and the proportion of the citizenry that is elderly is increasing. However, in most, if not all, developing countries the most significant effect has been on the other side of the chronological scale. Improvements in health care, infant mortality rates, and fecundity, accompanied by high birth rates, have led to explosive increases in the number of youths, so that in many Third World states half or more of the population is below the age of fifteen. Thus, in already difficult economic circumstances the proportion of that segment of the population which is particularly prone to recruitment for political activism is expanding quickly, thereby further complicating the task of government.[4] In many parts of the world, where progress was once at least a dream, the struggle now is to maintain what has been attained, to avoid regression.

The challenge facing the United States in the decade ahead is to decide how it is going to accommodate change, often disruptive change, in the developing world. The West no longer has all of the answers, not that it ever really did. Even if it did, it lacks the capacity to impose them. The important fact is that there is no deterministic or necessary connection between Third World political change and anti-Americanism. The question for the United States, then, is, Do these forces of change represent a threat to the national security of the United States?

Assessing the factors that contribute to change or instability in the Third World is at best a daunting task. The sources of political and economic change in the Third World are diverse and complex. The purpose of this chapter is to determine the extent to which these factors and the changes they may create should be considered threats to the interests of the United States. This assessment is conducted through the consideration of two of the most salient influences on Third World societies: religion and violence, specifically, terrorism. Should the religious movements influencing the developing world be considered hostile to U.S. notions of an acceptably stable international environment? Is terrorism a direct threat to U.S. interests that requires a substantial national response, or is it an endemic part of the forces of change in the Third World that need to be considered according to the specifics of each case?

This chapter considers the degree to which these two "nontraditional" influences in international affairs should be considered to be antithetical to the accomplishment of U.S. national interests. It is the contention here that these nontraditional influences are not inherently threatening to U.S. interests. However, they do not lend themselves to the conventional and comfortable conceptions of threat analysis that have attended the East-West debates of the post–World War II era; quite the reverse. Understanding the dimension of Third World political and economic activities requires a much more broadly based understanding of the factors involved and how they might affect U.S. interests and strategy than has heretofore been the case.

RELIGION AND POLITICS

Understanding Third World Politics

The American theory of pluralist democracy is not particularly useful for understanding politics in a non-U.S. setting.[5] Indeed, the competitive political party, the very epitome of democracy, is viewed suspiciously in some Third World settings. Islamic groups draw on a dogma that associates the political party with failed experiments in Western liberalism and view the party as a socially divisive political instrument. In Africa south of the Sahara, where one-party rule is more the rule than the exception, multiple parties are seen as an invitation for divisive tribal politics to emerge at the state level. Whereas pluralist theory argues that the basic units of politics are synthetic groups of shifting and overlapping membership, in much of the world the basic political units are social groupings of remarkable durability.

Third World politics are personalistic and intimate.[6] The informal group, not the political party or the interest group, is often the key political unit. Informal groups, defined by blood, ethnicity, or locality, are the locus for politics and patronage, as well as conspiracy. In oppressive settings the informal group is an ideal action set. It is hard to penetrate, and it is bonded by the most basic and enduring of ties.

Social mobilization does not push people away from the ties of family, lineage, and village but reinforces those ties. Even the presumed cauldron of modernity, the city, becomes an extension of the values of the countryside, and the engine of urbanization may be a misnomer; "ruralization" may be more apt. The stresses, strains, and crowding of the city revive, stimulate, and create new passions for real and artificial social identities.[7]

It needs to be emphasized that social identities are by no means fixed for all time; they are cultural constructions conditioned by the swerves and blows of history. It is extremely misleading to presume that man—whether in Cairo, Egypt, or Cairo, Illinois—carries within him a primordial nugget or essence that, when all of the pretenses of modernity are peeled away, somehow determines who he is really.

An apt example is the case of the Arab Shi'i Muslims, who have been encumbered with all sorts of unpleasant images in recent years. In fact, the Shi'a were not conscious of themselves as members of an overarching community of Shi'i Muslims until the recent decades, and even now there is by no means a unified sense of what it means to be a Shi'i Muslim, either in political or social terms. Identity is flexible and variable; it is hardly a permanent fact. As Hanna Batatu noted as recently as 1921: "Iraq's Shi'a did not constitute a closely knit body of people. Though sharing similar traits, they were split up, like the other inhabitants of Iraq, into numerous distinct, self-involved communities. In most instances, they did not identify themselves primarily as Shi'a. Their first and foremost loyalty was to the tribe and the clan."[8] The most far-reaching effect of the revolution in Iran nearly six decades later was that it gave the Shi'a a sense of themselves as part of a community that transcended provincial and national boundaries. Even so, the extent to which individual Shi'i Muslims in places such as Lebanon and Bahrain, not to mention Iraq, actively identified with their coreligionists in Iran has been much exaggerated.

This Iranian example is intended to imply that social mobilization in and of itself is directionless. It is political mobilization that mediates social mobilization, giving it direction and meaning. Thus, it matters a great deal that as men and women gain a sense of themselves as part of a larger or different community they do not leave behind the social institutions and ties that an earlier consensus of scholars predicted would be overwhelmed by modernity. In many of the developing countries, it is precisely those traditional institutions (temporal and sacred) which earlier were thought to be anachronisms that are challenging the secular modernizers.

The most precious resource of any regime is its legitimacy—that authority which rests on a cultural congeneracy of ruler and ruled.[9] Every government makes its claim for legitimacy in the form of a political formula justifying the rule of a monarch, a revolutionary class, or a popularly elected president. A political formula ceases to be compelling when the ruler or rulers, through neglect, incompetence, design, malfeasance, or happenstance, fail consistently or spectacularly to meet the cultural or material needs of citizens. When a government dissipates its legitimacy, it is naturally vulnerable to challenge. An example happened recently in Algeria, where the June 1990 electoral victory of the Islamic Salvation Front signified the transfer of legitimacy from the FLN (National Liberation Front), which for almost three decades had rested its legitimacy on its credentials as the revolutionary instrument with which Algeria gained its independence from France. But old glories don't fill empty stomachs; the transfer of power will follow naturally. The worldwide upsurge in religion owes less to renewed piety than to the fact that religious institutions offer a familiar and psychologically comfortable alternative to the status quo elites and their politics.

The Intersection of Religion and Politics

Religiopolitics, the intersection of religion and politics, is hardly the novel occurrence that headline writers and others would like us to believe.[10] Nor, despite the fact that some observers find the idea reassuring, are most religious activists driven to resist modernism or modernization.[11] Activists inspired by Islam, or Judaism, or Sikhism may seem to have emerged overnight, but the suddenness of their appearance has more to do with observers' inattention than to sporelike feats of growth. In much of the world, especially the Third or developing world, secularism has always been an *idée fixe* for Western-oriented intellectuals and visiting scholars. If, until rather recently, Western diplomats, journalists, and intellectuals exaggerated the appeal of secularism and underestimated the enduring significance of religion as a focal point for social identity, this view often only reflected their choice of company.

Religion has always been a focal point for social identity, and where politics are personalistic, informal, based on affinial or consanguineous ties, and local rather than national in their scope, it should not come as revelation that religion may define political behavior even if it does not organize it. As Ali Banuazizi notes, "Traditional ideologies seem to be at least as efficacious in articulating the demands of a movement for social change and in inducing collective action of a radical nature as any of their modern, secular counterparts."[12]

Whose Islam?

Unquestionably, the core symbol of Islamic fundamentalism is the late Ayatollah Khomeini, who won infamy in Western policy circles for fabricating an anti-American ideology, which, in turn, went some distance in justifying virulently anti-American acts of violence, such as the kidnappings in Lebanon and the broader wave of political violence that marked the Middle East from 1983 to 1986.

The potent ideology he developed could be aptly defined as neo-Shi'ism or revisionist Shi'ism in that it contains a number of innovations unfamiliar to classical Shi'ism, most especially the dogma of the *wilayat al-faqih* (the rule of the jurisconsult), whereby Khomeini's novel role qua ruling cleric was legitimated. It is a mistake to take Khomeini's neo-Shi'ism as a template or exemplar for fundamentalism, or even more self-deceptively, as indicative of Islam in general.

The omnipresence of Khomeini encouraged a simplified view of the Muslim world, one that takes inadequate account of the divisions between Muslims. In contrast to the tendency to think of Islam in terms of Sunni versus Shi'i, there are many ways to disaggregate Islam. Popular versus official variants of the religion are found throughout the *'ummah* (world community of Muslims); sufi (mystical) orders attract easily as many adherents as the so-called fundamentalist movements. Cultural distinctions are important, as in Java, where Islam is just one component in a syncretic religion. Natural history often decisively distinguishes one Muslim community from another, often along regional lines. And ethnic categories are notoriously important, as shown by the Arab-Persian divide between Iraq and Iran, as well as in Afghanistan.

In his vehement denunciation of the West, Khomeini was breaking ranks with some of the great thinkers of Islamic modernism—Muhammad 'Abduh chief among them—who went to lengths to link Islam and the West. Contemporary Muslim thinkers, more representative of majoritarian Islam than Khomeini, have emphasized ecumenical themes and have underlined the unity of Islam with both Christianity and Judaism. As Leonard Binder argues in *Islamic Liberalism,* Islam is not inherently anti-Western nor antiliberal.[13] Unfortunately, when the term *fundamentalism* is used in policy-making circles in Washington, it is usually intended to refer to Islamic fundamentalism, which, as if by definition, is taken to mean Muslim extremism. The basic mistake is thus made: a contemptible side effect of the revolution in Iran, an ephiphenomenon, is conflated with a range of religious and political behaviors that often have little to do with either Iran or extremism.

Revolutionary Greek Orthodoxy

The confluence of religion and politics is not new, nor is it unique to "exotic" religions such as Islam. Preindependence (prior to 1960) Cyprus illustrates some of the ways in which religious institutions and personalities, in this case the autocephalous Greek Orthodox Church, may effectively structure political action.[14] The Cypriot case is a rich example of a religious institution springing to the defense of a culture under challenge. Historically, the Greek Orthodox Church was marked by quietism and a decentralized authority structure. But under Ottoman rule the church emerged as the dominant social and, some would argue, economic institution on the island. As they did throughout the Levant, the Ottomans ruled through local religious authorities, so in Cyprus they recognized the authority of the church under the leadership of the ethnarch. The church buttressed its role by serving as the collector of taxes for the *muhassil* (Ottomon governor). The ethnarchy became the most authoritative and powerful institution on the island, and during the eighteenth century the ethnarch's power was said to rival that of the Turkish governor. The ethnarch served as the national leader and political spokesman for the Greek Cypriots.

Ottoman rule was replaced by British colonial rule following World War I. Unlike the Turks, the British were deeply committed to secularist norms and set out to undermine the church's authority. This policy, more than any other, fed the ardor of the Greek Cypriots for *enosis,* or union, with the mother of Hellenism, Greece. The Cypriot struggle against the British was an extraordinary one, since the declared goal was not independence. The movement toward *enosis* can be viewed primarily as the expression of a desire to reaffirm Greek Christian moral standards, which were being thwarted by British-sponsored secularism, as well as by the inexorable march of modernization.

The charismatic Archbishop Makarios was the very symbol of *enosis*. Bearded, berobed, and immensely popular, he used the trappings of his office with great skill. He had no political party; no political organization in the conventional sense. Historically, his role had been validated by the occupiers of his country, and major crises had erupted when the British attempted to limit his authority because they found it anachronistic and antimodern. Indeed, it was the organic connection between the church and the people that defined the identity of the majority of the Greek Cypriots. The hierarchical structure of the religious institution lent itself to directive control. Of course, described functionally, Archbishop Makarios seems a bit like a leading cleric in the Islamic Republic of Iran, but that rather makes the point.

The struggle against the British was pursued with bloody determination from 1955 to 1959, until in the Zurich agreement Great Britain agreed to the establishment of an independent Cyprus in 1960. Significantly, the campaign for *enosis* was reinitiated following independence and was only laid to rest following the disastrous events of 1974. In recent years, though the church remains a significant political force in the Cypriot republic, the death of Makarios in 1977 deprived it of a leader capable of mobilizing Greek Cypriots en masse, and the phase of intense religiopolitics has passed. Many Greek Cypriots reflect bitterly on that phase, which they evince as proof that clerics should stay out of politics.

It is instructive to note that the activism of the Greek Cypriots did not go unanswered by the minority Turkish Cypriot population, which responded to the radical proponents of *enosis* by creating their own organization, the Turk Mukavemet Teskilati (Turkish Defense Organization). This dialectical response has been mirrored again and again. The coptic response to Islamic militancy in Egypt is instructive.

Relevance for the United States

How are these examples relevant to the study of U.S. national strategy? Though policymakers sometimes seem loath to concede it, the goals of religious movements are sometimes, indeed often, not unlike the goals of secular interest groups and parties. So whether or not religious activism complements or contradicts U.S. policy interests needs to be decided on a case-by-case basis, not axiomatically. Populist religious movements often espouse social justice, if not democracy, and reject the staid religious institutions associated with the dominance of the state. The concept of *jahiliyya,* an Arabic word denoting the corruptness of the present government and society, plays a central role in the social critique by Islamic groups and is as much a critique of the religious establishment as of the secular authorities.

The resurgence of Islam is simply a manifestation of the changes that have marked the world, and especially the Third World, where the search for political meaning is especially poignant and relevant in a setting marked by repression, hunger, and injustice. The appeal of Liberation Theology—which has had a more geographically widespread impact than is commonly presumed—provides another example. For instance, Robert Bianchi notes that both Protestant and Catholic church groups in South Korea, influenced by the example of Liberation Theology, began to focus their campaigns for human rights on the struggling union movement during the late 1960s. This was in the context of more than a doubling of Christian adherents from some 4.5 million to about 10 million.[15]

The mixture of religion and politics in the developing world is not, and should not be perceived to be, inherently hostile to U.S. national interests. In fact, in many instances the integration of religion with politics promotes stability, such as in Saudi Arabia, for example. The real danger is that the pressures on Third World governments will not be easily met and that pandemonium will reign. It is by no means clear that the alternative should be either devalued or feared. Religious institutions may be the only force capable of holding some Third World societies together.

It is a simple fact that the energy of those involved in Islamic politics is principally directed, not at external policy issues, but at domestic power arrangements. Decidedly, the subject is not religion but politics. The issue is who rules and for what purpose. The unit being challenged is the state, not the West or the world. Iran's aspirations to speak for the 'ummah in opposition to the West should not be extrapolated to all religious activists, whether Islamic or not.

TERRORISM

It is often amazing to discover how little the world outside Washington is understood by the people in Washington who make decisions. The issue is not just knowing the name of a few countries in Africa, though it is always helpful to know a bit about geography, but appreciating the meaning of the changes taking place in the rest of the world. It is easy to think of the world in terms of good and evil, terrorists and victims, and to analyze it in terms of nonsense think-tank lingo such as "low-intensity conflict," a residual category subsuming an admixture of events that are most notable for their dissimilarity. Terrorism points up the problem.[16]

There can be little argument about the extent to which terrorism has continued to capture the attention of audiences and government officials around the globe, although terrorism is neither the most important nor the most dangerous problem facing civilized society. Terrorism both compels attention and inspires fear. As Raymond Aron wrote, its "lack of discrimination helps spread fear, for if no one in particular is a target, no one can be safe."[17]

The fact that terrorism, which physically touches very few people, has maintained its grip on the public's consciousness is a macabre tribute to the nature of the phenomenon. Indeed, it is easy to minimize the threat of terrorism, especially in contrast to risks more common in everyday life, such as traffic accidents, lightning, and even falls in the bathtub. Yet, terrorism does cut a wide emotional swath, even if the physical dangers are often more obvious than real.

For democracies, which are especially but by no means uniquely vulnerable, the risk of overreaction may be more dangerous than the threat itself. In this regard, the penchant of many "experts" to exaggerate and misconstrue the threat of terrorism is at best mischievous and at worst repugnant. Some of the writing on terrorism is more akin to special pleading and downright deception than dispassionate and objective analysis. Books and articles are filled with unsubstantiated claims that confound independent confirmation and play to public opinion rather than accuracy. Scholarly studies are not immune to this charge, and some of them are particularly egregious examples. The field seems to beg for exploitation, and one is sometimes prone to conclude that the entrepreneurs of terrorism studies are more numerous than the terrorists themselves.

Although there is no magic antidote to bad writing or muddled thinking on terrorism, there is much to be said for a clearheaded approach to the problem, especially if governments are to avoid falling in their own slippery language.

Defining Terrorism

Terrorism is a marvelous epithet with which to bludgeon or tar one's enemies. But the moral indictment is debased if it is used only to label acts of which we disapprove, while turning a blind eye to equally contemptible acts carried out by friends or allies for congenial goals.

Used in this way, it simply becomes a rubric for all forms of opposition violence.

The priests of the ten-second sound bite, in tacit alliance with policymakers impatient with details and analysis, have intoned "international terrorism" so frequently that sensible scholarship sometimes seems a mere heretical whisper. But like monolithic communism in the 1950s, the bugbear of "international terrorism" in the 1990s does not stand up well to close inspection. As many academics and government experts have long known, terrorism is not simply a cabalistic international phenomenon uniquely targeted against the free societies of the West. The phenomenon of terror-violence is not unique to the present era, nor is it practiced only by one's enemies. It is certainly not monopolized by a particular ethnic, ideological, or religious group. Moreover, terrorism is by no means a phenomenon that only emanates from the Third World.

Nineteenth-century examples notwithstanding, modern terrorists do not proudly don the label "terrorist." In fact, much of the writing by terrorists is precisely for the purpose of claiming that they are not the "real terrorists" and that what they are doing is therefore justified. But the tactic and the vocation of terrorism is unjustifiable not only on moral grounds but on practical grounds as well.

Terrorism is patently counterproductive. Rather than weakening the resolve of the target population, terrorists supply the argument—and all too often the methods—for their own eradication. The reaction in Europe and the United States to the downing of Pan Am 103 is illustrative. If nothing else, the destruction of Pan Am 103 has stiffened the resolve in many corners to catch the perpetrators and prevent a repeat performance.

Terrorism has a contagion effect. As Adam Roberts reminds us, legitimate counterterrorism campaigns all too often end literally as counterterrorism.[18] Terrorism breeds contempt for limits and inspires imitation. Consider the following pairings, each representing a case in which terrorism has inspired imitative acts of terrorism:

— Israeli Jew and Palestinian Arab

— Greek Cypriot and Turkish Cypriot

— Catholic and Protestant in Northern Ireland

Terrorism may be the product of popular struggles, but it is hardly a substitute for them. Indeed, all too often the use of terrorism stereotypes a community and inflicts heavy societal costs. Rather than enhancing international support for a community's claims, it corrodes sympathy and support. Consider the heavy moral baggage the Palestinian Arabs must carry as a result of past outrages. The Israeli view of the Palestine Liberation Organization (PLO) as a terrorist organization is not, as some Palestinians unfortunately still presume, merely a negotiating tactic or a negotiating scheme but the response of a population faced by attacks without moral limits. Conversely, the intifadah, a popular revolt with clear moral limits, has not yet erased the visceral fears of the Israeli public. (It is not too far afield to wonder how long it will take to erase the memory of the brutal Israeli response to the intifadah; these problems seem to come in pairs.)

For all of the justified indignation that terrorism arouses, it is altogether remarkable that the quest for a definition of terrorism has bedeviled diplomats and international lawyers. In fact, there is no internationally accepted definition of terrorism. The standard practice has been to proceed inductively, criminalizing specific acts such as air piracy, attacks on diplomats, or the theft of nuclear materials rather than attempting to define terrorism as an offense.

The perpetrators of abhorrent acts of violence appropriately earn opprobrium whether what they do is called terrorism or not. As the deluge of published pages on the subject testifies, no matter how precisely we strive to define terrorism, there is a zone of ambiguity where terrorism fades into political violence and warfare. This is why some observers even believe the term may be beyond repair. Some legal experts would prefer to drop the term entirely.[19] Often, conventional and adequately descriptive terms, such as *hijacking, kidnapping,* and *murder,* do suffice.

Yet, there is merit in solidifying a consensus on those acts of violence that are simply impermissible, but this will be impossible unless a parsimonious definition of terrorism is adopted. The central premise of this chapter is that there are some forms of terrorism that raise no arguments: they are morally obnoxious, pure and simple. The murder of innocents, the "tool of those who reject the norms and values of civilized people everywhere,"[20] is despicable by any humane standard, no matter what name is used to describe it, but it is precisely acts such as this that richly deserve to be labeled terrorism. Patent examples would include the anonymous car bomb exploded on a crowded shopping street in Beirut, random shooting in the Rome and Vienna airport departure lounges, the destruction of Pan Am 103, or wholesale slaughter of patients in a Mozambique hospital.

In fact, the problem with much of the commentary and thinking about terrorism is precisely that statesmen and scholars too readily accept the shopworn cliché that "one man's terrorist is another man's freedom fighter." If the term *terrorist* is used with the care and consistency urged here, one man's terrorist is simply another man's terrorist.

Even warfare has a framework of moral rules. Although these rules will necessarily fail to make warfare anything less than horrific, without them war would be even more horrendous. Noncombatant immunity is a basic principle of the laws of war. As a minimum standard, what is impermissible in war, specifically and especially the intentional targeting of civilians, should be impermissible outside of a war zone.

The clear delineation of an ethical boundary separating clearly objectionable forms of violence from other acts of violence is not only morally compelling but of practical utility as well, and as Stanley Hoffmann has noted, "Necessity is the mother of morality."[21] In a complex, increasingly intertwined world the minimal expectation must be that people can travel without fear of being blown up or raked by machine-gun fire.

There is little difficulty in agreeing on the protected status of civilian air transport, or civilian facilities at airports or rail stations, where the potential victims are literally innocents who have had the misfortune of stepping into harm's way. Hence, there is broad agreement in international law that acts such as skyjacking are in nearly all conceivable instances impermissible. Other clear-cut cases include attacks upon children, the elderly, and, usually, women. The intentional targeting of innocent noncombatant civilians—whether they are found in encampments, villages, towns, cities, or airports—is simply morally objectionable, and such wanton acts deserve universal condemnation.

Acts that one state denounces may be, and often are, justified by another. Some authorities stress the illegality of terrorism;[22] however, legality is a sticky point (and, unfortunately, often an irrelevant one in the international arena). Taken as a whole, the laws of a state may be morally commendable or morally reprehensible. To argue that an act is unlawful (a factual statement) is not the same as arguing that it is illegitimate (a normative conclusion). Paul Wilkinson distinguishes between those political systems in which the citizen may effectively voice his demands and those in which categories of citizens are disenfranchised. In the first category, political violence is both illegal and illegitimate, because the enfranchised citizen need not resort to violence to be heard and to enjoy the protection of the state. In contrast, in political systems in which the state is deaf to its citizens and residents, violence may be justifiable and legitimate even though it is deemed illegal.[23]

Although many "official" definitions have been proffered, one developed by the U.S. Department of State comes closest to capturing terrorism in most of its possible dimensions. The definition is particularly meritorious because it does not exclude states as sponsors or perpetrators of terrorism:

Terrorism is the threat or use of violence for political purposes by individuals or groups, whether acting for, or in opposition to, established governmental authority, when such actions are intended to influence a target group wider than the immediate victim or victims.[24]

The defect of the definition is that it does not clearly separate or delineate political violence from terrorism. In short, the very breadth and ambiguity of the definition ensures controversy, not consensus.

As defined above, terrorism may be employed in a variety of contexts, including widely sanctioned struggles, as well as regional conflicts. For instance, the right of a people to resist foreign occupation is widely, if somewhat erratically, upheld. Few observers outside the Soviet Union described the Afghan resistance fighters as terrorists, even though some of their attacks were decried as terrorism by the Soviets. So long as the Afghan mujaheddin directed their efforts against the Soviet presence in Afghanistan, right was literally on their side. By the same token, though agreement is less general, especially in the United States, the resistance by the Lebanese to the continuing Israeli occupation of a portion of southern Lebanon would be similarly sanctioned, despite Israel's penchant for describing those that attack its soldiers and client-militiamen as terrorists. However, when the Afghans or the Lebanese resistance forces broaden their campaigns to encompass protected categories of noncombatants, their actions tend to lose their privileged status. Whatever our politics, we can readily distinguish between attacks on soldiers occupying foreign lands and attacks on persons in universally accepted protected categories, such as children, or, more broadly, noncombatants.

Thus, in general, it makes more sense to concentrate on the moral legitimacy of the means than it does to concentrate on the technical legality of the ends. It is also sensible to attempt to focus on categories of objectionable acts that may be clearly distinguished from general political violence. Clearly, legal character notwithstanding, there is a big difference between an attack on a police station and an attack on a crowded shopping street.

Here the focus is upon the deliberate, unjustifiable, and random uses of violence for political ends against protected groups.[25] This is a functional and nonpolemical conception that has the merits of parsimony and universality. The perpetrators may be states, agents of states, or individuals acting independently. The qualifying condition is that in the eyes of the world their actions constitute uniquely abhorrent and morally objectionable attacks upon noncombatants.

Admittedly, the international system is biased in favor of the state (the alternative, at present, would be chaos), and states can often get away with heinous activities that nonstate actors would not even contemplate. But the fact that less can be done directly about the behavior of a state, particularly when it is acting within its own borders, by no means precludes a moral indictment, which often has more weight than might be presumed. Even, and perhaps especially, the most autocratic and ruthless governments are preoccupied by their image. Of course condemnation is a sword that can swing both ways. Thoughtful scholars such as Raymond Aron describe the Anglo-American carpet bombing of Germany in World War II as terrorism precisely because they were, by design, indiscriminate.

A sensible response to terrorism begins with the recognition that all states share an interest in protecting the political and social environment, just as the whole world shares an interest in preserving the quality of the physical environment. States that sponsor opprobrious violence usually disclaim their sponsorship, not just because of the risk of retaliation but to avoid censure. The weight of that censure must be increased.

CONCLUSIONS AND IMPLICATIONS

The terrorism example helps to underline the fact that global instruments are needed to deal with the political problems that lie ahead. Third World instability will not be mitigated by pummeling or squashing the forces of change. These forces have already exhibited striking resilience. Instead, it is imperative that the United States leave behind its cold war and realpolitik paradigm and begin to think in a global perspective. The scale of the problems demands nothing less.

This American "new thinking" about the Third World must be based on a realistic assessment of both interests and threats. The United States has legitimate and important interests throughout the Third World, interests whose protection will require innovative and insightful statecraft. The first step in protecting those interests is to recognize the inappropriateness of the traditional American outlook toward the Soviet Union.

For the foreseeable future, the Soviet Union will remain the major adversary of the United States simply because it is one of the two major military powers on earth, but there will be increasing opportunities for the Soviet Union and the United States to cooperate in the decade that lies ahead. The conflict in the Middle East is a major example, and terrorism is another. Both the superpowers stand to lose from a major confrontation in the Middle East, and both threaten to lose if the existing governments are changed into more hostile ones. The zero-sum-game thinking that has informed U.S. policy in the region must be put in the dustbin of anachronistic policies.

In fact, the vacuity of Soviet-centric policies is nowhere better illustrated than in the Middle East. For over four decades U.S. policy has been conditioned, not to say hobbled, by disproportionate concerns about the extension of Soviet influence in the region. Regional actors have exploited such concerns to their advantage, and they continue to do so with great adroitness. Arguably, it is only in the Gorbachev period that the Soviets have come forward with a coordinated and carefully conceived policy, accompanied, one must add, by an explicit desire to cooperate with the United States to dampen and solve regional disputes. Failing such cooperation, the tacit message is clear: the Soviets may finally become the formidable competitor that the United States has so long dreaded.

To be sure, U.S.-Soviet cooperation, if not collaboration, will not necessarily be welcomed by regional powers. Indeed, the very regional actors that have exploited the Soviet-American rivalry in the past will fear being exploited by any arrangement with even the scent of superpower condominium. But the problems of the region make cooperation compelling, especially for the United States. It is the novel task of the superpowers to take the lead in shaping a new pattern of behavior and to work assiduously to see that their exemplar gains universal acceptance.

For those of us living in the fortunate, profligate West, there may be an inclination to try and forget the Third World, as though it were an embarrassing romance. But the tasks that dog Third World governments—building coalescent societies, winning legitimacy, and meeting the basic needs of citizens—will not always respect borders, or be quietly resolved. In fact, it is a safe bet that the global agenda for the 1990s will be shaped largely by the imperative of responding to Third World crises.

The Decision-making Environment

4

The Political Economy of U.S. National Security Policy

AARON L. FRIEDBERG

Any effort to formulate an American national strategy for the 1990s and beyond will have to deal above all else with two critical questions: Do changes in economic conditions now require a major reassessment of U.S. foreign and defense policies? In particular, do economic factors now compel the United States to rewrite its alliance commitments and to withdraw a substantial portion of the military forces it presently has based overseas?

As the last decade of the twentieth century opens, an increasing number of observers seem to have reached the conclusion that the answer to these questions must be a resounding yes. The case for an economically driven retrenchment comes in two essential forms. Some analysts claim that in attempting to uphold its many overseas alliances and diplomatic commitments, the United States has been led into persistent and harmful fiscal imbalances. Others blame the extended strategic posture and unprecedentedly large defense budgets of the postwar period for disrupting the processes of investment and economic growth, thereby hindering the United States in its competition with the other, less heavily burdened industrialized countries.

The purpose of this chapter is to offer a systematic assessment of these two arguments and to consider their implications for the future of American national strategy. Have the large defense expenditures of the postwar period unbalanced America's finances and imperiled the nation's economic vitality? If so, what changes are likely to be required? If not, what are the sources of these misconceptions?

FISCAL IMBALANCES

The argument that U.S. global commitments are largely responsible for the fiscal imbalances of recent decades is made most clearly and force-

59

fully by David Calleo in *Beyond American Hegemony*. Calleo has long maintained that the existing structure of NATO is unnatural and, over the long run, unhealthy both for the United States and for its European allies.[1] Instead of an arrangement in which the United States bears the greatest share of the responsibility for Alliance defense, Calleo has consistently favored arrangements that would shift a larger portion of the burden onto the Europeans themselves. Calleo and others now conclude that a policy of "devolution" is not only desirable but essential if the United States wishes to preserve its own domestic health and to maintain the stability of the international economic system.

Although he bases his analysis primarily on a consideration of economic factors, Calleo actually begins with an important observation about the erosion in America's relative military power. After first toying with the idea of trying to match Soviet conventional power, American strategists in the early 1950s chose to rely instead on the clear U.S. advantage in nuclear weapons. If the Soviets dared to attack a U.S. ally, they should be met with crushing atomic and thermonuclear retaliation. Provided that the Soviets lacked any real capability for launching similar strikes on the United States, there was little reason to fear that they would ever initiate hostilities in the first place. As long as it retained its overwhelming nuclear superiority the United States could defend its allies (or at least deter attacks on them) without building large and expensive conventional forces. This policy of Massive Retaliation was, as Calleo puts it, a way of maintaining American "hegemony on the cheap."[2]

By the late 1950s, the Soviet Union was beginning to deploy forces capable of striking directly at the continental United States. As American invulnerability dwindled, so too did European confidence in the willingness of the United States to initiate nuclear war on their behalf. The shifting strategic balance seemed logically to push the burden of deterrence downwards onto the conventional forces of the United States and its allies. This was the reasoning adopted first by President Kennedy in the early 1960s and held to by successive administrations ever since.

Under Kennedy the United States began once again to expand its conventional forces while urging the Europeans to follow suit. This, in Calleo's account, is where the problems of the present really have their origin. With the exception of a brief period in the late sixties and early seventies, the last twenty-five years have been marked by a series of efforts by the United States to increase its conventional military power in order to compensate for a loss of strategic nuclear superiority. The problem is that compared with their nuclear counterparts, conventional forces are quite expensive. As a result, with the exception of the immediate post-Vietnam period, there has tended to be a strong upward pressure on American defense budgets. That pressure, combined with the increasing cost of government-funded social programs, has helped to create the deficits of the last three decades. Since 1961 federal outlays have been permitted to exceed revenues in every year except one (1969). This abandonment of the traditional principles of fiscal restraint was sanctioned first by a renewed faith in Keynesianism and then, in the 1980s, by the alluring assumptions of "supply-side economics."[3]

Most countries would be prevented from running indefinite budget deficits by the requirements of participating in the international economic system. Unless accompanied by tight monetary policy, deficit spending tends to be inflationary, and in an open world economy a state with a relatively high inflation rate will see money flow away from its national currency. As Calleo explains it, in most cases "the inflationary country suffers a balance-of-payments deficit and its currency begins to weaken against other currencies."[4]

In response to these pressures, an "ordinary" country would have to check inflation by balancing its budget or constricting its money supply. But America is no "ordinary" country. Thanks to its position at the center of the world financial system, the United States has been able to run a seemingly endless string of balance-of-payments deficits, paying with universally accepted dollars for the difference between what it takes from the rest of the world and what it provides.[5] Since the 1960s this situation has meant that the United States has been able to escape any external discipline on its increasingly unbalanced domestic fiscal policies. In doing so, however, the United States has caused serious economic problems for some of its most important allies and trading partners. In the 1960s and 1970s a combination of fiscal deficits and loose monetary policy meant that America was essentially exporting inflation (83–98). During the Reagan administration, continued deficits combined with tight money to produce relatively high real interest rates and a vast influx of foreign funds.[6] Once again, the dollar was propagating internationally the effects of American domestic fiscal irresponsibility.

The chain of causality that Calleo has identified may be summarized as follows: America's commitment to the defense of Europe leads to excessive defense spending, which contributes to persistent deficits, which encourage, in turn, international economic instability. The way to set things straight is to go to the source of the problem. The United States needs to cut deeply into its defense budget by significantly reducing its contribution to NATO. For starters the U.S. Army should disband five of the ten divisions it presently maintains for use in the European theater. Instead of five divisions on the Continent and five NATO-designated divisions in reserve at home, the Army should keep no more than three divisions on the ground in Europe and base the other two in the United States (165). Whatever gap this leaves in NATO's ground defenses can be made up by greater (and more closely coordinated) British, French, and German efforts. In addition to their expanded conventional role, the European powers will also have to field a more credible "indigenous deterrent" (169). This could take a variety of forms and might even include an independent German nuclear force (170).

Putting aside the question whether the changes Calleo proposes are either equitable (in terms of intra-alliance "burden sharing") or strategically desirable, are they, as he concludes, economically necessary? The crucial link in Calleo's causal chain is the second one, that connecting high defense spending with big budget deficits. If this link is strong, then the argument stands and the conclusions follow. If it is weak, then the situation may be more complex than it appears at first glance.

Budgetary outcomes are, of course, never the result of any one thing. They are instead a resultant of several sets of decisions taken simultaneously about expenditures, on the one hand, and appropriate levels of taxation, on the other. It therefore makes little sense to blame defense outlays alone for a particular deficit without reference to what was going on in other spending categories as well as on the revenue side of the budget ledger.

This said, it is clear that from the early 1960s to the late 1970s the connection between defense and deficits was extremely weak. While military outlays increased in absolute, current dollar terms, they did not grow nearly as quickly as did either total government spending or the economy as a whole. During this period defense actually fell as a percentage of total government outlays (from 50 percent in 1960 to 23 percent in 1980) and of gross national product (from slightly over 9 percent of GNP to 5 percent in the same twenty-year interval) (see figs. 1 and 2).

As defense went down in relative terms, from the mid-sixties onward nondefense spending rose dramatically. Between 1965 and 1980 nondefense expenditures (not including interest payments on the debt) increased from 50 percent of government outlays to 68 percent and from 9.5 percent of GNP to 17 percent. In the nondefense category, so-called entitlement programs (mostly Social Security, Medicare, pensions, and welfare) expanded most rapidly. Between 1965 and 1980 payments to individuals grew from 27 percent of total outlays to 47 percent and from 4.6 percent of GNP to 10 percent (see figs. 2 and 3).

While government expenditures on defense and nondefense programs together were increasing their share of GNP, federal tax revenues were holding more or less constant. Until the late seventies, budget receipts

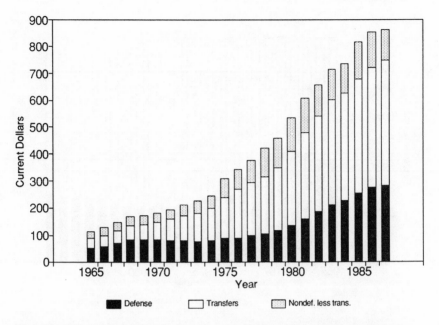

Figure 1. Government outlays by type: current dollars. Figures do not include net interest payments by the government. *Transfers* include items such as veterans benefits, Social Security benefits, Medicare, Medicaid, and Aid to Families with Dependent Children (AFDC). *Nondefense less transfers* includes government purchases of goods and services not directly used for national defense, such as roads, office buildings, and salaries for nondefense personnel.

Outlay figures for 1965–85 were taken from Tax Foundation, *Facts and Figures on Government Finance* (Washington, D.C., 1986). Outlays for 1986–87 were taken from Office of Management and Budget, *The United States Budget in Brief, Fiscal Year 1989* (Washington, D.C.: USGPO, 1989).

grew at the same rate as the economy and hovered at around 18 percent of GNP.[7] The product of all these trends was a series of increasing but still fairly minor annual budget deficits. Although they were generally bigger in absolute terms than those of the preceding decade, the deficits of the seventies were still comparatively small in relation to the size of the national economy, averaging only 1.7 percent of GNP each year.[8]

Except for Vietnam, the 1960s and 1970s marked the continuation of a larger historical tendency toward what one analyst has called the "waning of the warfare state" and the rise of an American "welfare state."[9] The general upward trend in budget deficits during this period was not the product of any one thing.[10] Spending of all sorts increased, and revenues did not keep pace. On the spending side, however, the expansion in social services played a far more significant part in un-

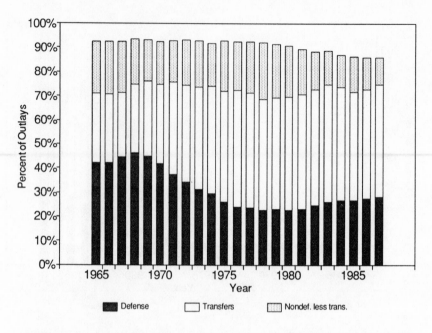

Figure 2. Government outlays by type: percentage of outlays. Figures do not include net interest payments by the government. *Transfers* include items such as veterans benefits, Social Security benefits, Medicare, Medicaid, and Aid to Families with Dependent Children (AFDC). *Nondefense less transfers* includes government purchases of goods and services not directly used for national defense, such as roads, office buildings, and salaries for nondefense personnel.

Outlay figures for 1965–85 were taken from *Facts and Figures on Government Finance*. Outlays for 1986–87 were taken from Office of Management and Budget, *United States Budget in Brief, Fiscal Year 1989.*

balancing the federal budget than did the much slower growth in defense outlays.

The connection between defense and deficits was far stronger during the 1980s than before, but once again, defense spending alone cannot be said to have caused the excess of expenditures over revenues. Under Ronald Reagan federal resources were shifted away from those non-defense programs that did not involve payments to individuals and toward defense and interest on the national debt. Between 1980 and 1987 defense increased its share of outlays (from 23 percent to 28 percent) and GNP (from 5 percent to 6.3 percent), while nondefense spending (less interest) fell from 68 percent of outlays to 58 percent and from 15.1 percent of GNP to 13.2 percent. Out of this total, transfer payments held steady (at around 47 percent of outlays and 10.5 percent

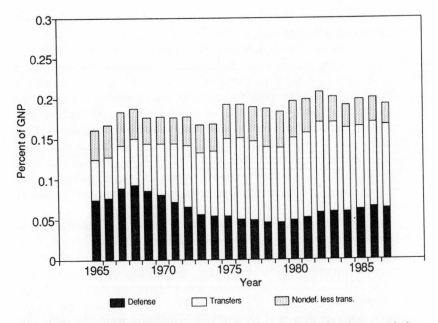

Figure 3. Government outlays by type: percentage of GNP. Figures do not include net interest payments by the government. *Transfers* include items such as veterans benefits, Social Security benefits, Medicare, Medicaid, and Aid to Families with Dependent Children (AFDC). *Nondefense less transfers* includes government purchases of goods and services not directly used for national defense, such as roads, office buildings, and salaries for nondefense personnel.

Outlay figures for 1965–85 were taken from *Facts and Figures on Government Finance*. Outlays for 1986–87 were taken from Office of Management and Budget, *United States Budget in Brief, Fiscal Year 1989*. GNP figures for 1965–82 can be found in U.S. Department of Commerce, Bureau of Economic Analysis, *National Income and Product Accounts, 1929–1983* (Washington, D.C.: USGPO, 1986); and for values thereafter, idem, *Survey of Current Business* (Washington, D.C.: USGPO, July 1986 and March 1988).

of GNP), and cuts were made in funding for such things as energy, education, community development, and public service employment.[11]

With no change in tax policy these shifts in expenditures might perhaps have produced substantial yearly budget surpluses.[12] Instead, in 1981 the Reagan administration chose to lower taxes, hoping in the process to stimulate economic growth and generate the revenues needed to make up any temporary gap between defense increases and nondefense cuts.[13] As is well known, a "supply side" dividend of the magnitude that had been predicted and presumably expected did not materialize. Tax receipts grew much less quickly than outlays, deficits skyrocketed, debt increased, and interest payments came to claim an increasing share of the national budget and of GNP.[14]

There is nothing about defense expenditures or even defense buildups that causes them inevitably to produce budget deficits. Imbalances result when governments are unable or unwilling to raise taxes or reduce other forms of spending sufficiently to pay for increased military outlays. Even a buildup as big and as fast as that of the early 1980s could conceivably have been carried out without producing massive fiscal imbalances.[15] If the Reagan administration had reduced taxes less or kept them constant, if it had accelerated defense spending more gradually or been more successful in slowing the growth of nondefense programs, it could have expanded U.S. military capabilities without increasing the size of the deficit.

The array of possible combinations of taxes and expenditures that might have permitted a fully financed buildup is virtually infinite. Similarly, the imbalances that now exist could, in theory, be brought down through a variety of differently mixed fiscal policies.[16] Making deep defense cuts would certainly be one way of approaching the problem. Given the magnitude of the present gap between revenues and expenditures, however, it is unlikely that such reductions would be sufficient, in and of themselves, to bring the federal budget more fully into balance. According to Congressional Budget Office projections, the deficit could remain at around $150 billion per year into the early 1990s.[17] According to some estimates, a 50 percent cut in U.S. ground forces in NATO would save $67 billion in annual expenditures.[18] As radical as it may seem at first glance, Calleo's proposal is therefore quite literally something less than a halfway measure.

Mere "devolution" will not be sufficient to get rid of the deficit; on the other hand, major changes in military strategy may not be necessary in order to achieve substantial savings on the defense budget. Simply by slowing the rate of growth in annual expenditures from 3 percent to 2 percent, for example, the Defense Department could trim an average of $40 billion annually from previously programmed spending.[19] Some civilian analysts have proposed even larger cuts.[20] Whatever the risks involved in trying to maintain existing commitments at a lower level of defense effort, a rational strategic planning process would have to weigh them against the possible dangers of a substantial pullback from America's present world position.

Unless the United States gets out of NATO altogether and cuts its military budget in half, dissolving the deficit will probably require some mix of tax increases and reductions in nondefense as well as defense expenditures. There is certainly no shortage of ways in which the federal government could enhance revenues, whether by "soaking the rich" and taxing "sinners," or by creating a new nationwide consumption tax, or by imposing charges for energy use and environmental pollution.[21] Some of these measures might even have economic and broader societal benefits, whatever their impact on the government's fiscal well-being.

Along with cuts in defense and increases in taxes, civilian spending could also be reduced in a variety of ways. Following the precedent set during the Reagan years, an administration might choose to slice even more deeply into nondefense, non-entitlement programs (the so-called discretionary items that make up around 16 percent of federal outlays). Further savings could also be obtained by restricting the costs of government operations.[22] Alternatively, President Bush or his successors could try to change the structure of entitlement programs that has been built up over the past thirty years. According to one recent estimate, fully 85 percent of the benefits from those programs are now provided on a "non-means-tested basis"; in other words, they are paid out to individuals regardless of their income.[23] The federal government undoubtedly could save a great deal of money if it provided less to those who are already relatively well off.[24] Controlling the rate at which benefits increase (rather than, as under present law, requiring that they rise automatically with the consumer price index) would also serve to slow the growth in social spending, and it could be argued that such changes would impose relatively little hardship on any individual recipient.[25]

In terms of simple bookkeeping arithmetic there is obviously no unique solution to the deficit problem. Whether the best way to proceed would be by cutting spending (on either defense or nondefense items or both) or increasing taxes or some combination of the two is a matter of societal choice; it is a political issue rather than a purely economic one.

Whatever their merits or drawbacks, none of the alternative measures mentioned above is so far-fetched as to be inconceivable. In any case, if the fiscal gap is to be narrowed in the years ahead, some changes in taxes and civilian spending are likely, with or without substantial shifts in foreign and defense policy. A major struggle over priorities is therefore quite probable. How that struggle is resolved will depend, among other things, on the coalition-building skill of the president, the balance of power in Congress, the influence of the various groups whose interests are inevitably affected by any major change in government fiscal policy, and the impact of unforeseen and unpredictable international events.

An American pullback from Europe may be strategically feasible; it may even be desirable as the perception of the Soviet threat in Europe wanes in the aftermath of the collapse of communist governments in

Eastern Europe. But it is not essential for financial reasons. The United States can put its budgetary house in order without drastic reductions in defense spending, and it may even be able to do so without radical tax increases or extensive cuts in existing social programs. Solvency and world power are not necessarily incompatible.

LONG-TERM EROSION

Even if America's present geopolitical posture can be maintained without harmful fiscal imbalance, it may be that doing so will still cause the country long-term damage. Over a sufficiently protracted period of time, pouring money into defense may weaken the U.S. economy and further erode America's international competitive position even if, year by year, it does not derange the nation's finances. That, at least, is the contention of Paul Kennedy's important and much-discussed book, *The Rise and Fall of the Great Powers.*

Stripped of its rich historical flesh, the skeleton of Kennedy's argument is actually quite simple. Looking back over almost five hundred years of history, Kennedy perceives a recurrent two-step process, driven forward ceaselessly by the engine of uneven economic growth.[26] During any given period, the dominant units of social organization (nation-states in the modern era) have increased their wealth at unequal rates, with some expanding more rapidly than others. This pattern of differential growth is a result of the fact that periodic "technological and organizational breakthroughs" tend to "bring a greater advantage to one society than to another."[27]

Although the correlation has not always been exact or immediate, states that have grown wealthier than their competitors have also tended, over time, to become more powerful in military terms. The reasons for this increase in military power are easy to see. As Kennedy explains it: "Once their productive capacity was enhanced, countries would normally find it easier to sustain the burden of paying for large-scale armaments in peacetime and maintaining and supplying large armies and fleets in wartime" (xvi). Given that "wealth is usually needed to underpin military power" (xvi), it seems obvious that the more wealth a country has in relation to its neighbors, the greater its potential for obtaining military advantage over them.

Historically, the wealthiest and strongest states have tended to expand their political influence. The superior military might that these countries can generate gives them the capacity to conquer and colonize "peripheral" areas (as Spain, the Netherlands, France, and Great Britain all did in their time) and to defeat other major powers (as the United States has done in the twentieth century). Riding the wave of economic development, one state after another has risen to "great power" status. But rising is only half of the story. The ascent of any given country, no matter how powerful it may be at its peak, does not bring the process of economic progress to a close. The same forces that, for a time, work to the advantage of one state compared with all the others rarely will continue to do so for very long. Countries that are left behind during one cycle of development and growth may be able to reassert themselves and perhaps even to pull ahead in subsequent phases. In time the biggest, fastest-growing states will have their chance to become the world's leading military powers.

Historians, economists, and political scientists have long noted the crucial role of wealth in promoting the accumulation of military power.[28] In explaining the decline of the mighty, however, Kennedy postulates the existence of a less commonly recognized mechanism. As they grow richer and stronger, states typically acquire interests and commitments beyond their own borders. These may take a variety of forms ("dependence on foreign markets and raw materials, military alliances, perhaps bases and colonies"),[29] and at first they may be relatively easy for a rapidly growing country to defend. With shifts in the locus of economic leadership, however, this happy coincidence of capabilities and commitments is unlikely to last. As Kennedy describes the beginning of this next historical stage: "Other, rival Powers are now economically expanding at a faster rate, and wish in their turn to extend their influence abroad" (xxiii). As this happens, the dominant state will find itself feeling increasingly vulnerable. In order to defend its home territory and, even more urgently, its external interests, the world leader will have to undertake larger and more costly defensive efforts. Ironically, these exertions may actually weaken a country rather than make it stronger and more secure. As more is spent on defense, the once-dominant power's rate of overall economic growth will slow even further, thereby accelerating the process of relative decline and worsening the country's strategic problems. According to Kennedy: "If too large a proportion of the state's resources is diverted from wealth creation and allocated instead to military purposes, then that is likely to lead to a weakening of national power over the longer term" (xvi).

In Kennedy's view the United States has recently entered the second, downward portion of its trajectory as a "great power." By the beginning of the twentieth century the United States had surpassed all other states in such measures of economic capability as steel production and energy consumption (200–202). On the eve of World War I, Americans were enjoying a per capita income greater than that of any other industrialized state (243). Still, despite its crucial role in determining the outcome of that conflict (271), for domestic political reasons the United States remained a latent, or "offstage," superpower (320), reluctant to play the military and political role to which it was entitled by its economic prowess.

Only the colossal upheaval of World War II proved sufficient to draw America permanently onto the global stage. Emerging in 1945 with enormous economic and military advantages over all possible rivals, the United States began finally to follow a course that, as Kennedy puts it, "could come as no surprise to those familiar with the history of international politics. With the traditional great powers fading away, it steadily moved into the vacuum which their going created; having become number one, it could no longer contain itself within its own shores, or even its own hemisphere" (359).

Whether the United States jumped or was pulled into its new role matters little. Within a very brief period the country had abandoned its isolationist traditions and acquired a vast assortment of overseas interests and outposts (389–90). These were easy enough to defend at first, but soon the United States began to encounter problems similar to those of all previous "number one" nations. As the Soviet Union and the countries of Europe and Asia recovered from World War II, America's economic edge began to dwindle. Yet, from the early 1950s onwards the nation's overseas commitments remained largely unchanged.

By the 1970s the United States was beginning to find itself increasingly in a situation of "imperial overstretch" or "strategical overextension" (515). Given the scope of its responsibilities, the persistence of the Soviet Union as a major military power (although one that is itself faced with severe economic problems), and the rising costs of weapons systems, the United States has been forced to spend considerable sums on defense (515–23). At the same time, the massive American economic lead of the 1940s and 1950s has been eaten away at a very rapid rate. As a result, the U.S. capacity to carry all its assorted burdens is "obviously less than it was several decades ago" (529).

In Kennedy's view the United States is now caught on the horns of a familiar dilemma. If it reduces military spending, it will wind up "feeling vulnerable everywhere." If it attempts to sustain "a very heavy investment in armaments," it can buy greater security in the short run, but in the process it may "so erode the commercial competitiveness of the American economy that the nation will be less secure in the long term" (532–33). Although Kennedy does not spell them out in detail, the implications of all this for American foreign policy seem clear enough. The United States cannot preserve its existing strategic position, nor can it completely reverse the relative erosion in its power. The best that can be hoped for is that American statesmen will "manage" that

erosion so that it "takes place slowly and smoothly, and is not accelerated by policies which bring merely short-term advantage but longer-
term disadvantage" (534). Kennedy does not say so, but the successful
"management" of relative decline would appear to require a withdrawal
by the United States from all or some of its present commitments and
a redirection of the resulting savings from military expenditure to civilian
investment. Only in this way can the country hope to hold onto even
its "natural" share of the world's wealth and power, which should
probably be "16 or 18 percent" as compared with the 40 percent it
had acquired by 1945 (533).

At the heart of Kennedy's general argument—one that he seeks to
make not only about the United States but also about the great powers
of the past—is the question whether and under what conditions defense
spending may inhibit economic growth. This question is, as Kennedy
notes, "a highly controversial one . . . and the evidence does not point
simply in one direction" (531–32). Indeed, according to a recent survey,
"The literature offers no clear and simple answer to the question: Does
defense spending have an impact on economic performance?"[30]

The relationship between defense and growth may depend in part
on a state's level of economic development. Although their views are
controversial, some analysts believe that less developed countries need
not suffer and can actually benefit from high levels of military spending.[31] In the short term, at least, the impact of defense expenditures is
also a function of domestic economic conditions.[32] An identical expansion in military budgets could stimulate a flagging economy or
produce inflation in one already operating at close to full capacity.[33]
Using various statistical techniques, a number of researchers claim to
have found a correlation over the long run between large military budgets and low levels of investment or economic growth, but the validity
of these results has been questioned by other analysts.[34]

Kennedy is interested, of course, not in all countries under all conditions, but in great powers and especially those that have entered into
a period of economic decline. On the crucial question concerning what
part military expenditures may play in bringing on that decline, Kennedy
is somewhat vague. At some points he seems to suggest that the difficulties produced by defense spending are simply a function of time and
level of effort. Thus he maintains that "the historical record suggests
that if a particular nation is allocating over the long term more than
10 percent (and in some cases—when it is structurally weak—more that
5 percent) of GNP to armaments, that is likely to limit its growth rate."[35]
More typically, he argues that defense becomes a problem only during
certain phases of a great power's development, particularly when it has
already begun to experience some erosion in its relative economic and

military power. At that point, what he calls "excessive arms spending" or a "top-heavy military establishment" (made necessary by strategic overextension, which, in turn, was made possible by an earlier, relatively rapid accumulation of national wealth) "will hurt economic growth" or "may slow down the rate of economic growth" (444–45).

In the end, Kennedy's reflections on the relationship between defense spending and decline come down to a simple and seemingly incontestable observation: once a leading power has begun to slip economically, for whatever reason, it will find it increasingly difficult to sustain large (still less, rising) defense burdens. As Kennedy explains it, declining powers are like aging people: "If they spend too much on armaments—or, more usually, upon maintaining at growing cost the military obligations they had assumed in a previous period—they are likely to overstrain themselves, like an old man attempting to work beyond his natural strength" (540).

It may not be possible, at this point, to make any more powerful, universal generalizations about the economic impact of defense spending. Nevertheless, it may be that the effects of such spending can be determined with precision in particular cases. For the United States, the questions are both empirical and theoretical: First, have the substantial peacetime military expenditures that the United States has undertaken since 1945 caused (or at least substantially contributed to) its relative economic decline? Second, if continued, will those expenditures inevitably cause further erosion in the U.S. position?[36]

Although their significance has been contested, the raw facts of American decline are by now widely accepted.[37] The U.S. share of gross world product, world trade, and production of industrial manufactured goods has diminished substantially since the end of World War II.[38] This alone, of course, is not evidence that there is anything wrong with the American economy. In 1945, with the rest of the world in ruins, the United States enjoyed an unnaturally large advantage over all other countries. As the world recovered, the American margin was bound to shrink, and, indeed, that very recovery was a principal aim of postwar U.S. policy.[39]

"The real question," as Kennedy explains, is not " 'Did the United States have to decline relatively?' but 'Did it have to decline so fast?' " and, he might have added, will it continue to decline so rapidly in the future?[40] There were surely good reasons to expect that in the initial postwar era the American economy would grow more slowly than those of its recovering rivals and that the United States would therefore lose part of its initial, overall advantage. What is disturbing from the American point of view is that in some cases the difference in growth rates persisted long after the war was over. Throughout the sixties, seventies, and into the eighties U.S. GNP, GNP per capita, and manufacturing productivity all grew far more slowly than those of Japan. Compared with the performance of the European countries, American performance was more mixed, with the United States regaining some advantages by the seventies and eighties.[41]

Three different arguments are made in support of the contention that America's comparatively unimpressive postwar economic performance was due to its relatively high level of defense expenditures. Each of these assertions centers on the alleged impact of defense spending on investment. The first argument, or as economist Lester Thurow describes it, the "quantitative" version of the argument, is simply that military expenditures "crowd out" private investment.[42] This claim follows from an examination of the national income identity in which a state's GNP is defined as equal to the combined value of its private consumption, private investment, total government spending (including both defense and nondefense expenditures), and net exports.[43] Clearly, for a given level of national income, if one of these categories goes up, then some or all of the others will have to come down. Assuming for a moment that consumption, nondefense government spending, and net exports are fixed, if defense spending increases, then investment must decline. But because investment is the engine of future economic growth, as it diminishes, so too will the rate at which national income expands. Under certain conditions, therefore, high levels of defense spending may lead to slower growth.

Even in the abstract this connection is obviously not simple or direct. Increasing military expenditures will not lead automatically to diminished investment if, for example, private consumption falls or government spending on nondefense items is reduced by an equivalent amount. On the other hand, cutbacks in military spending will not necessarily promote more rapid economic growth. Reductions in one form of government spending might be made up by increases in the other variety or, perhaps, by an upsurge in private consumption. In either case, there would be little or no increase in private investment and, assuming for the moment that government spending cannot act as a form of investment, little acceleration in the rate of overall economic expansion.

Since the end of World War II the United States has spent relatively more on defense than its major allies.[44] During the same period the portion of American national income devoted to investment has also been comparatively low.[45] To conclude that the first fact is uniquely responsible for the second would be to overlook another crucial piece of the equation. In postwar America both military spending *and* private consumption have been relatively high.[46] Instead of asserting, as Thurow does, that the United States has "essentially taken defense out of investment ever since World War II," it would be more reasonable to say that if investment has suffered, it has been at the expense of both defense and private consumption combined.[47]

If levels of consumption had been lower in the past, the United States could have sustained higher levels of investment along with actual rates of defense expenditure. Looking to the future, increases in the level of private investment could be achieved through cuts in the share of national income devoted to defense or nondefense government programs or by reductions in the levels of private consumption.[48] Such shifts in the flow of national resources could be encouraged by cutbacks in government spending or changes in the tax laws intended to discourage consumption and promote savings and investment or by some combination of the two.[49] In any case, claims to the contrary notwithstanding, there is no ironcast tradeoff between defense and investment. As economist Charles Schultze has pointed out: "There is no reason in principle why we cannot design the taxes needed to support defense spending so as to depress consumption rather than investment. If we do otherwise, the resulting fall in investment is our own choice and not something inherent in defense spending."[50]

Even if a "quantitative" investment problem can be avoided, there may still be a second, "qualitative" one. Despite descriptions of defense spending as just another form of consumption, the military actually invests billions of dollars each year in research and development.[51] This work, like its counterpart in civilian industry, requires the efforts of highly skilled scientists and engineers. If there were only a fixed number of such people in the United States, and if, for whatever reason, they preferred involvement in military over civil programs, then commercial research could possibly suffer, and along with it the entire economy. This, according to Lester Thurow, is precisely what has happened throughout much of the postwar period. "The best and the brightest among America's engineering and science prospects tend to enter military R&D," he claims, because "it is simply more fun." In this way, "the large U.S. military establishment handicaps future civilian economic success."[52]

Despite such assertions there is little evidence of a past military "brain drain."[53] Far from being fixed, the number of scientists and engineers has actually grown considerably since the 1960s.[54] The fraction of the total involved either directly or indirectly in defense work is a matter of definition and a subject of debate. A recent survey suggests, however, that the percentage has actually declined significantly during the seventies and eighties.[55] The same study also found no indication of a shortage in scientists and engineers, even at the peak of the Reagan buildup, and no evidence that the "best and the brightest" were being drawn from civilian to defense work, whether by higher salaries or the promise of greater intellectual stimulation.[56] In fact, judging by some recent studies, it is government, not industry, that is now most concerned about attracting first-rate technical personnel, thanks largely to limits on salaries imposed by the civil service pay system.[57]

Assuming that a shortage of talented labor for nondefense projects did exist, reducing the military budget would not be the only way to deal with the problem. Instead of cutting defense R&D (thereby freeing researchers to take on work in the civilian sector that is now presumably going undone), the federal government might try to further expand the total skilled manpower pool by providing more support for education and technical training.[58] Increasing the supply of scientists and engineers could make it possible for more defense and nondefense research to be done in the United States.

The third variant of the argument linking defense, investment, and growth centers on "spinoffs" and "tradeoffs." Since the end of World War II, the U.S. government has spent a great deal of money on R&D. In 1987 federal R&D expenditures were around $60 billion, roughly half the combined national total of government and private-sector spending on research.[59] Of this sum, fully 69% went to defense-related projects, 18% more than in 1977.[60] Some observers believe that whatever their impact on American military strength, these expenditures produce little of value for the economy as a whole.[61] If money from defense were transferred to civilian R&D, it is claimed, the results would be enhanced productivity, greater competitiveness, and faster economic growth.

The question of how much "spins off," "spills over," or "trickles down" from military R&D to civilian industry is a contentious one. Even many skeptics acknowledge, however, that defense-related research often has produced indirect and sometimes unintended commercial benefits.[62] If the federal government were to eliminate spending for defense research, and if the funds freed up as a result did not find their way into other forms of R&D, the net impact on the U.S. economy would probably be negative. On the other hand, there is little reason to think that spending on military R&D is the most efficient way of promoting progress in nondefense sectors. In the words of one noted authority on science policy, "If economic spin-off is what is desired, it is better to stimulate it directly than to try to derive it indirectly from military spending."[63]

Even if government-funded defense research produced no spinoffs at all, it would not necessarily be doing any harm to the economy as a whole. The real concern about military R&D is, therefore, that it has opportunity costs, that it must somehow be displacing either nongovernment research on civilian projects or government-funded nondefense research or both. As has already been discussed, defense R&D could conceivably cut into the civilian sector by drawing away skilled manpower and driving up research costs. Although there appears to be little direct evidence, it is possible that this may have happened in the past and that if the government had supported less military research, more work would have been done by industry on civilian applications.

It is also at least conceivable that if the federal government had spent less over the years on defense R&D, it could have devoted more funds directly to work with purely civilian applications. Given the pressures of the strategic competition with the Soviet Union and the traditional American aversion to central planning and government economic intervention, such a shift in priorities was probably not very likely. Similar, although possibly less stringent, constraints will no doubt continue to apply for some time to come.[64] A one-for-one transfer of defense R&D dollars to carefully chosen, government sponsored projects aimed at commercial innovation might well have a beneficial impact on American economic performance. But any sharp move in this direction would certainly arouse concerns and political opposition on both national security and economic grounds.

Without necessarily either cutting defense R&D or adopting a full-fledged national "industrial policy" aimed at picking commercial "winners and losers," the federal government could spend more on supporting basic science and on promoting certain research projects intended to have widespread and immediate civilian application. In addition to whatever it did directly in these areas, the government might also take steps designed to encourage private industry to invest more heavily in its own R&D programs.[65] Finally, assuming that some military research continues into the foreseeable future, that work might be conducted in ways aimed at maximizing civilian "spinoffs."[66] The question whether in the past such "spinoffs" have, on balance, outweighed the likely opportunity costs of government-sponsored defense research must remain an open one. Regardless of the answer, however, there are no grounds for asserting that such research must inevitably be a net drain on the economy.

In conclusion, it seems clear that general assertions about the relationship between military expenditures and economic decline (and general theories built on that supposed connection) must be approached with considerable caution. The suggestion that persistent, high levels of defense spending can do a country serious economic damage is probably correct. The crucial question, however, is, How much is too much? On this issue the economic evidence is inconclusive.

In the American case, large peacetime defense expenditures, combined with a range of other factors (including relatively high levels of consumption and, perhaps, an inadequate supply of skilled scientific manpower and insufficient spending on civilian R&D), may have helped to retard and distort postwar economic growth. It also seems quite likely that things having little or nothing to do with defense have had an equal and probably a far greater role in shaping the events of the past four decades.[67] Military expenditures alone did not cause that portion of America's relative decline which may have been, in some sense, avoidable. And defense cuts by themselves cannot be expected to produce dramatic improvements in future U.S. economic performance.

Even if the United States hindered itself in the past by spending between 5 percent and 10 percent of its GNP on defense, it does not follow that attempts to continue a similar level of effort would lead inescapably to equivalent harm. If the federal government were to adopt policies aimed at promoting savings, productive investment, education, and scientific research, there is no reason why such defense budgets could not be combined with rising productivity, steadier growth, and enhanced international competitiveness.

CONCLUSIONS

The argument presented here can be stated concisely: the United States can continue to spend from 5 percent to 10 percent of its GNP on defense without unbalancing its finances or hastening its relative economic decline. Doing so will, however, have costs, some of which the nation's citizens have been reluctant to pay in the past. These may include higher taxes, lower levels of private consumption, and proportionately smaller quantities of government spending on nondefense programs. All of these changes will involve some measure of pain, and that pain will not, in all likelihood, be felt equally by all groups in society. As a result, the formulation of anything resembling a coherent national strategy—one in which the military, diplomatic, and economic elements are successfully integrated—will involve a great deal of debate and contention. Indeed, the obstacles to such a strategy have much more to do with politics than they do with economics. Agreed action will require something approaching a consensus concerning both what kind of society Americans desire at home and what role they believe their country should play in the world.

Because of the considerable costs, there is every reason to want to restrict military expenditures to the lowest possible level. Even if the United States can spend, let us say, 6 percent of its national income on defense, it is important to ask whether such spending is actually necessary. This is a question of strategic judgment and so lies outside the scope of this chapter. Nevertheless, because claims that the United States is not now living within its means are usually followed by proposed solutions, a few brief remarks are in order.

Many of the present advocates of retrenchment agree with the widely accepted view that the Soviet Union has, in the past, posed a real threat to the security of the United States and its allies. Earlier American exertions intended to deter attack or to defend against it if it came were, it is generally agreed, neither foolish nor malicious. The point is simply that for economic reasons, those exertions have become too burdensome. Two escapes from this dilemma have recently been proposed, the first centered on the Soviet Union and the second on America's overseas allies.

Whatever has been true in the past, it is sometimes argued, thanks to the initiatives of Mikhail Gorbachev, the United States may now be in a position to dissolve its longstanding differences with the Soviet Union and bring the cold war to a final, happy conclusion. Short of this, opportunities may presently exist for major, negotiated, money-saving reductions in conventional and nuclear forces on both sides. Through the *deus ex machina* of arms control, the United States should be able to maintain something like its present strategic position, albeit at greatly diminished cost.

There is every reason to hope for a world in which the Soviet Union and the United States will no longer be hostile political rivals and potential military opponents, but there is no reason to expect it to arrive any time soon. Gorbachev may sincerely intend to undertake a radical departure in Soviet foreign policy, and he may hope to preside over a new and more relaxed era in East-West relations. Whatever his intentions, however, Mr. Gorbachev may not last, and American policy should not be based on the assumption of his personal political survival. Even if he does succeed in retaining his power, and even if the rosiest Western expectations about his objectives prove accurate, the Soviet Union will continue to pose a substantial, potential military threat to the United States and its allies. A less expansive Russia will still be a great Eurasian military power, its very existence weighing on the independence of the neighboring countries of Europe, Asia, and the Middle East. Thus, the need for a powerful military counterweight will remain, even if the level of the balance can be reduced and stabilized.[68]

Although the two are by no means mutually exclusive, the most frequently proposed alternative to arms control is increased burden-sharing. While the United States has declined in relative economic terms, its allies are among those who have risen. As this country has become less capable of paying for the defense of its allies, they have become increasingly able to take care of themselves. Even if the threat remains constant, it is claimed, a U.S. withdrawal from its commitments in Europe and Asia can be matched by an equivalent expansion in local forces. Western security need not be diminished as the United States pulls back from the posture its has maintained since 1945.[69]

Like "good" arms control, "better" burden-sharing is something to be hoped for rather than relied upon. In Europe, where the threat (in the form of substantial, nearby Soviet forces) is most immediate and the need for relief is greatest from the American point of view, the potential for expanded allied effort is also quite limited.[70] Whatever the political and economic constraints on defense spending in the United States, they are likely to be even more stringent in Europe, where levels of taxation and nondefense expenditures are already much higher. It is possible that a unilateral American withdrawal could be followed by increased European efforts, but Western European perceptions of a significantly diminished Soviet threat make it much more likely that such a move would leave NATO weaker and more divided than it is at present.[71] If a substantial departure of U.S. forces takes place under cover of a new detente, it is especially difficult to see why the Europeans should feel obliged to burden themselves with larger defense budgets. There might be little short-run danger in this, but over the long term Western Europe could be left more vulnerable than it has been for most of the last forty years.

The situation in the Far East is the reverse of that prevailing in the West. There the direct military threat is lower, while the margin for increased allied participation, in the form of larger Japanese defense expenditures, is quite large. Even at 1 percent of GNP Japan is already spending more in dollar terms than many of the NATO countries. If that fraction is doubled or tripled over the next decade, Japan will be well on her way to becoming a major military power. For the moment, the domestic political constraints on such an expansion remain considerable, and it seems unlikely that Japan will reemerge as a true "great power" before the early decades of the next century. Whether it is in the U.S. interest to encourage such a transformation is also a question that deserves more detailed, thoughtful, and frank discussion.

Over the next decade American statesmen will be preoccupied with working their country out of the difficulties into which it has been led by the policies of the recent past. In particular, an attempt will have to be made to reduce the existing budgetary and trade imbalances without, on the one hand, provoking a precipitate withdrawal from overseas commitments or, on the other, setting off a destructive series of intra-alliance squabbles.

Looking beyond the next few years, it seems likely that the United States will have to try to remain as the leader of an oceanic alliance of industrial democracies. Despite the erosion in its relative power, there is, quite simply, no one else who can do the job. This does not mean that the United States should attempt to preserve all existing arrangements without modification. There is certainly room for some redistribution of burdens within the alliance, but this should be accomplished gradually, particularly in light of the uncertainties inherent in the political developments in Eastern Europe and the prospect of a reunified Germany. Meanwhile, the United States is going to have to try both to maintain a moderate, sustained military program and to reinvigorate its domestic economy. These are conflicting but not completely incompatible goals. Recent discussions of the connection between economic and military power serve as a reminder that the two are, in fact, inseparable. Assuming sound policy, it should be possible to have ample quantities of the second without sapping and ultimately destroying the first.

5

Congress and National Strategy: The Appropriate Role?

GEORGE C. EDWARDS III

Because of its significance to the nation and the world, the making of U.S. national security strategy is a topic of the utmost importance. The process of developing and implementing national security strategy has numerous facets, but the most controversial issue may be the appropriate role of Congress. A number of scholars, especially those grounded in the realist tradition of foreign policy, tend to view congressional involvement in the making of national security strategy as largely unhelpful. In this sense, Congress might be viewed as the most significant constraint on the ability of the United States to formulate and execute a coherent and rational national security strategy. Congressional assertiveness in the 1980s, broad claims of executive power made by the Reagan administration, and the dispute created by the Iran-contra affair have stimulated even more interest in this venerable question.

The purpose of this chapter is to determine the appropriate role, if any, of Congress in the development of U.S. national security strategy. This issue suggests two broad sets of questions. The first relates to determining the appropriate role of Congress in the American political system and, consequently, in the making of national security strategy. Three specific questions are relevant here: What powers does the Constitution allocate to Congress for setting national security strategy? What role has Congress played historically? and, What role does the public want Congress to play in national security policy?

The second set of questions relates to the effectiveness of Congress in making national security strategy. Although Congress has the authority to act in the realm of strategy, it could very well be that the nation is not well served when Congress chooses to do so. Here one might ask what advantages the executive has in the realm of strategy; how well each of the branches has performed; and what advantages accompany (or might accompany) extensive congressional involvement.

Addressing these questions provides the framework for this chapter. Is extensive congressional involvement in making national security strategy appropriate, inevitable, or even desirable? Our assessments of the issues related to the role and effectiveness of Congress in national security matters will provide the basis for an answer to that fundamental question.

Before proceeding, however, it is necessary to note that there is no widely accepted definition of *national strategy,* and usually the term is used without clarification.[1] For purposes of this chapter, *strategy* refers to the major thrusts of national security policy, including decisions regarding the allocation of resources to national defense, the distribution of resources among components of the national defense sector, U.S. commitments to other nations, and the use of force.

THE ROLE OF CONGRESS IN MAKING NATIONAL SECURITY STRATEGY

Congress's Constitutional Authority

The place to begin an examination of the appropriate role of Congress in determining national security strategy is with the Constitution. The essential question here concerns the authority of Congress to make national security strategy. If national security strategy is outside its jurisdiction, then all other questions about its proper role are moot. An examination of both the Constitution and case law suggests that one is hard-pressed to support an argument that there is no constitutional basis for congressional involvement in national security.

There is little question that the Constitution allocates to Congress a central role in determining the major elements of national security policy if Congress so chooses. There is no serious dispute over Congress's power to determine what strategic weapons systems the United States will develop and deploy; what international commitments the United States will enter into (even executive agreements may not be contrary to congressional legislation); the size and organization of the armed forces the United States maintains; the rules under which the United States engages in international commerce; both the assistance the United States extends to other nations and the sanctions it levies against them; and whether or not the United States engages in war. All of these decisions would properly be included in our definition of strategy.

The difficulty that precludes a smooth division of responsibility between the executive and the legislature is the fact that the Constitution established a system of shared, not separate, powers in national security as well as in domestic policy matters. The Constitution's peculiar merging of powers between the executive and the legislature prevents either branch from acting unilaterally on most important matters. This allocation of responsibilities is based upon the framers' apprehension about the concentration and subsequent potential for abuse of power. The founding fathers, for example, divided the powers of supply and command in order to thwart adventurism in national security affairs. Congress can refuse to provide the necessary authorizations and appropriations for presidential actions, while the chief executive can refuse to act, for example, by not sending troops into battle at the behest of the legislature.

Several witnesses, including former President Reagan's national security adviser, Vice Admiral John Poindexter, testified in the Iran-contra hearings that the executive branch could circumvent congressional limitations on the president by resorting to the use of nonappropriated funds. Such an argument is based more on desperation than on an understanding of the constitutional system. Relying on nonappropriated funds would destroy the system of checks and balances that is at the heart of the American system of government and unite the sword with the purse, exactly what the framers feared. Moreover, it would invite corrupting quid pro quos as presidents are tempted to reward countries that provided funds with trade concessions, weapon sales, or other assistance.

The Constitution does not vest authority to make foreign policy in the president. The express language of the Constitution assigns both the president and Congress a central role in national security matters. Although the president is commander in chief of the armed forces, he was given that power primarily to assure civilian control of the military, not as a license to determine national security strategy unilaterally.

Supporters of the view of a restricted role for Congress in national security policy continuously refer to the 1936 case *United States v. Curtiss-Wright Export Corporation*.[2] They are fond of quoting the assertion expressed in the decision that the president is the "sole organ" of the United States in foreign policy.

An examination of the context within which the case was decided allows one to appreciate the narrowness of the Court's finding. In two famous cases decided in 1935, the Court struck down statutes because they delegated excessive legislative powers to the president in domestic policy matters.[3] *Curtiss-Wright* dealt with a law passed by Congress empowering the president to forbid the sale of munitions to warring Latin American nations, with such limitations and exceptions as he should determine. The Curtiss-Wright Export Corporation, prosecuted for attempting to smuggle weapons into Bolivia, argued in its defense that the law was an unconstitutional delegation of power to the executive.

The case provides a weak basis for claims of independent executive power, since the central question in the case was Congress's efforts to delegate its power to the executive. The resolution of the case only shows that Congress can delegate its powers broadly to the president in the field of foreign affairs. It does not support the notion of inherent or extraconstitutional powers for the president.

Proponents of presidential supremacy in the field of foreign affairs also are fond of quoting Justice George Sutherland, the author of the opinion, whose obiter dicta (really little more than a justice's elegantly stated personal opinion) accompanying the case claimed the existence of "plenary and exclusive powers of the President as the sole organ of the federal government in the field of international relations." This claim of extraconstitutional powers for the president in the field of foreign affairs echoed positions Sutherland had taken as a U.S. senator; it was not supported by his colleagues in the Senate at the time, and it has not been supported by the Supreme Court either then or since.

Sutherland's position appears weak on other grounds as well. He distinguished between domestic and foreign policy matters, arguing that powers of external sovereignty passed directly from the English monarch to the national government, where they reside for use by the president. Scholars have repudiated this notion as simply bad history.[4] Moreover, even if this assertion were true, the Constitution still divides the power of external sovereignty between the president and Congress.

The famous phrase "sole organ" comes from a speech John Marshall made as a congressman in 1800. Sutherland distorted the historical record when he cited Marshall as saying the president "is the sole organ of the nation in its external relations, and is its sole representative with foreign nations." Those were Marshall's words, but they do not represent his meaning. He was simply supporting presidential power to carry out policy already determined by the two branches. He was merely saying that in executing a treaty the president was the "sole organ" of the nation. He never argued that the president was the exclusive maker of foreign policy.

Subsequent Court decisions have established the fact that Sutherland's positions were unrepresentative of the Court as a whole. Justice Robert H. Jackson noted in the 1952 steel seizure case that the most that can be drawn from *Curtiss-Wright* is the intimation "that the president might act in external affairs without congressional authority, but not that he might act contrary to an Act of Congress" and that much of the opinion was dictum.[5] In 1981 a federal appellate court rejected the notion that *Curtiss-Wright* constituted a blanket endorsement of plenary power in foreign affairs.[6]

There is an important distinction between being the sole representative of the country abroad and being the sole maker of foreign policy at home. No one disputes the power of the president to develop and execute national security strategy. The real issue is the president's independent power to determine it. Congress is not an illegitimate intruder into making national security strategy; it is a full, constitutional partner.

The Historical Record of Congressional Participation

A second question relating to the role of Congress in making national security strategy concerns the historical record of its involvement. The history of American national security policy is a long one, and any detailed review would far exceed the limits of this chapter. We can safely conclude, however, that except during the period of the Civil War, Congress was at least a full partner in making national security policy throughout the nineteenth century, often dominating the White House. From the turn of the twentieth century until World War II, the president and Congress competed for leadership in national security matters, with conflicts over issues ranging from the ratification of the Treaty of Versailles to the Neutrality Acts of the 1930s.

After the war the president seemed to be the unmistakable locus of national security policy making. Analysts commonly look back thirty or forty years to the period following World War II and call for a return to an era of "consensus" and "bipartisanship" in foreign policy and national security strategy. Typically such commentators hope that the president can regain his "lost" position of dominance over Congress in national security matters.

This wish is based on a misreading of history, however. Consensus on the basic strategy of containing the spread of communism and the perception of an aggressive adversary in the Soviet Union masked underlying tensions over national security policy. Moreover, the policy innovations of the maintenance of a large standing force in peacetime and the threat of nuclear missiles (whose delivery times required a virtually instant decision on retaliation, preempting broad consultation) increased the prominence of the president, especially in his capacity as commander in chief of the armed forces.

Nevertheless, in the words of two of the closest students of national security policy making, Richard Neustadt and Ernest May, the oft-cited bipartisan national security policy consensus of the Truman and Eisenhower years was "almost pure fantasy." The era was characterized instead by "bitter, partisan, and utterly consensus-free debate."[7] During the height of the cold war, presidents did less well with Congress than the conventional wisdom suggests and had to work very hard for the victories they won.[8] One need only remember the difficulties Eisenhower faced on matters ranging from mutual security aid to the Bricker amendment. Partisan voting on national security matters was high.[9]

Thus, calling for a return to an era that never existed has little merit. Presidential dominance of national strategy during peacetime is, at best, a historical anomaly. The apparent increase in congressional assertiveness in national security affairs since the mid-1960s is merely a continuation of the characteristic pattern of executive-legislative relations throughout American history.[10]

Public Opinion on Congressional Involvement

The third question relating to the role of Congress in making national security strategy concerns the attitude of the American people. Even if Congress has discretionary authority to participate fully in crucial decisions about national security policy, the public might want it to defer to the chief executive.

Such is not the case, however. The American public expects the president to be responsive to public opinion and to be constrained by majority rule in Congress. A substantial number of polls taken over more than four decades show that the public overwhelmingly desires Congress to have final authority in policy disagreements with the president, and it does not want the president to be able to act against majority opinion.[11]

Even in the area of national security, the public is not necessarily deferential to the president. It had more confidence in the judgment of Congress than in that of the president on the question of entry into World War II and on reorganization of the Defense Department in the 1950s—even when the president at the time was former General of the Army Dwight Eisenhower.[12]

In 1973, 80 percent of the people supported a requirement that the president obtain the approval of Congress before sending American armed forces into action outside the country.[13] With the public's support that year Congress passed the War Powers Resolution over the president's veto. The purpose of this law was to limit substantially the president's flexibility to continue the use of U.S. forces in hostile actions without the approval of Congress.

In 1987 only 24 percent of the public responded that they trusted President Reagan more than Congress to make the right decision on national security policy. Sixty percent had more confidence in Congress.[14] Only 34 percent of the public agreed that the president should be allowed to conduct secret operations in foreign countries without notifying anyone in Congress. Sixty-one percent disagreed.[15] In the same year, 63 percent of the public desired the president to obtain the approval of Congress to keep U.S. ships in the Persian Gulf. Only 33 percent wanted him to be able to make the decision himself.[16]

In sum, although Americans might be attracted to strong leaders in the White House, they feel most comfortable when Congress has a central role in determining national security policy.

CONGRESSIONAL EFFECTIVENESS IN MAKING NATIONAL SECURITY STRATEGY

Advantages of the Executive Branch?

Even if Congress has the power to be a full participant in national security matters, it does not follow that it should exercise its discretion to be involved. Some argue that the nature of national security policy and the nature of Congress are such that Congress cannot exercise wise judgment and thus ought to defer to the president.[17]

In theory, the executive has several advantages over the legislature in establishing national security policy. Congress is not structured primarily to make decisions; instead, it is structured to encourage open deliberation and the articulation of diverse views. The executive branch, on the other hand, has a more hierarchical and more specialized organization with greater potential for employing secrecy, speed, expertise, and coherence in the development and implementation of public policy.

Congressional effectiveness is sometimes posed as one of the inevitable tradeoffs between democracy and efficiency. The costs of democracy are aggravated by the fact that congressional leverage often depends on blunt instruments, such as cutting off funds or rejecting or amending carefully negotiated international agreements. Moreover, Congress's role may constrain the president's flexibility in negotiations and reduce his ability to provide other nations assurance of U.S. policy.

The characteristics of Congress do not differ between domestic and foreign policy, but advocates of a dominant role for the president argue that national security policy is distinctive because information is less readily available and the costs of failure to produce a coherent policy are greater. The argument is, first, that because most members of Congress lack expertise in foreign policy, they should rely on specialists in the national security community. Yet, typical members of Congress are not specialists in health care, Social Security financing, economics, or agriculture, and no one argues that they should be especially deferential to the executive branch in these areas. Then why should they defer in national security matters? National security policy is certainly complex, but it is not more sophisticated than matters about which Congress routinely makes decisions.

The response might be that national security is different because it is so important, at times involving matters of life and death and fundamental freedom. Yet it is just because national security is so fundamental that Congress needs to be involved. It is especially on the most significant of issues that the people ought to be represented. It is crucial that broad perspectives, diverse views, and full discussion of the possible consequences of alternatives and the likely tradeoffs involved in choices among policies occur. Sometimes it is essential for Congress to nudge a reluctant administration in a direction, such as toward arms control negotiations.

The nuclear mystique can be blinding. If the nature of a situation, such as a nuclear attack, precludes a role for Congress, then Congress in effect defers to the president. It does not follow that Congress should defer when there is more time for deliberation. Members of Congress are no less able than officials in the executive branch to listen to experts on the Strategic Defense Initiative (SDI). In addition, they are better positioned to represent the will of the people and to consider the true costs of such a policy, including the tradeoffs with other policies.

Those who decry a role for Congress because it produces inconsistency in policy often are really only complaining about failing to obtain support for their policy proposals. When Congress failed to appropriate any or all the funds the president requested for aid to the contras, SDI research, or the MX missile, did the Reagan administration cease its support of these initiatives in the interests of continuity in policy? Of course not. Instead it continued to fight for the funds, hoping thereby to create a discontinuity in policy.

The Performance of the Executive Branch

As I have suggested, proponents of executive dominance in making strategy argue that such an approach is the only way to impart coherence and rationality to the system. The question, then, is whether Congress interferes with what otherwise would be a coherent and rational policy-making process in the executive branch? Examination of the policy areas where executive dominance has been observed suggests that such an argument has little basis in reality.

Defense spending. In the 1980 presidential election campaign, Ronald Reagan proposed a 5 percent increase in real defense outlays. Jimmy Carter's last budget, submitted to Congress just before Reagan took office, proposed the same figure. According to one of the new president's top economic advisers, Reagan responded by revising his own budget proposal upward to 9.4 percent per year for his first term to demonstrate a stronger commitment to defense than his predecessor had shown. Consistent with this lack of analytical rigor was the concomitant lack of substantive review in the White House of U.S. foreign policy objectives and military commitments.[18]

Certainly Ronald Reagan had little idea of how to best spend the money. He relied heavily on the Department of Defense, especially on Secretary of Defense Caspar Weinberger. Yet the Department of Defense had not developed a program to spend the money, and there was little effective review in the Office of the Secretary of Defense. Instead the budget request was "little more than a stapled package of the budget requests from each service." Moreover, Reagan would consider defense options from no one but Weinberger, and he would not listen to arguments over the content of defense programs. Further insulating the president from careful policy analysis was Weinberger's refusal to permit the Office of Management and Budget to review the defense budget.[19] Thus, instead of first determining national security strategy and then seeking the funds to implement it, the president simply demanded money.

There is good reason to think that as a result, much of the money was not well spent. According to one Pentagon budget officer in the Office of the Secretary of Defense, "Carter had given us a lot. The Weinberger team came in and said, 'Add more. Find room to add. Find places to put more money.' "[20] In addition, the public learned the hard way that items ranging from minesweepers, to planes for supporting ground troops, to factories producing material for nuclear weapons were neglected.

A good argument can be made that the buildup was wasteful as well as incoherent. According to former Assistant Secretary of Defense for Manpower, Installations, and Logistics Lawrence J. Korb, the rapid increase in defense spending "overwhelmed the acquisitions system and made it impossible for DoD's contracting personnel to monitor the procurement process effectively."[21] Ideology rather than analysis drove the president's decisions. The same people that argued that we should not throw money at social problems did exactly that when it came to matters of national defense.

In addition, when Congress called a halt to increased defense spending in the second Reagan term, the administration did not deal with the strategic implications of this fact of life in its proposals for future spending. For example, it continued to plan on a 600-ship navy even though its budget would only support a 550-ship force. Instead of thinking strategically, it stretched out procurement, driving up unit costs and denying the armed services needed spare parts, ammunition, and support equipment.[22]

Such a process of decision making does not inspire confidence in the competence of the executive branch. It is difficult to conclude that Congress should be especially deferential to the executive on budgetary matters in the face of this experience.

The Iran-contra affair. On January 17, 1986, President Ronald Reagan signed a document, technically called a "finding," that paved the way for the United States to secretly sell arms directly to Iran in hopes of obtaining the release of American hostages held in the Middle East. This finding also created the opportunity to generate profits on the arms sales that could be, and were, diverted covertly to the contras fighting the Nicaraguan government.

The finding was presented to the president by his national security adviser, Vice Admiral John Poindexter. It had a cover memo, prepared by Lieutenant Colonel Oliver North, but the president did not read it. Although the memo pointed out that the plan was opposed by the secretaries of state and defense, their views were not included, nor were justifications for the assertions of success contained in the memo. Eleven days earlier, not realizing that it was only a proposal for discussion, and before the National Security Council meeting he called to discuss it, the president had signed a similar finding that had not been fully staffed.[23] As is well known, the administration took steps to ensure that Congress was not involved in the process. According to the president's chief of staff, when the president was first told of the Israeli idea of selling Hawk missiles to the Iranians, Reagan asked few questions and none that were probing.[24]

The policy was a failure, and it undermined America's strongly asserted policy of not trading arms, or anything else, for hostages. When details of this policy decision began to emerge that November, there was a broad public outcry, and the president fell substantially in the polls, his political clout lost. Things got even worse when the diversion of funds to the contras came to light. At this point the president fired North, accepted the resignation of Poindexter, and had to face a year of congressional hearings and a critical investigation by a special commission he appointed to examine his handling of the matter.

In a speech to the American people, President Reagan responded to the Tower Commission report: "A few months ago I told the American people I did not trade arms for hostages. My heart and my best intentions still tell me that's true, but the facts and the evidence tell me it is not."[25]

A spate of books written by top officials in the Reagan administration (detractors term them "kiss and tell") revealed what others had long suspected: Ronald Reagan was a peculiarly detached decisionmaker. Having strong views on the basic goals of public policy, he left it to others to implement his broad vision. Aides prepared detailed scripts on index cards for his use in meetings, and he even consulted astrologers on scheduling matters.[26]

In the future, do we really want to argue that Congress should defer to an executive who makes decisions in such a fashion? one who may not even know what decision he has made? one who may not grasp the specifics of policy alternatives (or, more recently, one who refers to policy direction as "the vision thing")? one who may not evaluate adequately their likely consequences? one who may be very much a prisoner of his premises?

The Performance of Congress

A question related to executive performance in making national security strategy is that of the record of congressional involvement. Has Congress inhibited the development of strategic policy? Has it systematically thwarted executive proposals? An examination of the major strategic national security policy initiatives of the 1980s suggests that this has not been the case.

One of the principal elements of national defense strategy in the 1980s was the largest peacetime increase in defense spending in history. Leaders of the Reagan administration often referred to it as a cornerstone of their national security policy. At least in the first Reagan term, Congress acquiesced in the buildup. In the second term, it called a halt to increased expenditures. Given what we know about the manner of defense spending during this period, perhaps Congress should have acted sooner.

Congress was equally compliant regarding specific components of defense strategy. As part of its defense buildup, the Reagan administration placed a high priority on modernization of the strategic triad. The development and procurement of weapons systems normally poses little problem for the White House, and the 1980s saw a continuance of this trend. The B-1 bomber, the D-5 submarine-launched ballistic missile, and the B-2 (Stealth) bomber all received the support of the legislature.

The one exception to the pattern of congressional support for strategic weapon systems was the MX (Peacekeeper) missile. The essential reason that the president did not receive all that he wanted is straightforward: members of Congress objected when the people living where the missiles would be based opposed locating the missiles nearby. In a democracy, the people have a right to a say in national security policy, and Congress provides a valuable service in being sensitive to the trade-offs involved in various policy options.

Another major strategic innovation in the 1980s was adding a defensive capability to nuclear strategy. The president persuaded Congress to appropriate billions of dollars for SDI, although he did not receive all he wanted. There were several factors at work here, including general fiscal constraints, disagreement over both the strategic implications and the practicality of SDI, and a response to the administration's interpretation of the ABM Treaty of 1972. Regarding the latter, the president claimed that the United States was not bound by the interpretation of the treaty advanced by the Nixon administration when it presented it to the Senate for ratification. Not only would the administration's re-interpretation undercut the treaty, but it would also undercut the constitutional power of the Senate in treaty ratification. Nevertheless, SDI did move forward, while Congress continued to evaluate it cautiously. By 1988 both major-party candidates for president indicated at least some skepticism about the program. Even the Reagan administration acknowledged that it had advanced unrealistic arguments on behalf of SDI when it was first proposed. Thus, an independent congressional review of SDI was a valuable contribution to national security.

In the realm of U.S. military operations, the president also received the support of Congress most of the time (Libya, Grenada, Panama, Saudi Arabia). There was more congressional resistance to the stationing of troops in Lebanon, but it would be difficult to argue that the executive branch had a coherent policy in this arena. A more aggressive congressional posture might have prevented a disaster from occurring.

U.S. proxy interventions in Afghanistan, Cambodia, and Angola (after 1985) also received congressional support. Aiding the contras in Nicaragua was a different story of course, but this was a visible policy that was broadly debated and was consistently opposed by a majority of the American people. It is difficult to argue that Congress should ignore the people's wishes under such circumstances.

In addition, Congress supported both the deployment of intermediate-range nuclear missiles in Europe and then the treaty to remove them. It supported adding offensive capability to conventional defensive strategy (the Maritime Strategy of the Navy), and it supported the Army's AirLand Battle doctrine.

In sum, Congress supported most executive branch initiatives in national security strategy while raising significant questions about a few of them. In no case did it absolutely refuse to support the president. Even the contras in Nicaragua received aid, including military assistance. It would be difficult to make the case that Congress acted irresponsibly or fundamentally altered U.S. national security strategy. On the other hand, a strong case can be made that the legislative branch contributed to more effective analysis of strategic options. It is interesting that many of those criticizing congressional involvement in national security policy do not raise the issue of Congress's lack of deference to President Carter on the SALT II treaty.

The charge is often made that Congress is too parochial to make decisions regarding national security strategy. Yet as the examples above illustrate, narrow constituency interests rarely impinge on broad strategic matters. In the few instances where they do (as in the case of the MX missile), their opposition tends to reflect deep skepticism within the body politic. In such cases, Congress provides a valuable check on the executive, just as the founding fathers desired.

In addition, who can seriously argue that executive branch decision making is devoid of parochialism? Have presidents been significantly less supportive than Congress of Israel? Is opposition to aid for the contras an example of parochialism, or is support for them? We typically cannot even determine unequivocally what the national interest is. It begs the question to define it as whatever policy the executive proposes.

Using Congress in Making Strategy

At the end of his report to Congress on national security strategy in January 1988, President Reagan concluded that an effective national security strategy "must be a cooperative endeavor" of both the president and Congress.[27] In 1975 Secretary of State Henry Kissinger declared, "The executive accepts that Congress must have both the sense and reality of participation: foreign policy must be a shared enterprise."[28] Neither of these statesmen was overly fond of congressional involvement, but both recognized its principal advantage: it provides enhanced legitimacy to policy decisions and an accompanying perception of strong political will.

In a system of decentralized power the executive branch cannot determine national security strategy on its own. Although the executive should be relatively unhindered in the conduct of foreign policy, Congress has a central role in the making of it. When members of Congress feel they have been excluded from their proper role in the formulation of foreign policy, they have a tendency to turn to micromanagement to reshape that policy in its implementation. As former Senator J. William Fulbright put it, "When the President, for reasons with which we can all sympathize, does not invite us into his high-policy councils, it is our duty to infiltrate them as best we can."[29] In contrast, when senators and representatives have been consulted on a policy, they are more likely to feel they have a stake in it and less likely to oppose the president out of frustration at being excluded from crucial decisions.

If there is one lesson that defense officials carry from the war in Vietnam, it is the necessity of including Congress as a central participant in setting national security policy. Rather than resisting congressional involvement, it is simply smart politics to make Congress a partner in the enterprise. Those who are not involved in the takeoff are much less likely to defend a rough landing.

CONCLUSION

A prominent congressional role in making national security strategy may be distressing to some observers, especially those who value continuity, secrecy, and dispatch in the conduct of national security policy. Yet efficiency is not the only criterion for evaluating policy making. If it were, the United States should hold a constitutional convention immediately. Historical perspective is useful here. Congress has been intimately involved in national security matters from the beginning, and this involvement is what the American people desire and what the framers intended. It is by no means clear that the executive branch has a monopoly on wisdom or that national security policy cannot benefit from a deliberative process, even at the cost of speed and secrecy in action.

Moreover, it is not apparent that congressional involvement in national security policy has been costly to the nation's long-run interests. Although every reader can cite cases in which Congress may have acted unwisely, there are an equal number of instances in which the executive branch can be safely accused of the same failing.[30] At the same time, there are few examples of instances in which the president has simply been unable to act in an emergency because of systemic constraints. The War Powers Resolution, the most notable effort of Congress to constrain the president formally, has not proven to be a significant restriction, and systematic evidence shows that presidents have not reduced the use of force in international relations over the past decade.[31]

Congress and the public are most likely to be concerned with national security affairs when the issues involved are salient to them. Their participation is entirely appropriate, because such matters are usually at the core of defense and foreign policy. It is difficult to articulate a view of democratic government that does not accord citizens and their elected representatives a central role in important matters of national security policy. In addition, chief executives in a democracy need the support of the people if they are to successfully establish and implement policies that require sacrifice and moral commitments.

Based upon the issues addressed in this chapter, one must conclude that extensive congressional involvement in making national security strategy is appropriate, inevitable, and usually desirable. The question that remains is, What will be the nature of that involvement in the 1990s? Although predictions about congressional behavior are inherently unreliable, it does appear that two broad trends are in evidence.

First, although Congress as an institution will not retreat from its current level of extensive involvement in national security strategy affairs, it is unlikely that it will seek to steal the initiative from the president in most cases. Questions of institutional capability aside, there remains a great deal of reluctance within Congress to take the lead on questions of national security strategy (witness the reaction, even within Congress, to former Speaker Jim Wright's involvement in Central American diplomacy in 1987 and 1988),[32] although there is much more willingness to constrain the president when members of Congress believe that his initiatives are clearly inconsistent with the preferences of their constituencies or their ideologies.

Second, Congress will continue to insist upon full autonomy on budget matters, an issue that will become increasingly contentious if defense spending continues to decline in real terms. It is reasonable to expect that Congress will be more prone to micro-manage a smaller defense budget.

Of course, this continued congressional involvement will cause proponents of presidential government to continue to grumble over congressional "meddling" in foreign and security policy. But the enlightened citizen should keep his eye on the important criterion rather than the trivial: Is the quality of national security decision making improved as a result of the enhanced deliberation that accompanies congressional involvement in the process? The answer is usually yes.

PART III

Alternative Strategies for the United States

6

Discriminate Deterrence

THE COMMISSION ON INTEGRATED
LONG-TERM STRATEGY

THE CHANGING SECURITY ENVIRONMENT

Defense planning in the United States has centered for many years on a grand strategy of extraordinary global sweep. The strategy can be stated quite simply: forward deployment of American forces, assigned to oppose invading armies and backed by strong reserves and a capability to use nuclear weapons if necessary. Resting on alliances with other democratic countries, the strategy aims to draw a line that no aggressor will dare to cross.

The durability of this strategy is remarkable. American forces have now been deployed in Central Europe for 40 years. They have been in the Republic of Korea for 35 years. The Atlantic Alliance has now outlasted all multilateral peacetime alliances in modern history.

The strategy has had considerable success. All the Alliance members are still free countries. Soviet forces have not attacked Western Europe, and North Korean forces have not again attacked South Korea.

But the strategy has also had some setbacks. Soviet power has by-passed the lines we drew and has pushed into Southern Asia, the Middle East, Africa, the Caribbean, and Central America. In a world that is less bipolar than it once was, the strategy has not helped much in dealing with hostile countries (Iran, for example) outside the Soviet bloc. In Europe itself there are signs of severe strain. The Alliance has not succeeded in matching Soviet conventional forces on the continent, and for many contingencies our threat to use nuclear weapons against them has become progressively less credible in light of the growth in Soviet nuclear forces.

The Commission is not proposing to replace the strategy. We believe in forward deployment of American forces, in backing them with strong reserves, and in retaining the nuclear threat to help defend our allies. But we also believe that the strategy needs to be brought into line with contemporary realities. . . .

In taking a long-term perspective, the Commission is not assuming the permanence of today's international security environment. Indeed, we believe that the environment may change dramatically. Twenty years hence America may confront a vastly more complex environment, including some new major powers and new kinds of weaponry and alliances. Some possible changes are already discernible at several points on the strategic landscape, and several in particular seem worth focusing on:

The rise of Japan and China. In some measure, military power reflects economic power. Japan's economy is now the second largest in the world and is apt to continue growing. In the decades ahead, a key question affecting the strategic balance will be whether Japan exercises its option to become a major military power. Even if it does not, it may be influencing the strategic environment simply by its investment decisions. A Japanese decision to help in the development of Soviet technology, for example, could help to increase the Soviet military potential. On the other hand, additional Japanese economic assistance to U.S. allies and friends (e.g., the Philippines, Turkey, Egypt) would benefit our security.

Over the next 20 years, the Chinese economy may well grow faster than those of the United States, of Europe, or the Soviet Union. By 2010 China may have the world's second or third largest economy (the Soviet Union is now third). It may well become a superpower, in military terms, though still behind the Soviet Union and the United States. Large uncertainties attach to China's future.

A world with three or four major, global military powers would confront American strategic planners with a far more complicated environment than does the familiar bipolar competition with the Soviet Union. In any such multipolar world, the United States would have to manage relations with several different global powers and form appropriate coalitions with them. Wars might break out between powerful nations not aligned with the United States. Alliances might shift. The next 20 years will be a period of transition to this new world of several major powers.

Soviet economic difficulties. The U.S.S.R.'s persistent economic difficulties, and the regime's efforts to deal with them via "restructuring," are huge imponderables for U.S. defense planners. Whatever the long-term prospects for Soviet economic growth, progress in the near term is apt to be modest. It is also unclear what, if anything, higher rates of economic growth would imply for Soviet foreign policy. In any event, we cannot base our long-term strategy on uncertain forecasts about a more benign Soviet foreign policy. Change is possible, but it would have to show itself in concrete actions that reduce the dangers to our interests.

What about the possibility that continuing economic weakness might mean a reduced Soviet threat? In the long run, the Soviet leaders would have difficulty maintaining the country's present military position if economic reform fails. Still, nobody can be sure how even a resounding failure would play out. Failure might drive the regime to seek legitimacy in military successes abroad, or even to try gaining control over foreign resources. In combination with the U.S.S.R.'s growing ethnic tensions, economic failure might even trigger efforts by some parts of the Soviet empire to loosen their bonds.

Changes in military technology. Dramatic developments in military technology appear feasible over the next twenty years. They will be driven primarily by the further exploitation of microelectronics, in particular for sensors and information processing, and the development of directed energy. These developments could require major revisions in military doctrines and force structures. The U.S. leads in developing many of the relevant technologies, which may be a source of concern to the Soviets. But the Soviet military establishment is already engaged in a major effort to understand the military implications of new technologies, and appears to have concluded that revolutionary changes in the nature of war will result. The much greater precision, range, and destructiveness of weapons could extend war across a much wider geographic area, make war much more rapid and intense, and require entirely new modes of operation. Application of new technologies to both offensive and defensive systems will pose complicated problems for designing forces and assessing enemy capabilities.

The precision associated with the new technologies will enable us to use conventional weapons for many of the missions once assigned to nuclear weapons. The new technologies will work to strengthen the ability of our ground and air forces to defeat invasions. Particularly important in this connection is the prospective use of "low-observable" (Stealth) technology in combination with extremely accurate weapons and improved means of locating targets. In the years beyond 2000, this combination will provide new ways to stop invading forces at great distances from the front lines.

But high tech is not an American monopoly. Since the mid-1960s, Soviet gains in nuclear weapons have gradually deprived us of a strategic edge that served to compensate for the Soviet advantage in conventional forces threatening Western Europe. In light of this revolutionary change it became increasingly important for the Atlantic Alliance to counter the Soviet numerical superiority in tanks, armored personnel carriers, artillery pieces and other equipment with the broad qualitative superiority of its systems. But the Soviet military establishment is striving to match or even surpass our weapons technology, and will increasingly do so unless we increase our research efforts.

Soviet military industry is already producing vastly improved armor for tanks. They have made enormous strides in submarine technology. The Soviets are sure to stay well ahead in their research on chemical and biological weapons, where they have practically no U.S. competition. Particularly ominous is the large and rapidly growing Soviet capability for military use of space in support of conventional warfare, in combination with vigorous research efforts on several technologies relevant for space warfare.

Soviet qualitative gains might be extended for several reasons. At present, for example, the United States has fewer scientists and engineers working on military technology. The U.S. budgets for defense research and procurement have been lagging the Soviet effort and may continue to do so. Western controls on the transfer of technology (the effectiveness of which has varied over time) might again become less effective. And, based on past performance, we can assume that any agreements limiting the testing of military technology would be observed far more rigidly in the United States than in the Soviet Union.

The worldwide diffusion of advanced weapons. The relationship between the major and minor powers will change by the early 21st century. Today the United States and the Soviet Union can often decisively influence the military postures of smaller states by making weaponry available or denying it. In the years ahead, weapons production will be much more widely diffused, and the superpowers (especially if there are three or four) will have less control over transfers of advanced systems. Many lesser powers will have sizable arsenals. These will often include chemical weapons and short-range or even medium-range missiles. Several large and mid-sized countries that used to be listed among the less-developed countries—India, Brazil, South and North Korea, Egypt—are now building sizable arms industries.

The next twenty years could also see the production of atomic bombs in many countries not now possessing them. Because of the spread of nuclear reactors and the technology associated with nuclear energy, many countries are in possession of fissile material or the means to produce it. This creates a potential for some of the countries, including several that are relatively poor and less industrialized, to build arsenals of a dozen or more atomic bombs. In the next century, forty or more countries in Europe, Asia, the Middle East and elsewhere will have the technical wherewithal to build such arsenals within a few years. Today, fortunately, nearly all countries other than the five avowed nuclear powers hesitate to launch programs for building nuclear weapons. (A few go about it furtively and slowly.) In some regions, increasing arms competition or a prolonged war might undermine this extraordinarily important restraint and might even bring to a shattering end a half-century of non-use of nuclear weapons.

The arsenals of the lesser powers will make it riskier and more difficult for the superpowers to intervene in regional wars. The U.S. ability to support its allies around the world will increasingly be called into question. Where American intervention seems necessary, it will generally require far more cooperation with Third World countries than has been required in the past. Furthermore, American efforts to influence military outcomes in regional wars will call for use of our most sophisticated weaponry, even though this could compromise its effectiveness in a U.S.-Soviet war.

Deteriorating U.S. access. One long-term trend unfavorable to the United States concerns our diminishing ability to gain agreement for timely access, including bases and overflight rights, to areas threatened by Soviet aggression. We have found it increasingly difficult, and politically costly, to maintain bases in the Third World. Many of our friends there become vulnerable to nationalist charges that they are surrendering sovereignty by allowing us to use ports, airfields and other territory; even overflight rights for U.S. aircraft have become controversial in some friendly countries. Our current basing agreement with the Philippine government expires in 1991, at which point our stay there becomes subject to a one-year termination notice. The 1979 Panama Canal treaty and its supporting agreements specify that all U.S. bases in the area be closed down by 1999. Both treaties allow for renegotiation, but it is far from certain that we will be able to retain a base support structure in either country. The use of our bases in the Azores may also become more restricted.

The United States will continue to need bases because the need will remain to deter or defeat aggressors at distant points overseas—typically at points much closer to our adversaries than to us. Meanwhile, the Soviet Union, which begins with the advantage of greater proximity, has enormously strengthened its airlift and sealift capabilities; in addition, it now meets little resistance to its overflights in many parts of the world. Reversing the relationships of the fifties, the Soviets could now put large forces into the Middle East quite rapidly, while the United

States cannot do so without more help than we have been getting from our allies there.

The emergence of new threats in the Western Hemisphere. The absence of significant security threats close to home has helped free the United States to play a global military role in the years since 1945. This situation might change if more pro-Communist regimes come to power in the hemisphere. If the Sandinista regime consolidates its power in Nicaragua and continues to receive Soviet support, hostile Communist regimes might gradually become established elsewhere in Central America—for example, in El Salvador, Honduras, and Panama. Any such trend could be expected to endanger control of the Panama Canal and threaten the political stability of Mexico. These developments would force the United States to divert far more of its foreign policy resources and defense assets to the Caribbean region, leading to a reduced American role in NATO.

One overriding message in all these imponderables is the need for flexibility in the U.S. defense posture. We will presumably continue to face Soviet challenges at various points on the periphery of the U.S.S.R., but we must also expect a broader range of challenges in the Third World. The demands on U.S. forces may well be growing at a time when budgetary constraints are limiting the size of those forces. The challenge will be to defend our interests in many different places, even while lacking the resources to offer much peacetime support to our allies and friends there. Plainly the Pentagon must give preference to more mobile and versatile forces—forces that can deter aggression by their ability to respond rapidly and discriminately to a wide range of attacks.

THIRD WORLD CONFLICTS AND U.S. INTERESTS

Nearly all the armed conflicts of the past forty years have occurred in what is vaguely referred to as the Third World: the diverse countries of Asia, the Middle East, Africa, Latin America, and the Eastern Caribbean. In the same period, all the wars in which the United States was involved—either directly with its combat forces or indirectly with military assistance—occurred in the Third World. Given future trends in the diffusion of technology and military power, the United States needs a clear understanding of its interests and military role in these regions.

The overarching common feature of our military involvement in the Third World has been rancorous disagreement about the nature of our interests. We have disagreed not only about whether we should be involved (as in Nicaragua), but even about whether we were supporting the right side (as in Mozambique). Our failure in Vietnam still casts a shadow over U.S. intervention anywhere, and other setbacks—notably those we suffered in Lebanon—have left some predisposed to pessimism about our ability to promote U.S. interests in the Third World. Our ability to persevere in such wars is always questionable.

The tools and tactics of American involvement are severely circumscribed. In addition, we are sometimes constrained by the need to "save" forces or advanced technologies for a possible confrontation with the Soviet Union—even though our potential adversaries in the Third World are themselves acquiring increasingly sophisticated weaponry.

These conflicts in the Third World are obviously less threatening than any Soviet-American war would be, yet they have had and will have an adverse cumulative effect on U.S. access to critical regions, on American credibility among allies and friends, and on American self-confidence. If this cumulative effect cannot be checked or reversed in the future, it will gradually undermine America's ability to defend its interests in the most vital regions, such as the Persian Gulf, the Mediterranean and the Western Pacific.

In the coming decades the United States will need to be better prepared to deal with conflicts in the Third World. The preparations will not be expensive. But they require new kinds of planning, since they often call for missions, force structures, and equipment not now available in the U.S. inventory.

U.S. difficulties in dealing with this violence constitute a major reason for its persistence. Our adversaries tell themselves that they often run little risk when they attack U.S. interests or allies in the Third World, especially if the warfare is of low intensity and protracted, and if they use guerrilla forces, paramilitary terrorist organizations, or armed subversives. If we do not improve our ability to counter this lesser violence, we will surely lose the support of many Third World countries that want to believe the United States can protect its friends, not to mention its own interests. Violence in the Third World threatens our interests in a variety of ways. It can imperil a fledgling democracy (as in El Salvador), increase pressures for large-scale migration to the United States (as in Central American wars), jeopardize important U.S. bases (as in the Philippines), threaten vital sea lanes (as in the Persian Gulf), or provide strategic opportunities for the Soviet Union and its proxies.

The Soviet Union and its allies have often backed terrorism and insurgency around the world. They have skillfully exploited pervasive poverty and nationalist resentments in many regions, and their methods of political control provide a useful model for Third World dictatorships seeking to gain and hold power. Still, the Soviets have problems of their own in these regions. It is increasingly well understood that Communist economics offers no passport to development: the contrast between North and South Korea carries a powerful message, and so do the economic disasters of Ethiopia, Angola, Mozambique, and Cambodia. Right now something like 500,000 insurgents have taken up arms against Soviet-supported regimes (which are in the aggregate supported by perhaps 400,000 Soviet, Cuban, and Vietnamese troops).

Many of our problems in the Third World are centered on what is now called "low intensity conflict." The term refers to insurgencies, organized terrorism, paramilitary crime, sabotage, and other forms of violence in a shadow area between peace and open warfare involving large units. To defend its interests properly in the Third World, the United States will have to take low intensity conflict much more seriously. It is a form of warfare in which "the enemy" is more or less omnipresent and unlikely ever to surrender. In the past we have sometimes seen these attacks as a succession of transient and isolated crises. We now have to think of them as a permanent addition to the menu of defense planning problems.

Thinking of low intensity conflict as protracted war should lead us to a number of changes, some fairly obvious. We will have to make sure that our security assistance is targeted on countries that face long-run threats, and we will need to be seen as reliable in providing them with steady amounts of aid over time. In security assistance, as in defense spending generally, consistency over time is often more important than the actual budgetary level.

We also need to think of low intensity conflict as a form of warfare that is not a problem just for the Department of Defense. In many situations, the United States will need not just DoD personnel and materiel, but diplomats and information specialists, agricultural chemists, bankers and economists, hydrologists, criminologists, meteorologists, and scores of other professionals. . . .

The strategic concepts laid out here to deal with low intensity conflict could be funded with about 4 percent of the defense budget, requiring annual outlays of perhaps $12 billion. This amount could be provided under current Defense Department budget levels without significantly impairing our ability to prosecute higher-intensity wars. Indeed, in the long run, any such shift in emphasis would enhance our situation relative to that of the Soviet Union.

Third World conflicts in the future will call for many different responses by the United States, but it is possible to specify some guidelines for U.S. strategy. We see a strategy built on six basic propositions:

1. U.S. forces will not in general be combatants. A combat role for U.S. armed forces in Third World conflicts has to be viewed as an exceptional event. Some exceptions will doubtless occur, as in 1983 in

Grenada and in 1986 in Libya, and it would be self-defeating for the United States to declare a "no use" doctrine for its forces in the Third World. But our forces' principal role there will be to augment U.S. security assistance programs. Mainly that means providing military training, technical training and intelligence and logistical support.

2. The United States should support anti-Communist insurgencies. In carefully selected situations, where important U.S. objectives would be served and U.S. support might favorably affect outcomes, the United States should help anti-Communist insurgencies, especially those against regimes threatening their neighbors. . . .

3. Security assistance requires new legislation and more resources. U.S. economic and security assistance—the foreign aid programs to assist U.S. friends and allies in reducing the underlying causes of instability—have proven inadequate and inflexible. Congress has repeatedly underfunded Administration requests, and has earmarked as much as 86 percent of military assistance for five countries (Egypt, Israel, Greece, Turkey, and Pakistan). . . .

4. The United States needs to work with its Third World allies at developing "cooperative forces." Regrettably, we have a lot to learn from the Soviet Union in this regard. Soviet efforts to advance and defend their interests in less developed countries are typically supported by a familiar cast of characters from the Soviet bloc—Cubans, Nicaraguans, Vietnamese, North Koreans, and East Europeans. These cooperating forces are led and financed by Moscow, even when not tightly controlled from there. Support may also be available from quasi-allies such as Libya or the PLO [Palestine Liberation Organization], whose interests sometimes diverge from those of the Soviet Union, but who are available for heavy duty on other occasions. The entire operation carries enormous advantages for the Soviet Union, both in minimizing its own risks of confrontation with the West and in making available troops that blend readily into the environment.

In this area, the United States has some large competitive disadvantages. Because they are dictatorships, Soviet client states can secretly order aid missions and military units abroad and disguise their missions there. The United States and its friends and allies cannot ordinarily move troops around so cavalierly.

Still, some allies have substantial reasons for joining in a cooperative-forces program. They can point to our mutual interests in open societies and in containing or reversing Soviet gains in the Third World. They will expect to improve their own military capabilities, and perhaps their regional political and economic influence, in the process. We could hope to develop some mobile forces available for duty in particular regions, or even outside them—somewhat on the model of the Republic of Korea troops or the Philippine Task Force that helped the United States in Vietnam.

5. In the Third World, no less than in developed countries, U.S. strategy should seek to maximize our technological advantages. In some cases, technologies developed for fighting the Soviets will be enormously useful. Here too we will want to use smart missiles that can apply force in a discriminate fashion and avoid collateral damage to civilians. Advanced technologies for training will also offer us more effective ways to help friends cope with terrorism and insurgency. . . .

High tech is not always the answer. Some Air Force transports and Army helicopters are far too big, expensive and complex for many allies. Providing canned field rations and a means of manufacturing boot soles may be more important to the mobility of a Third World army than advanced aircraft.

6. The United States must develop alternatives to overseas bases. In some contexts, to be sure, bases will continue to be critically important—especially when our problem is to defend against possible Soviet aggression. But we should not ordinarily be dependent on bases in defending our interests in the Third World. We have found it increasingly difficult, and politically costly, to maintain bases there.

Here again our technology can help us. Low-cost satellites in space can in some measure replace the communication and intelligence-gathering functions of overseas bases. We can build very long-endurance aircraft for surveillance, manned or unmanned. We also have some impressive naval options. Located in international waters, or in an ally's territorial waters but still out of view, our operations can be far more secure than those on land bases. Among the approaches studied, one of the most interesting is the use of standard merchant container ships to support specially configured units, with the containers carrying all military equipment needed.

WARS ON THE SOVIET PERIPHERY

The conventional forces of the Soviet Union, like its nuclear forces, represent awesome power. Nowhere on the periphery of the country today is it credibly threatened by invasion. At several points around the periphery, the U.S.S.R. and its satellites could plausibly expect to win conventional wars and occupy other countries' territory. The prospects of its neighbors in any such wars would vary with their prior defense efforts, with their alliance ties (especially to the United States), and with geographical differences.

Soviet neighbors in the Far East are in some ways best off. Japan is favored by geography (and also helped by the relative modesty of Soviet amphibious-warfare capabilities). The Republic of Korea is strongly defended, and its ability to resist conventional attacks from North Korea should increase; but the defense of South Korea will have to be achieved under the shadow of possible Soviet intervention. U.S. assistance will continue to be required to deter such outside intervention in support of a North Korean attack.

At other points on the periphery, the conventional balance will continue to favor Soviet forces. They would be favored in an attack on Northern China, say, or one limited to the Nordic areas of Europe. A broad attack on Western Europe would be more problematical, but there too the balance of conventional forces favors the Soviet Union. It would be more in the Soviets' favor if they attacked in the Persian Gulf area.

It is sometimes assumed that the Soviet Union would never attack in the Gulf region alone—that any such attack would surely be part of a larger assault on Europe, or that it would inevitably spread there. The assumption is unwarranted. The turbulence of the region, the importance of its oil to Western countries for the foreseeable future, the severe limitations of countervailing force in the region—all these factors combine to make it plausible that Soviet leaders might seize an opportunity to intervene—for example, by taking advantage of an "invitation" to support a new revolutionary regime. Success would confer a major economic and geostrategic advantage on the Soviet Union and deal a possibly decisive blow to the unity of the Western alliances. History and common sense both suggest that if indeed they attacked, the Soviets would try to limit the war to one or a few of the Gulf states, where their strategic advantages are greatest. The Soviets have not in the past attacked all their objectives at the same time; in 1939 they attacked Poland, then occupied the Baltic States, then attacked Finland; and Stalin ended the Berlin blockade before the Soviet-supported attack by North Korea on South Korea.

The West's ability to counter threats to the Gulf area has declined substantially since the 1950s, even as the area's strategic importance has grown. Thirty years ago, the United States and Britain could respond to a crisis there with overwhelming power. A broad Alliance consensus, combined with our superior airlift and access to bases in the region and along the way, would have enabled us to move in our forces (mostly from Europe) well before the arrival of Soviet forces. Their airlift capabilities then were relatively primitive, and their aircraft were routinely denied the right to fly over Iran and other countries in the region. . . .

Not all the trends are unfavorable. In the past seven years, U.S. airlift and sealift capabilities have increased by roughly 50 percent. There are ways for us to build on this improvement and increase our ability to defend the Gulf. However the defense will depend critically on our having substantial air power in the region. Having bases close to the Gulf will increase our ability to concentrate tactical air forces in addition to those which could be provided from our aircraft carriers. American air power would in fact present a formidable threat to the Soviet troops invading a Gulf state, who would necessarily be massed at various points in Iran, Afghanistan, or their bases in the Trans-Caucasus.

Present strategy recognizes the potential of our air power but requires us to depend on an uncertain prospect: that if an attack seemed imminent, we could then get the needed bases. But hints of an attack, and the intimidating crisis atmosphere presumably accompanying them, could make our allies more reluctant than ever to call us in. Our major problem, then, is that, except for carrier-based aircraft and long-range land-based aircraft, we have no assured timely access for our air power. The challenge is to get some.

Turkey, a NATO member, adjoins the major Soviet military area threatening the region. Building up Turkey's defense capabilities, particularly those for air defense, would cast a strong shadow over any Soviet planning for operations in the Gulf region. The other NATO allies, by clearly demonstrating an ability and resolve to resist a Soviet attack on Turkey, can further intensify this Soviet dilemma.

In addition, we should continue to encourage other friends there—Saudi Arabians, for example—to help improve U.S. access and make bases available in an emergency for the only power that can defend them. Considerable progress has been made along these lines in recent years, but more is needed. The threat we will face in the region is that the Soviet Union will be able to put enormous forces on the ground rapidly, before we have a chance to block them. . . .

In developing a strategy for dealing with Soviet conventional power, we take note of a truism: in the nuclear age, no conventional war involving combat between U.S. and Soviet forces would be unaffected by nuclear weapons. The war would inevitably be planned and fought in the shadow of nuclear threats.

Strategies for conventional war in Europe return repeatedly to this theme. The U.S. and its allies have frequently stated that their forces in Europe are not equipped to sustain themselves in combat beyond a certain number of days, and that they would then have to turn to nuclear weapons.

However, a fateful ambiguity enshrouds this declaration. Sometimes it has seemed as though NATO plans to use battlefield or even theater-wide nuclear weapons for their direct effect in repelling the Soviet invasion. At other times, NATO officials posit a different strategy—

that what NATO really intends in threatening to use nuclear weapons is to point up the perils of escalation and, in effect, concentrate the minds of Soviet leaders on the apocalypse at the end of that road.

If the latter is really the Alliance's message, would it remain credible? Can NATO rely on threats of escalation that would ensure its own destruction (along with that of the Soviet Union) if implemented? These disturbing questions, which are scarcely new, have again been raised squarely in recent European debates, many of them triggered by the negotiations to eliminate intermediate nuclear forces from the continent. NATO plainly needs a coherent strategy that will be viable for the long haul. . . .

In recent years, the Warsaw Pact forces have substantially narrowed NATO's qualitative advantage. Moreover, the Soviet Union would choose the point of the attack, the place where the quantitative superiority is most relevant. The defense's disadvantages would be additionally complicated by the Soviets' ability to present ambiguous threats in many different areas at once. And here again, Soviet planners could play on the likely reluctance of some NATO members to take decisive defensive measures that might look "provocative" in a crisis.

The Pact is now well positioned to launch a surprise attack, and in the coming decade it could enhance this capability. Its forces are arrayed so that they do not need a great deal of final preparation or reinforcement from the Soviet Union. Speed is emphasized in Pact combat training. The attackers would be aiming for a blitzkrieg, expecting to break through forward defenses quite rapidly and destroy much of NATO's nuclear force before it could be used. A number of analyses suggest that the Pact's forces could move deep into Western Europe within ten days or so, before many, or perhaps any, U.S. troop reinforcements were on the continent.

To be sure, there would be several disadvantages to the Soviets in a surprise attack organized along these lines. In particular, it requires them to depend heavily on East European forces. This dependence should work to deter Moscow, and the deterrent effect could be enhanced if NATO took more advantage of the fact that most of Eastern Europe would be an unwilling accomplice in any Warsaw Pact attack.

So the Soviets might mobilize before an invasion and rely much more heavily on their own forces, even if this meant that the attack lost an element of surprise. In that case, a critical question would be whether the Alliance took advantage of the warning signals, which would doubtless be ambiguous—or declined to react promptly for fear of exacerbating the crisis.

Significant improvements have been made in recent years in U.S. capabilities for conventional defense in Europe. The most important of these have been the higher readiness and improved morale of military personnel. In addition, we have strengthened command and control systems and introduced some advanced munitions. Other equipment has been upgraded significantly. . . . For the future, the strengthening of a non-nuclear defense of Europe should be centered on the vigorous procurement of advanced conventional weapons and advanced technology for training. NATO must move again to reassert the technological superiority that has always been a major "comparative advantage" of the Western powers.

The Alliance's posture could be transformed by new military technologies. Among the most important: those distributed, advanced processors promising new effectiveness for command and intelligence functions, those involved in accurate standoff weapons, in new target acquisition systems for these weapons, in "low-observable" (Stealth) systems for aircraft and other vehicles, and for improved ballistic missile and air defenses. The number of advanced standoff weapons required if they are to have a decisive effect on a full scale engagement between NATO and the Warsaw Pact would be substantially greater than those we now plan to acquire; they would, however, replace many of the hundreds of thousands of "dumb" bombs that would be required in their absence. Smaller numbers could be highly effective in more restricted engagements, particularly in NATO's central region. These advanced weapons do not come cheaply; still, their cost would remain only a small fraction of current Alliance spending—small enough so that their acquisition could be accomplished by reallocating funds among NATO's programs, if necessary.

The advanced weaponry would help NATO implement its plans for the so-called Follow-on Forces Attack (FOFA), a doctrine formally embraced by the Alliance in 1984. The central idea of FOFA is that a purely static and shallow defense has no hope of repelling an invasion— that the Alliance must instantly launch air strikes against the enemy's follow-on forces in the rear. But air strikes would not be enough. A credible conventional defense must also include plans for NATO ground forces to mount counter-offensives across the NATO–Warsaw Pact border (which would, of course, have been violated by the Pact's invasion). Even more important, Alliance preparations for war should include specific plans to exploit Eastern Europe's potential disaffection from the Soviet Union.

Even if NATO makes dramatic improvements in its conventional defenses, the Alliance will still want nuclear weapons (including weapons based in Europe) for at least two reasons. First, because nuclear weapons discourage the massing of forces in any attack. Second, because

NATO's ability to respond with controlled and effective nuclear strikes would minimize the Soviets' temptations to use such weapons in discriminate attacks of their own on key elements of the Alliance's conventional capability.

However, there should be less ambiguity about the nature of this deterrent. The Alliance should threaten to use nuclear weapons not as a link to a wider and more devastating war—although the risk of further escalation would still be there—but mainly as an instrument for denying success to the invading Soviet forces. The nuclear weapons would be used discriminately in, for example, attacks on Soviet command centers or troop concentrations. The Alliance's nuclear posture, like its posture for conventional war, will gain in deterrent power from new technologies emphasizing precision and control.

There would be powerful incentives for Soviet planners to make sure that any nuclear attack on NATO forces was selective and discriminate. An attack of this kind would seek to exploit the fact that NATO forces, unlike the Soviet forces, are not prepared to fight a combined nuclear-conventional war. In particular, the Alliance is dependent on a small number of air bases and its vulnerable command system.

Although Soviet military power in East Asia is less formidable than in the Gulf region or Europe, it has been growing and, in combination with North Korean forces, poses a threat to South Korea. The threat is also of deep concern to Japan and other countries. The growing Soviet military presence in South Vietnam, together with uncertainty about the future of the U.S. bases in the Philippines, raises the possibility of a major strategic shift in Southeast Asia.

The U.S. force presence in this region is an important deterrent against attack; it contributes to discouraging Soviet aggression in other regions; and it has the virtue of not being highly costly. The bulk of our strength is in flexible naval forces, usable in any theater. As in the case of forces for Europe, these will benefit from the addition of smart, standoff weapons based on new technology. While the numbers required for possible wars in Asia would be less than those in Europe, an extended reach for these weapons would be even more critical in Asian contingencies.

The ability of the Japanese and South Korean forces to contribute to a conventional defense is steadily improving, and they complement U.S. forces in important ways. Japan's air defenses and ability to control the straits through which the Soviet Pacific fleet must move could bolster our ability to deal with a wide range of contingencies in the Pacific. And improving Japanese air defenses, increasingly coordinated with our naval force operations, enhance the effectiveness of those forces.

THE EXTREME THREATS

United States defense planning has long been dominated by two extreme contingencies. The first is a massive conventional attack against NATO by the Warsaw Pact, directed primarily at taking over Western Europe. The second, even more apocalyptic, is an unrestrained Soviet nuclear attack on U.S. strategic forces and other military targets in the West, many of which are located in or near cities. The first contingency leaves essentially no ally the chance to opt out; the second leaves the United States no incentive to exercise restraint.

Many NATO officials see a crucial connection between the two extreme contingencies. In the event of a conventional attack by the Warsaw Pact, they envisage an Allied conventional defense backed by the threat to use nuclear weapons. While the outcome of the conventional campaigns would of course affect the terms for ending the war, these officials do not expect these campaigns to be decisive in halting a Soviet attack. What they ultimately count on to stop the invasion, and make possible a peace on terms acceptable to the Alliance, is Soviet fear of an ever-widening nuclear war. They see the prospect of a "nuclear exchange"—one that would destroy both the Soviet Union and the United States—as NATO's ultimate leverage in defending against conventional attack. In the last analysis, then, the deterrent against the massive conventional attack is the same as the deterrent against the all-out nuclear attack.

A strategy that depends on this "nuclear exchange" has serious limitations. At best, it is useful only in dealing with those extreme contingencies. An excessive focus on these contingencies diverts defense planners from trying to deal with many important and far more plausible situations in which threats of nuclear annihilation would not be credible.

Apocalyptic showdowns between the United States and the Soviet Union are certainly conceivable in the nuclear age, but they are much less probable than other forms of conflict. Even when Soviet forces move into other countries, Soviet leaders are likely to indicate that their objectives are limited. They will try to behave in ways that give the West a stake in restraint and prudence. Over the last forty years, the Soviet regime has shown no signs of gravitating toward all-or-nothing gambles, much preferring instead to make gains by successive, incremental advances, below the threshold at which nuclear war would be a possibility. . . .

The Alliance must obviously plan for the extreme contingencies. But excessive emphasis on them can leave us unprepared for other and more likely kinds of aggression. The massive, worldwide, conventional attack by the Soviet Union is frequently characterized as a "worst case" scenario, and many assume that if we can defend against such attacks then surely we can also handle the "lesser included cases." But such reasoning misleads us. A geographically limited attack could exploit advantages that the Soviets gain from their internal lines of communication; they could bear down on one or more weakly defended U.S. allies while providing incentives to opt out for those not attacked. The attack would not look like a lesser case, but like a quite different case, in some ways much more difficult to deal with.

An emphasis on massive Soviet attacks leads to tunnel vision among defense planners. Assuming that any attack would rapidly become worldwide and necessarily involve most of our allies, planners have neglected the problem of Alliance disunity in a selective attack (the opting-out problem). They have not given enough thought to our prospects for exploiting tension within the Soviet empire (and giving the East Europeans some reasons to think about opting out). They have overemphasized war on Europe's central front, where the threat to use nuclear weapons might be more credible, and neglected planning for the possibility of Soviet assaults on the flanks, in Norway or Turkey.

Because they are so ingrained in the traditional thinking about defense, the extreme contingencies also warp decisions at a deeper level. They provide an inadequate conceptual framework for the Pentagon's decisions on defense priorities, requirements for weapons systems, or arms control criteria.

The dominant role of the extreme contingencies became especially perverse when they were packaged together in public debates with certain other ideas about nuclear deterrence. These ideas became influential in the West by the end of the 1960s. The core idea: that nuclear forces of the United States and the Soviet Union could be locked into a relationship of "stability" in which "mutual deterrence" made any war between the two sides quite impossible. There could be no war because war would inevitably lead to the use of nuclear weapons, which would mean the destruction of the two sides, which meant in turn that neither side would ever start a war. Nuclear weapons were inherently unusable.

This doctrine presents large difficulties. If deterrence really depended on mutual vulnerability, then NATO's foundation idea—that an attack on one is an attack on all—would be overboard. In the long run, the doctrine could not even deter selective attacks on the United States. It would be seen as a bluff, and the bluff would be called.

The criticism above is scarcely original. Extreme versions of the doctrine of mutual vulnerability as a guarantor of "stability" have been assailed for their contradictions ever since they first surfaced. Yet such views have, incredibly, retained an extraordinary hold over political and military elites in the West, especially in Europe.

We have argued here that the most extreme threats are also the least likely. It is obviously essential to keep them that way—to continue the inverse relationship between the intensity and the probability of the threats. However, this relationship is not a law of nature: it depends on things we do, or fail to do. If we slide into postures leaving us weak at higher levels of warfare—or leaving us with no higher-level response that leaders of democratic countries could reasonably make in a crisis—then our adversary will be encouraged to raise the level of violence, or to threaten to do so. Threats against us of mass destruction would look much more plausible.

What should the United States do to minimize the likelihood that the more extreme case—the all-out nuclear attack—will come to seem more probable? The answer is reasonably clear. Deterrence against any such attack requires the assured survival not only of powerful retaliatory forces, but also of the command and communications system that controls them. We must continue to ensure that Soviet leaders will never think they could launch a surprise nuclear attack of such effectiveness that it would prevent even a "dying sting" by a mortally wounded United States. For the U.S. retaliatory response to such a Soviet attack, our surviving forces need not be capable of destroying the entire range of military targets in the Soviet Union. If our civil society were destroyed, it would not matter much whether Soviet military targets were destroyed promptly or comprehensively.

To deter more plausible Soviet nuclear attacks, however, we also need survivable forces that could respond with discriminating attacks against military targets. The Soviet military has made clear its enormous interest in the new technologies of guidance and precision, and will have the capability to destroy military targets in the United States with low-yield nuclear weapons. We plainly cannot be caught without a similar capability.

In addition, we should continue moving toward a posture that includes defenses against ballistic and cruise missiles. Too much of the national debate about the Strategic Defense Initiative centers on the degree of perfection attainable in a system finally deployed. Even partial ballistic missile defenses can reduce an attacker's confidence in the success of his missile attack on our command centers and military forces. Relatively thin defenses may be effective against missile attacks by minor powers, many of which may have nuclear weapons in the years ahead. Such defenses might also help to forestall catastrophe in the event of an accidental missile launch, since retaliatory threats will not work against accidents. We should recognize that a limited initial deployment of ballistic missile defenses can be of value for several important contingencies, and we should pursue research and development aimed at such initial capabilities.

To deter the more plausible Soviet attacks, we must be able not only to respond discriminately, but must also have some prospects of keeping any such war within bounds—of ensuring that it does not rapidly deteriorate into an apocalypse. The revolution in micro-electronics (and photonics), along with advances in certain space technologies, have multiplied the modes of telecommunications available to command centers and generally made survivable command and control much more achievable. They have made possible the creation of a command system based on multiple centers, protected by its redundancy. The image of a "decapitated" nuclear force should become extinct. The assumption that command and control would instantly collapse in a nuclear war has led some proponents of "stability" through mutual vulnerability to favor launches of our strategic missiles as soon as U.S. warning systems signaled a Soviet missile launch. The concept involves a reckless gamble with fate. It must be banished from our long-term strategy.

INFLUENCING SOVIET ARMS POLICY

For the foreseeable future, the United States will have to compete militarily with the Soviet Union. Oddly enough, some Americans regard that statement as controversial. They see our past efforts to compete as part of an "action-reaction cycle" that has triggered a mindless and futile "arms race," leading to ever greater numbers of increasingly destructive weapons.

The facts are in sharp contrast with this view: in 1967 the U.S. had a third more nuclear weapons than it does today. The total explosive power of U.S. nuclear weapons today is only one quarter of the peak reached in 1960. The average warhead yield of U.S. nuclear weapons today is only one-fifteenth its 1957 peak. Even on the Soviet side, while the total number of nuclear weapons has been steadily increasing, the total explosive power and average warhead yield have both been declining since the mid-1970s.

It should not be thought that the decline in the U.S. nuclear arsenal was achieved at the cost of military effectiveness. Rather, it resulted mainly from technical innovations that made it possible to substitute conventional weapons for nuclear weapons in most anti-air and anti-submarine roles. Additional reductions should be achievable as new technology makes it practical to use conventional weapons to attack many ground targets that currently require nuclear weapons. This trend runs exactly counter to the notion of a "qualitative arms race" which sees innovation as the principal cause of the "nuclear arms race."

As we integrate our national security strategy and our arms negotiation policy, it is worth remembering that past reductions in the U.S. nuclear stockpile, undertaken in pursuit of our unilateral strategic objectives, have been larger than the total reduction in the number of Soviet warheads that would be accomplished together by the INF [Intermediate Range Nuclear Forces] treaty and the 50 percent reduction hoped for from START [Strategic Arms Reduction Talks].

In fact, the Soviet-American military competition has not been much of a race. The pattern of the past forty years is more accurately characterized as a steady, slow-paced, relentless military buildup on the Soviet side and an erratic, inconsistent, up-and-down performance by the United States. Only our side has been reactive: we have let defense slide in periods when no threat seemed imminent, then turned around and launched a buildup after an external challenge — as in Korea (1950), Berlin (1961), Vietnam (the 1960s), and Afghanistan (1979). During the 1960s and 1970s, Soviet strategic spending grew steadily, but U.S. spending on strategic forces declined by 67 percent, while the myth of the arms race flourished.

Since we need to compete with the Soviet Union, we need to emphasize strategies for doing so more effectively — strategies that will continue to capitalize on our inherent advantages in technology, that maximize the return on our military investment, and that lower returns to the Soviets on their huge investments. By learning how to compete effectively, we can improve our chances of negotiating useful arms agreements.

We need to promote military programs in which the United States has a special competitive advantage vis-a-vis the Soviets. One example is "low-observables" (Stealth) technology, which will make aircraft and other military vehicles harder to target. The "competitive" case for investing heavily in Stealth is not just that we are ahead in the technology but that deploying it will render obsolete much of the enormous Soviet investment in air defense. Following on Secretary Weinberger's 1987 initiative, the Defense Department should seek out other programs that offer the United States a special competitive advantage.

The military strategy described throughout these pages has to include an arms control strategy. The link between national security and arms control might seem obvious and noncontroversial: good arms control agreements will give us more security, possibly at lower cost. But many people prefer to think of arms control as somehow taking place on a different plane from that of defense planning. A great deal of political rhetoric encourages them to believe that the ultimate point of arms control is not so much military as political. For many Americans and

Europeans, the lure of the agreements is that they enable us to engage Soviet leaders in a "process," expected to develop a "momentum" of its own, that will lead to understanding about other contentious matters and serve broadly to reduce international tensions.

This perspective could be a recipe for disaster. When arms control agreements are valued mainly for the international good will they are expected to generate, and only secondarily for their effects on arms, then our political leaders will always be under pressure to reach agreements by making concessions on arms. Moreover, if an existing agreement is valued primarily as an expression of good will toward the Soviet Union, then it is much more difficult for American leaders to express concern about cheating by the Soviets, since these expressions will inevitably be translated on the political stage as a lack of interest in furthering the new relationship.

The problem of cheating is hard to handle in a democracy. Proposed arms deals cannot be evaluated solely on the assumption that the Soviet Union will automatically comply. We must also ask whether we could cope with a major violation or sudden abrogation of the agreement. In particular, we need to anticipate the effect on our security of a delayed or uncertain U.S. response to substantial violations. To begin with, our arms agreements must be capable of yielding evidence, in the event of a major violation, that will be sufficiently unambiguous to enable the U.S. Government to decide on an adequate response. Such a decision would be painful for both Congress and the Executive Branch, for it would mean that our hopes for arms control had been set back and that costly remedies were urgently needed. The more significant the arms agreement, the more important a U.S. capability to deter violations, or promptly to redress the damage arising from major violations. To this end we must maintain a standby capacity for surging defense production.

A good arms agreement will be consistent with our long-term military strategy. This means we want agreements that (a) do not assume nuclear vulnerability is a desirable condition for the American people, (b) do not assume that accuracy is an undesirable attribute for American weapons, and (c) do not assume that defense against nuclear attacks is more threatening than offense. Agreements should be negotiated with an awareness that they could restrict our forces and technologies for decades.

For the foreseeable future, it will not be realistic to pursue agreements to eliminate all nuclear weapons, or all chemical weapons. The huge Soviet advantage in conventional forces makes it likely that the Alliance will need some nuclear weapons to defend Europe for many years to come. A ban on chemical weapons could not be verified.

Soviet arms control proposals often favor limits on testing of new technology. Such limits impede us in maintaining our technological advantage. Mutual testing restraints, even if enforceable, must be examined carefully to make sure they would indeed serve our interest. The United States relies on technological advantages to compensate for quantitative inferiority, so test limitations would rarely work in our favor. The ultimate problem about such limitations is that they make it harder to continue developing the new technologies associated with accuracy and precision. Tests of less destructive but more accurate conventional arms can help us to develop forces that will reduce our reliance on nuclear weapons.

Nuclear arms agreements should be centered on verifiable reductions in offensive weapons. A substantial reduction in the nuclear missile forces of the U.S.S.R. and the United States would make it much easier for both sides to develop and deploy effective missile defenses. Such a long-term reduction in nuclear weapons could serve the security of all nations, provided at least two conditions are met:

1. For the foreseeable future, the U.S. verification system and the U.S. capability for responding to violations must be able to prevent (or be able to cope with) major Soviet cheating.

2. The threat of nonnuclear aggression against our allies and other vital areas must be greatly reduced, in part, perhaps, through conventional arms reductions.

The United States might gain substantially from arms agreements focused on conventional forces. Agreements to reduce U.S. and Soviet forces stationed in Europe might improve Alliance security. Their value would depend on the readiness and ability of the Alliance to respond promptly to a reintroduction of Soviet forces, even under ambiguous circumstances and considering Soviet geographic advantages in bringing force to bear, not only on NATO's central front, but in particular at the flanks. However, to make significant cuts in defense budgets, it is necessary to demobilize conventional forces, not merely to remove them from Europe. Indeed, such agreements are the only kind that might lead to significant cuts in defense budgets. Agreements limited to nuclear weapons affect only a small fraction of U.S. and Soviet military expenditures.

An agreement that imposed considerably larger cuts on the preponderant Soviet conventional forces, and mandated the destruction of their heavy equipment (tanks and artillery), could improve Alliance security unambiguously. Such an agreement would work to reduce the Soviet geographic advantage and avoid excessive dependence on NATO's ability to respond quickly to ambiguous warning. It is conceivable that

Soviet leaders might agree to some such deal to reduce the pressures of defense spending on their beleaguered economy.

MANAGING TECHNOLOGY

Although U.S. strategy has depended heavily on our technological superiority since World War II, American technology today is less superior than it used to be. Even some Third World countries are becoming independent producers and users of high tech. The Soviet Union is gaining in a number of areas, while continuing to acquire Western technology both legally and illegally. In addition, the Soviets have worked hard at ensuring that their acquisitions are applied rapidly to priority military missions. Their military research budgets have exceeded those of the United States and have continued to increase steadily.

U.S. budgeting for research and development has been constrained and uneven, and from the mid 1960s to the late 1970s, the technology base was substantially eroded. During the period 1965–1980 U.S. spending on military research and development declined about 20 percent. In 1965, estimated Soviet spending on military research and development was about 65 percent of the U.S.'s, but by 1980 it had grown to more than 150 percent of U.S. spending. In the 1980s, a turnaround for the United States began, but more recently our spending on the technology base was cut back again.

At the same time, the substantial R&D undertaken by U.S. defense industry (reimbursed in part by the Department of Defense) has changed significantly in its character. While this effort was highly innovative in the 1950s and 1960s, it has become increasingly conservative in the 1970s and 1980s. Today, it has become far more an effort to reduce technical risk than to innovate. In some measure the Pentagon is responsible for the new emphasis. The main criterion for reimbursement used to be the innovativeness of the work; today the controlling question is apt to be whether industry's R&D is sufficiently related to an ongoing weapons program.

The underlying trends are disturbing. In a growing number of basic technologies with important military applications, the United States may lose its superiority over the Soviet Union. Moreover, in translating scientific knowledge into deployed military systems, the Soviet Union has recently been far more successful than we have. Our current approach is piecemeal and haphazard. The procurement process is rigid, slow, confrontational, and micro-managed in ways that endlessly work against the efficient use of our resources.

Even more important is the difference between the U.S. and the Soviet approach in relating decisions on new weapons systems to a long-term strategy. It has become apparent from Soviet arms control decisions over the last 20 years, as well as from the way in which Soviet arms have been fielded, that Moscow's decisions on new military systems have been guided by a long-term strategy to a far greater extent than ours.

Defense Department officials try to minimize program risk by writing excessively detailed specifications, which unfortunately guarantee that compliance will be expensive, technically conservative, and uncreative. Throughout the acquisition process, such risk is avoided by focusing on today's technologies and on familiar old operational concepts—even though the system being procured will typically be needed for many years into the future. To be sure, conservatism in procurement has also been fostered by the past absence of an integrated long-term strategy. In its absence, the system keeps responding to only a few standard contingencies and overlooking many likely demands on U.S. forces in the future.

Fixed-price R&D contracts have been another obstacle to advanced technology. Such contracting has several pernicious effects. It leads contractors to commit themselves without a proper plan for follow-up, which greatly increases the likelihood of overruns and slipped schedules. These in turn lead the harried Defense Department program manager to minimize technological risk in a project, which he typically does by steering clear of the cost and schedule uncertainties associated with leading-edge technologies.

For the coming years, we will need an acquisition process that fosters cohesion, speed, and incentives for innovation. The Defense Department has made a fair amount of progress toward revitalizing the acquisition process by implementing the recommendations of the Packard Commission. But the reforms need to be moved further, preferably with Congress a partner in the process—and exhibiting some self-restraint on micro-management.

Conservatism in procurement has meant a dearth of "new-new" projects—efforts to develop systems incorporating both new technologies and new operational concepts. Successful past examples of such efforts are the long-range bombers, nuclear submarines, and solid-propellant missiles of the 1950s. (Stealth may turn out to be a more recent example, provided it will be coupled with new operational concepts.) These were all highly successful, but a defining characteristic of new-new efforts is that success surely cannot be predicted with much certainty. Which is precisely why such projects have been rare in today's age of micro-management.

The main reason for the dearth of projects incorporating both new technologies and new military operations is the way in which the Pentagon tends to establish requirements for military systems. A few major innovations, combining both new strategic concepts and new technologies, have recently been instituted from the top down—that is to say they have been driven by a Presidential decision, or a decision of the Secretary of Defense. An example of the former is SDI in 1983; examples of the latter are Stealth and cruise missile development in the 1970s, and conventionally armed cruise missiles in the 1980s. But the majority of R&D and procurement projects originate at the working level of the Services. The CINCs (Commanders in Chief of Unified and Specified Commands) can identify needs related to their missions. This role of the CINCs has recently been strengthened, but the dominant role in setting new requirements still rests with the Service staffs.

The process of generating requirements for R&D and procurement must be guided by a long-term view of U.S. strategy and of the technological opportunities. The process should not only tolerate but actively seek out new concepts for meeting our basic strategic needs through new systems and new operational tactics. We must overcome the "horse cavalry syndrome" familiar from military history. A number of options are available to the Secretary of Defense for encouraging strategic innovation and imparting a long-term perspective in the requirements process. For example, when we have identified an innovative, high priority project that combines new technology with new operating concepts, we may want to set up a special "fast track" on which risk-takers suffer fewer penalties.

We cannot assume that all programs currently planned for the 1990s will in fact be fully funded. This means that defense planners will likely face some wrenching decisions about trade-offs. They will want to maintain spending on many systems now in engineering development, yet they will also find it difficult to cut personnel-related costs. All of which suggests that the Defense Department will have trouble in fully replacing its aging 'capital stock. It is not yet possible to predict how these trade-offs will play out and whether (to mention a particularly tough decision) they will result in force-level cutbacks.

We can, however, decide now which programs should be given the highest priority in the new long-term strategy. In general, these include programs that strengthen our ability to respond to aggression with controlled, discriminate use of force. They also include programs that in diverse ways work to promote flexibility and widen the options available to future Presidents. We would also assign a high priority— higher than it has been getting in recent years—to spending in the accounts for basic research and advanced development.

Among the programs meeting these criteria, four seem especially urgent:

1. the integration of "low-observables" (Stealth) systems into our force posture;
2. "smart" weapons—precision-guided munitions that combine long range and high accuracy;
3. ballistic missile defense; and
4. space capabilities needed for wartime operations.

Returns to national security will be especially high in these areas, and Congress and DoD must work to ensure that the systems have adequate funding and become operational as soon as possible. . . .

The technologies mentioned above are by no means the only ones needing extensive development, but they afford a powerful reminder of the extent to which our long-term strategy depends critically on investments in military science. The "rusting" of the technology base in the past couple of decades is a deeply disturbing trend. The United States badly needs an aggressive effort, informed by a long-term strategy, to strengthen science and technology programs.

MANAGING THE DEFENSE BUDGET

Budgeting for national security is apt to be especially difficult in the decades ahead. The integrated long-term strategy proposed in these pages will provide a guide to some difficult budget decisions the country will be making in this period.

The resources available for defense will probably be constrained more than in the past, principally by concern over the national debt and pressures for social spending (the latter driven, for example, by the aging of the U.S. population). These constraints are likely to increase risks to our national security. The United States came into the Eighties suffering from the cumulative effects of many years in which our military investment was below that of the Soviet Union. Despite our spending turnaround in the first half of this decade, we have yet to eliminate the gap that opened up in the 1970s.

National security does not have much of a "natural constituency" in the United States, and Congress has repeatedly demonstrated that in the absence of a crisis it is prone to cut back on defense—and then to spend heavily when the next crisis comes along. In the years since World War II, the United States has never had a period of more than six years in which defense spending increased in real terms every year. Defense dollars will continue to buy less so long as we remain in this stop-go mode.

Congress and the Executive Branch should aim at steady, moderate growth in the defense budget and avoid these extreme fluctuations. As a modest first step toward smoothing out our spending, the Defense Department has been supporting a move to a two-year budget cycle, and the Congressional committees concerned with the armed services and with the budget have agreed that the proposal makes sense. Such a budget would help both government and industry to plan more realistically for procurements. It should also help to make various defense accounts less vulnerable to changes resulting from short-term political considerations. It would still not give the United States the formidable stability that has long marked Soviet defense investment, but it would be a highly positive development.

Given the continuing threat represented by large Soviet forces with the advantage of interior lines of communication, our current defense budget is none too large. The spending required to sustain that posture has recently absorbed around 6 percent of our country's output, which is at the lower end of the historic defense/GNP ratio. Only in the mid-1970s has spending fallen below 6 percent. Yet we now face the prospect of the spending levels again declining below 6 percent. . . .

If we hold at around a 6 percent share of GNP, the United States will be able to increase real defense spending at the long-term growth rate of the economy—3 percent or so a year. At that rate, we could acquire the systems needed to maintain the current worldwide posture, cope with some occasional new threats, and retain some needed flexibility. We could also incorporate the capabilities called for in this report. But if defense cutbacks continue, and we drift to lower levels of GNP share, something will have to give.

Precisely because the years ahead are likely to be austere, we need a long-term strategy that tells us how to rank our priorities. We need to be clear about which programs we want to protect in periods when budgets are being cut. Meanwhile, we also need to plan better for the occasional periods of expansion. So long as the country remains afflicted by stop-go spending, the Pentagon will need plans for taking maximum advantage of the next crisis-driven surge in spending.

Defense budgeting decisions inescapably require resource allocations to deal with present and future risks. A decision to invest incremental dollars in operations and maintenance rather than to initiate procurement of complex weaponry is implicitly a judgment that near-term threats outweigh those for the long term. These abstract considerations are especially relevant to budgetary decisions in periods of cutbacks.

When spending decisions are not clearly linked to a strategic vision, then there will be heavy pressures to maintain force size and take the cuts out of modernization. Any steady pattern of that sort would be incompatible with the strategy we propose, which depends heavily on procurement of advanced weaponry. The preceding [section] described several of the programs we believe to be especially important to our proposed strategy. As indicated in the [section], heavy investment in basic research—the longest lead-time of all—is essential.

In past years, defense planners have generally identified ships, aircraft, and other major platforms as the long lead-time items requiring the most protection in periods of budget stringency. More recently these "platforms" have become enormously expensive and are being introduced less and less often. The Air Force introduced ten new fighters in the 1940s, six in the 1950s, two in the 1960s and two in the 1970s; we now look for only one fighter to be introduced in the 1980s and 1990s combined.

To a considerable extent, then, we recommend that modernization in the years ahead take new forms, with a particular emphasis on the auxiliary systems which can be changed more frequently than can the expensive major "platforms." These systems include the intelligent subsystems and munitions carried on the platforms. Not necessarily carried on the "platforms," but helpful in informing and directing their use, will be modernized sensors, command, control, and communications. If indeed we can afford fewer major weapons "platforms," then we must equip those we have so as to maximize their effectiveness and flexibility. U.S. forces are small relative to those of the Soviet Union. To maximize their effectiveness, we should ensure that our active forces are prepared to deter or resist the most plausible kinds of Soviet attacks—those that are highly selective and have limited objectives—and are not configured only against massive and widespread attacks on the West as a whole. We must maintain the readiness, sustainability, and mobility of active forces sufficient, at least, to meet the likeliest attacks. With the over-all size of the active forces possibly being reduced, we may have to rely more heavily on cadre units and reserves as a base for mobilization.

As noted elsewhere in this report, security assistance programs are of great importance, and we must get rid of the endless restrictions placed on the dwindling amounts of available funds. A case can be made that a dollar spent on security assistance buys more security for the United States than a dollar spent anywhere else. In comparison to the amounts involved in supporting our own forces or procuring new weapons, security assistance is cheap, and we call on Congress to recognize that modest expenditures in many Third World countries can dramatically improve our long-term strategic position.

Our budgetary strategy should also provide for continuing and strengthening the Defense Department's planning for a "surge capability." In a world of stop-go budgeting, we need better ways of spending the money when the light suddenly turns green—when, say, Congress responds to some sudden threat or crisis by making substantial new funds available. The Defense Department should continue its advance planning to make the best use of such a surge. It should develop the capacity to expand production of critical equipment, for example, and to stockpile long-lead items that might represent bottlenecks in a buildup. It should also try to assemble "human resource" inventories pointing to expertise of various kinds that would be needed at such times. With planning, we can develop sizable surge capabilities with relatively modest investments.

CONNECTING THE ELEMENTS OF THE STRATEGY

The Enduring Aims of U.S. Policy

We live in a world whose nations are increasingly connected by their economies, cultures, and politics—sometimes explosively connected as in the repeated vast migrations since World War II of refugees escaping political, religious and racial persecution. It is a world in which military as well as economic power will be more and more widely distributed and in which the United States must continue to expect some nations to be deeply hostile to its purposes.

The United States does not seek to expand its territory at the expense of the Soviet Union or any other country. Nor do any of our allies present a danger of an invasion of the Soviet Union or the territories it dominates. The Soviets, nonetheless, insist that we, our allies and other countries, the weak as well as the powerful, do threaten attack. Such Soviet suspicions or assertions have been inherent in their system of rule: they need to posit a hostile world to establish the legitimacy of their regime. We would, needless to say, welcome a basic change in their antagonistic stance.

However, even if "perestroika" and "glasnost" signal an intention to make that change, it will not be easy to accomplish. Moscow's suspicion and hostility are rooted in 70 years of Soviet and 400 years of Tsarist history. Relaxing their hold on the countries they dominate on their borders can threaten their control of dissident nationalities within their borders. We should not deceive ourselves. The Western democracies cannot do much to advance the process simply by persuading the Soviets that we are not about to attack them, or by trying to shed any capability for offense—and thus for counterattack. Such efforts would merely reflect misunderstandings of the internal role played by external threats in Soviet rule; and might encourage aggression. The Soviets feel threatened by the autonomy of the free countries on their border.

The United States has critical interests in the continuing autonomy of some allies very distant from us—in Europe and the Mediterranean, in the Middle East and Southwest Asia, in East Asia and the Pacific, and in the Western Hemisphere. We use bases, ports and air space in helping these allies defend themselves and one another. In some cases, where the danger to them from an adversary close by is especially great, it has been a durable element of U.S. strategy to deploy our forces forward. We do this, however, at the invitation of allies who are sovereign and independent of us and on conditions that they name. They can always ask us to leave. In some cases they have; and unlike the Soviets, we have always complied.

The fact that we lead sovereign allies who can differ from us in their interests in various circumstances and places has direct implications for defense; it means that even where there are gathering but ambiguous signs of danger to our common interests, getting a cohesive allied response and bringing it to bear in time to block the danger may be difficult. A dictator, or an involuntary coalition dominated by a dictatorship, has less trouble in preparing to launch military operations. And the Soviets are not, and will not be, the only danger to our interests.

In the changing environment of the next 20 years, the U.S. and its allies, formal and informal, will need to improve their ability to bring force to bear effectively, with discrimination and in time to thwart any of a wide range of plausible aggressions against their major common interests—and in that way to deter such aggressions.

We need to bring a longer view to the necessary day-to-day decisions on national security. The next two decades are likely to exhibit sharp discontinuities as well as gradual changes with effects that are cumulatively revolutionary: major new military powers, new technology, new sources of conflict and opportunities for cooperation. To cope with these changes, we will need versatile and adaptive forces.

An Integrated Strategy

Because our problems in the real world are connected and because budgets compel trade-offs, we need to fit together strategies for a wide range of conflicts: from the most confined, lowest intensity and highest probability to the most widespread, apocalyptic and least likely. We want the worse conflicts to be less likely, but that holds only if our weakness at some higher level—or the lack of a higher level response that democratic leaders would be willing to use—does not invite such raising of the ante. For genuine stability, we need to assure our adversaries that military aggression at any level of violence against our important interests will be opposed by military force.

More violent wars grow out of less violent ones, and locally confined aggression (e.g., a Soviet invasion of the Persian Gulf) could drastically alter the correlation of forces. And one cannot completely separate "internal" and "external" conflicts. The shadow of Soviet intervention could affect the outcome of an internal succession crisis in Iran for example. (In the past the Soviets have used a puppet "Free Azerbaijan" to cloak their preparations for intervention in Iran and Eastern Turkey, which they appear to regard as strategically linked.) Even terrorism can have a large effect on our ability to meet greater dangers by destabilizing vulnerable allies, dividing allies from each other, and dividing public opinion at home.

Policy statements on deterring and on fighting aggression should fit together. We cannot dissuade an attacker if he believes we are not willing as well as able to fight back. Our will is called into question by frequent statements about "mutual deterrence" that imply that we want the Soviets to be able to deter the United States unless the United States has been attacked. Such statements undermine the essential pledge that we will use conventional, and if they fail, nuclear weapons in response to a Soviet attack directed solely at an ally. Similarly, the Soviet leadership might be misled by statements, heard in Europe, that even winning a conventional war would be "unacceptable." If such statements mean that fighting with nuclear weapons would do less harm to civilians than precisely delivered conventional weapons, or that such conventional weapons would cause "more harm to civilians than World War II," they are plainly wrong. If they mean that the West would be unwilling to use either non-nuclear or nuclear weapons, then they suggest we would not respond at all and so erode our ability to deter an attack. The issue is about how effectively to deter a non-nuclear or a nuclear attack. We and our allies would rather deter than defeat an aggression, but a bluff is less effective and more dangerous in a crisis than the ability and will to use conventional and, if necessary, nuclear weapons with at least a rough discrimination that preserves the values we are defending.

Offense and defense (both active and passive) complement each other at any level of conflict. Just as our offensive capabilities can discourage an adversary from concentrating to penetrate defenses, so active defense and passive defenses (such as concealment and mobility) are mutually reinforcing.

Decisions on military systems are interconnected and ought not to be dealt with piecemeal. The connections must be reflected in arms negotiations, in force planning and in the definition of military "requirements" during the acquisition process.

The Need to Consider a Wider Range of More Plausible, Important Contingencies

Alliance policy and weapons modernization, as already mentioned, have focused largely on the two extreme contingencies of a massive Warsaw Pact conventional attack and an unrestrained Soviet nuclear attack aimed at widespread military targets, doing mortal damage. The first contingency diverts allied attention from obligations underlying the basic premise of the Alliance—that an attack on one possibly vulnerable ally is an attack on all—and it ignores the Soviet interest in inducing other allies to opt out. The second contingency assumes the Soviets would have little concern about inviting their own self-destruction, since it would leave us no incentive to exercise discrimination and restraint.

However, Soviet military planners have shown an awareness that if the Politburo uses military force, it has a strong incentive to do so selectively and keep the force under political control. They do not want their nuclear attack to get in the way of their invading forces or destroy what is being taken over. And above all, they do not want to risk the destruction of the Soviet Union. They recognize as revolutionary for the nature of war the ongoing revolution in microelectronics which makes possible the strategic use of non-nuclear weapons. Their 40 years of investment in protecting their national command system, as well as their careful attention to the wartime uses of space and other means of command and control, show they are serious about directing force for political ends and keeping it under control. If we take the extreme contingencies as the primary basis for planning, we will move less rapidly toward a more versatile, discriminating and controlled capability.

It will always be possible to slip mindlessly toward such an apocalypse, so we will always need to deter the extreme contingencies. But it does not take much nuclear force to destroy a civil society. We need to devote our predominant effort to a wide range of more plausible, important contingencies.

Changes in the Security Environment

Our central challenge since World War II has been to find ways, in formal and informal alliances with other sovereign states, to defeat and therefore deter aggression against our major interests at points much closer to our adversaries than to us. "Military balances," i.e., matching numbers of NATO and Warsaw Pact tanks, guns, anti-tank weapons, etc. (even adjusted for qualitative differences in technology) fail to reveal the problem. The issue is not simply one of distance, but of timely political access en route to and in a threatened area, and of getting cohesive, preparatory responses by sovereign allies in answer to ambiguous signs of gathering danger.

The Atlantic Alliance has a problem of cohesion. In dealing with countries like Nicaragua or Libya, it is perhaps not surprising that the allies differ in how they conceive their interests. But even on NATO's flanks and in the Persian Gulf, where the vital interests of our European allies in blocking a Soviet takeover are more direct and massive than ours, the problem has been worsening. In recent base negotiations, Spain and Portugal have shown little concern for their role in reinforcing Turkey or allied forces in the Gulf. And some NATO countries on the Northern Flank, with small military forces of their own, have opposed measures that would help timely reinforcement for themselves; they justify this opposition on the far-fetched grounds that the Soviets need reassurance that they will not be the victims of an unprovoked attack. The increasing number of European advocates of "Non-Offensive Defense" would carry reassurance further by eschewing all "offensive" weapons. That would not prevent enemy attack, but it would prevent counter-attacking.

While our timely access has deteriorated sharply since the 1950s, the Soviets have used their internal lines of communication to improve greatly their ability to bring conventional force to bear quickly at points on their periphery and have systematically improved their access to air space and bases near their periphery. As a result, in some vital theaters such as the Persian Gulf, their ability to bring force to bear has improved dramatically while ours has declined in absolute terms. In the next 20 years and in other theaters of conflict, increasingly well equipped smaller powers as well as new major military powers are likely to give us still stronger incentives to develop a more versatile and discriminate force.

We have developed a variety of precise weapons, both long and short range, and have taken important steps to improve the robustness and effectiveness of our command, control, communications and intelligence as well as the training of our forces. Cumulative advances in microelectronics have already had a revolutionary impact on the possibility of increasing the effectiveness of attacks on military targets while confining effects largely to these targets. The advances have enormously improved the possibilities of large scale battle management and the maintenance of political control. In the next decade or two, they will do so even more. Most importantly, these cumulative changes have made a single, or a few, nonnuclear weapons effective for many missions previously requiring thousands of nonnuclear weapons, or nuclear ones.

As stated elsewhere in this report, we would depend heavily on space systems for the control and direction of our conventional forces needed to defeat a Soviet invasion, and the Soviets would use their own satellites as an essential support for their invasion. Each side would have strong reasons to defend its own space system and to degrade the other side's.

The dynamism of our private sector gives us an inherent advantage in realizing the benefits offered by the new technologies. Nevertheless, we and our allies have often lagged in actually fielding the capabilities needed to meet the increasingly formidable dangers presented by the growing strength of the Soviets and other potential antagonists.

Wars on the Soviet Periphery and in the Third World

We and the Soviets will have very large incentives to exploit the greater effectiveness and discrimination of conventional weapons afforded by the new information technologies and to confine destruction so as to give the other side a stake in keeping destruction within bounds. If nuclear weapons were used, both sides would have even larger incentives to rely on technologies of control, since losing control then would be most disastrous. Both sides have devoted growing efforts to ensure the survivability of their command and control under wartime conditions.

The equipment, training, uses of intelligence, and methods of operation we have developed mainly for contingencies involving massive worldwide attacks by the Soviet Union do not prepare us very well for conflicts in the Third World. Such conflicts are likely to feature terrorism, sabotage, and the "low intensity" violence. Assisting allies to respond to such violence will put a premium on the use of some of the same information technologies we find increasingly relevant for selective operations in higher intensity conflicts. The need to use force for political purposes and to discriminate between civilian and legitimate targets is even more evident here. In particular, we will need optical and electronic intelligence, communications and control, and precise delivery of weapons so as to minimize damage to noncombatants. We will need advanced technologies for training local forces. These will be important both for obtaining local political support and support in the United States and elsewhere in the West.

The Northern and Southern Flanks of NATO are more weakly defended than the Center. Both are of critical importance for the Center's defense, but both suffer from political problems which inhibit reinforcement in a timely manner. Defense of the Northern Flank depends critically on rapid reinforcement from the U.S. and the rest of NATO;

yet increased restrictions on U.S. and NATO activities in Norway limit our ability to bring force to bear quickly in defense of the region. In the south, Turkey is of key importance both in the defense of U.S. and other naval forces in the Eastern Mediterranean and defense of our interests in the Persian Gulf. Turkey's critical importance should be recognized by increasing security assistance from the U.S. and from other members of NATO as well as countries such as Japan that have a vital interest in the areas Turkey would help to defend.

In the Persian Gulf itself, the great distances and political difficulties involved in obtaining timely access must be overcome to mount a credible defense of the region. Improvements in technology, and a greater allied willingness to share the political risks of getting such access, would greatly improve our ability to deter attacks.

Both South Korea and Japan will be increasingly able to defend themselves against a conventional invasion. The U.S. presence in both countries works to discourage possible dangers, such as Soviet (or Chinese) intervention or use of nuclear weapons, and should be continued, not least because it is also of great importance in increasing our capability to deal in a timely way with threats elsewhere in the Western Pacific.

It has long been the policy of the Atlantic Alliance that if non-nuclear force proves inadequate, we must be prepared to use nuclear force to stop a conventional invasion. But this force should be effective and discriminate—kept under control rather than a suicidal bluff. We need in any case the ability to deter plausible nuclear attacks on U.S. and allied forces. This should include a large role in defending common interests outside national boundaries and outside Alliance boundaries where, as in the Persian Gulf, allied critical interests clearly coincide with our own. A larger nuclear role in the defense of other European allies, which has been suggested for the British and French, will require, as in our own case, an effective and discriminate nuclear force capable of use to defeat a Soviet invasion into allied territory. The French and British now have options to move in that direction.

The Coherent Use of Resources for Security

We have lagged in fielding weapons systems needed to cope with the increasingly capable forces of the Soviet Union and lesser adversaries of the Third World. As the Packard Commission has stressed, this lag has to do with cumbersome and unstable acquisition and R&D funding procedures and the lack of adequate and early testing. To overcome this lag, we should turn to faster prototyping and testing of systems that would make our forces more versatile and discriminate.

Equally important, however, will be clearly defined "requirements" that are related to a coherent national strategy. "Requirements" guided by a long-term strategy are critical to getting the most out of a given budget.

The increasingly widespread latent dangers with which we and our allies must cope do not justify the belief that we can safely hold our defense budget level, much less reduce it. However, if tighter budgets impose an increase in risks, we should, for the near term, accept a greater risk of the unlikely extreme attacks, in order to bring about a reduced risk of the more probable conflicts, both now and in the future. Instead of giving priority to buying various types of large "platforms," we should seek continued improvement in the sensors and command, control and intelligence systems which can multiply the effectiveness of our ships and aircraft. And we must provide the resources needed to maintain the training, morale, and excellence in leadership of the men and women in the armed forces.

Arms Agreements and the Continuing Problem of Bringing Discriminate and Timely Force to Bear against Aggression

Carefully designed and enforceable arms agreements can help reduce the risk of war by diminishing military threats for a range of plausible contingencies while preserving, or facilitating, our capacity to keep the application of force discriminate and effective. Recent proposals by the Soviets and some in the West to stop the testing of missiles, nuclear warheads, anti-satellite systems and active defenses have been based on the premise that this would slow the qualitative arms race that is assumed to drive a quantitative arms race. However, such restraints frequently would have the opposite effect to that intended; they would make the job of getting a credible deterrent harder. . . . A well-designed agreement on self-defense zones in space could make it easier to protect the space-borne sensors, and command, control and communications systems. An agreement that would drastically reduce the Soviet advantage in non-nuclear force has been proposed by leaders in both American Parties and by many prominent Europeans. Its purpose would be to make more equal the ability of NATO and the Warsaw Pact to bring timely, effective force to bear at critical danger points. It would thus address the basic East-West asymmetries due to geography and the greater Soviet conventional effort.

The strategy recommended in this report should guide arms negotiations as well as national and Alliance decisions on defense. Such a strategy of discriminate deterrence seems in any case more capable of building a community of interests with adversaries over the long run than reckless threats to annihilate their populations. Our arms control policy must be connected coherently to a viable, long term Alliance strategy.

7

U.S. Grand Strategy for the 1990s: The Case for Finite Containment

STEPHEN M. WALT

As the United States approaches the twenty-first century, a major debate on U.S. grand strategy has begun.[1] Since World War II, the main objective of U.S. grand strategy has been to prevent territorial expansion by the Soviet Union while simultaneously avoiding a major war.[2] Although both ends and means have varied over time, the central elements of this strategy—commonly known as "containment"—have been military alliances with Western Europe and Japan and the deployment of U.S. armed forces in Europe and the Far East.[3] Despite initial misgivings and occasional flurries of criticism, the strategy has enjoyed substantial popular support, largely because it has worked so well.

In recent years, however, containment has come under increasing attack. The sources of discontent are easy to identify: the relative decline of U.S. power,[4] the resurgence of America's allies, the collapse of Soviet-sponsored regimes in Eastern Europe, and the possibility that *glasnost* and *perestroika* may significantly alter the Soviet threat. Given these developments, it is not surprising that the fundamental principles of postwar U.S. grand strategy are being debated more vigorously now than at any time since the beginning of the cold war.[5]

THE STRATEGIC DEBATE

Alternative Views

Proposals for change are remarkably diverse, in both the ends they seek and the means they would employ. At the risk of oversimplification, the main alternatives can be divided into several distinct schools of thought. At one extreme is what we might label *world order,* whose proponents argue that other states do not pose the main threat to U.S. interests, that the real dangers are nuclear war, ecological decay, and

136

persistent global poverty. Because they believe that a system of independent states cannot manage these common problems, they favor a fundamental transformation of the existing state system. The United States should direct its efforts toward the creation of a more humanitarian "world order" through disarmament, moral education, greater reliance on international law, and strengthened international institutions (such as international peacekeeping forces). The implications for U.S. grand strategy would be enormous: in the unlikely event that this approach were adopted, military power and alliance commitments would be of minor importance.[6]

A second grand strategy is *neo-isolationism.*[7] This strategy assumes that the United States has few, if any, security interests beyond its borders, that threats to these interests are modest, and that very limited means (a modest army, a coastal navy, and a small nuclear deterrent) are sufficient to protect them. Neo-isolationists argue that U.S. allies are capable of defending themselves, that U.S. alliance commitments rest on escalatory threats that lack credibility, and that continued economic prosperity will require reducing U.S. defense expenditures. These writers advocate the rapid dissolution of U.S. alliance commitments, a drastic reduction in U.S. defense spending, and a return to hemispheric or continental defense.[8]

A third school advocates a policy of *disengagement* by reducing (but not eliminating) the U.S. military commitment to Western Europe. These writers argue that U.S. security interests have shifted since the early cold war; in their view, although deterring Soviet expansion is still important, the current focus on Europe is an anachronism. Some analysts favor reducing the U.S. role in Europe in order to devote greater attention to the Third World or the Pacific Rim; others favor withdrawal in order to reduce U.S. defense burdens. Unlike the neo-isolationists, these writers acknowledge that Europe is still a vital U.S. interest and that the United States should play a role in preventing Soviet expansion. However, they also believe that U.S. allies can do more for their own defense, thereby allowing the United States to reduce or redeploy its own military forces.[9]

There are important differences between these various schools (and among different representatives of each one). However, most of these analysts favor reductions in the global role of the United States, and most see this adjustment as an unavoidable response to the relative decline of U.S. power. As one would expect, this view is challenged by analysts from the other end of the political spectrum. For example, many hardline analysts advocate a strategy of *global containment.* This strategy also seeks to contain Soviet power, but it argues that this goal should be pursued on a global basis. This conclusion rests on the assumption that the emergence of pro-Soviet regimes anywhere in the world provides a positive increment to Soviet power. Efforts to prevent or reverse such a development are therefore justified as necessary for U.S. national security. These writers also argue that the United States faces a diverse and growing array of other threats (such as international terrorism) that can best be met by further increases in U.S. military capabilities and by a greater willingness to use these forces.[10]

The final alternative is *rollback*, which seeks to eliminate communist influence worldwide. Although it resembles global containment, this strategy rests primarily on ideological beliefs rather than security considerations. Supporters of rollback argue that the main goal of U.S. foreign policy should be the triumph of democracy over communism. The objective is not simply the containment of Soviet or communist power (though that is obviously important) but the eventual elimination of Marxist influence worldwide. This strategy also prescribes active U.S. support for anticommunist forces (including rebel groups such as the contras or pro-U.S. dictatorships) even if U.S. security interests are not involved.[11]

Finite Containment

Each of these proposals is misguided. As an alternative, I present the case for a strategy of *finite containment*. This strategy resembles the traditional strategy of containment outlined by George Kennan, Hans Morgenthau, and Walter Lippmann, which concentrated on containing direct Soviet expansion on the Eurasian landmass.[12] In addition to maintaining a robust nuclear deterrent, this strategy would preserve the United States' present alliances with Western Europe, Japan, and Korea (at roughly the current level of ground and air forces), along with the U.S. commitment to protect Western access to Persian Gulf oil.

Finite containment is not a continuation of the status quo, however. For most of the cold war, U.S. grand strategy has leaned toward "global containment," with occasional attempts to "roll back" Soviet clients.[13] Unlike global containment, finite containment seeks to prevent Soviet expansion only in the "key centers of industrial power." Thus, with the partial exception of the Persian Gulf, finite containment rejects a substantial U.S. military role in the Third World. And unlike rollback, finite containment does not entail a global crusade against Marxism-Leninism. The United States would remain a global military power under this strategy, but it would permit a number of reductions in U.S. military capabilities. Among other things, this strategy would help alleviate the United States' current fiscal problems without jeopardizing vital U.S. interests.

The Need for Systematic Analysis

Despite the growing attention that U.S. grand strategy has received, the debate has not been conducted in a systematic way. In particular, the beliefs and assumptions that support different positions are rarely identified or evaluated. As a result, this debate has yet to produce a clear consensus or even a serious exchange of views.

In an attempt to alleviate this problem, in this essay I present a way of thinking about U.S. grand strategy that may help participants in this debate organize their discourse more effectively. I do so for two reasons. First, merely presenting the case for a single alternative is not enough; one must also show why it is superior to other options. Second, the best way to compare the relative merits of alternative strategies is to examine the assumptions and key beliefs that underlie each one. Grand strategy identifies the objectives that must be achieved to ensure the security of the state and specifies the political and military actions that are most likely to lead to these goals. Ideally, a state's grand strategy should be based on empirically grounded hypotheses about the nature of contemporary international politics.[14] These hypotheses enable national leaders to evaluate the threats and opportunities they face and to make contingent predictions about the effects of alternative strategic choices.[15]

It follows that the best way to assess the merits of different strategies is to evaluate the different assumptions and hypotheses upon which they are based. In fact, the only systematic way to select a strategy is by comparing its theoretical and empirical bases with those of the principal alternatives.

In this essay I attempt to perform precisely this task. Fortunately, the disputes that divide different strategies are amenable to systematic research; indeed, some of them have already been given careful attention. By identifying the most important disputes and by examining the existing state of our knowledge on each one, I seek to narrow the range of debate and outline an agenda for future research on this topic. Even more important, by examining the core beliefs that underlie the debate on U.S. grand strategy, I reveal why finite containment remains the best alternative.

Key Questions

In the remainder of this essay I examine four key issues that divide the different schools of thought on U.S. grand strategy. The first issue is the location of key areas of vital interest: which regions are critical to U.S. security (and why), which states threaten them, and what does this imply for U.S. strategy? The second issue is the *offense-defense balance*: is conquest easy or difficult, particularly in the regions that matter? Third, what are *Soviet intentions*: how hard will it be to deter the Soviets from attacking key U.S. interests? Last, what are the *causes of alignment*: can the United States count on allied support, and what factors will encourage this tendency?

These questions are crucial because competing views about U.S. grand strategy usually rest upon different beliefs about one or all of these issues. How one answers these questions will determine the interests it is necessary to defend, the identity and magnitude of possible threats, and the steps that must be taken to ensure adequate allied support. Taken together, the available evidence on each one supports the strategy of finite containment. Let us therefore consider each question in turn, noting both where disagreements exist and how these disputes should be resolved.

IDENTIFYING VITAL INTERESTS

When formulating a grand strategy, the first step is to identify the key regions that comprise the state's vital interests. For strong states, which enjoy the luxury of worrying about more than just the defense of their own territory, the identification of vital interests will depend primarily on the distribution of global power. The distribution of power identifies which regions contain important assets and the states that possess the means that threaten these regions. To identify key U.S. interests, therefore, we must first specify the sources of power in contemporary international politics.

Defining Power

For most experts, national power is a function of material assets such as size of territory, population, military power, industrial capacity, and resource endowments.[16] These factors are often related (in the modern era, military power is based largely on industrial capacity), and taken together, they determine a state's capacity to defend itself, especially in war. Because no supreme authority exists to protect states from each other, the capacity to wage war is the ultimate guarantee of independence and the ultimate source of influence in the international system.[17] Moreover, it is a state's combined capabilities that are important; states that lack critical elements of power will be more vulnerable than states that possess a complete array of capabilities.[18] There is no precise formula for weighing the different sources of power (which leads to recurring disagreements over the relative importance of different components), but most writers on strategy agree that national power ultimately rests on a state's material assets and capabilities.[19]

This conception of power is not universally accepted, however. Both the world order idealists and the neo-conservative advocates of rollback tend to focus more on ideas and ideology than on the physical capabilities of different states. Because they believe that the United States and its allies are threatened more by global problems than by other states (such as the Soviet Union), world order theorists pay little attention to the relative capabilities of different nations. For them, the main threats require a fundamental transformation of the state system; the power of individual nations is thus less important than the power of ideas. In their view, once mankind learns new values (such as nonviolence, equality, and cooperation), the dangers inherent in the present system will be eliminated.[20]

At the other extreme, advocates of rollback view contemporary international politics as a quasi-religious conflict between communism and democracy. For these writers, ideology is more important than the physical elements of power; interests are identified not by comparing capabilities but by examining political beliefs. By this logic, states that embrace U.S. values deserve support, states that do not are suspect, and states that embrace Marxism are automatically enemies.[21] Coexistence with communism is assumed to be impossible, which justifies efforts to undermine or overthrow all communist or Marxist regimes.[22]

Ignoring the material elements of power raises several problems for these two schools of thought. Even if world order idealists are correct to remind us that global problems now threaten all states, they ignore the fact that states still threaten each other as well. Moreover, the record of past efforts to erect moral barriers to war is not encouraging, and the various norms these writers extol would have to command universal acceptance before the danger of war would decline. By ignoring the distribution of power, these writers cannot tell us how to preserve peace or defend existing interests while their new "world order" is being created. By itself, therefore, this approach offers few insights for U.S. grand strategy.

At the other extreme, advocates of rollback err by exaggerating the importance of ideology in international politics and by ignoring the role of national power. To begin with, they overstate the ability of either superpower to export its ideology to other societies. Historically, no ideology has ever attracted a universal following, and neither superpower shows signs of doing so today.[23] In addition, because true democracies are a minority, basing U.S. foreign policy solely on ideological criteria would place the United States in opposition with most nations of the world and would make it more likely that some would seek protection from the Soviet Union. At a minimum, such a policy would alienate U.S. allies that have little desire to support such a crusade. The costs and risks of an ideological foreign policy explain why even radical states soon learn to compromise their ideological convictions when more serious interests are involved.[24]

Most important of all, the ability to promote ideological principles is itself a function of economic and military power.[25] Communist ideology would be largely irrelevant if Albania were its chief sponsor; it is Soviet power that makes communism seem dangerous to the United States, not the specific content of the ideology itself. Thus, even if ideological beliefs matter in certain circumstances, the relative power of their proponents matters far more.

Why Containment?

The distribution of power, defined in terms of relative capabilities, identifies regions that are strategically vital and the states that pose the greatest threats to these areas. This insight provides the principal basis for containment. As Hans Morgenthau and Walter Lippmann noted several decades ago, the common theme of U.S. foreign policy has been to oppose any power that threatened to dominate Eurasia, whether it was Wilhelmine Germany, Nazi Germany, or the Soviet Union since 1945.[26] The rationale for this principle is straightforward: as a continent-sized state lying far from the other major centers of world power, the United States could be seriously threatened only if a single state or coalition were able to control the combined resources of the Eurasian landmass. Such an accumulation of power would dwarf U.S. capabilities, thereby placing U.S. security in jeopardy.[27]

The strategy of finite containment follows precisely the same logic. In George F. Kennan's original formulation, the key aim of containment was to prevent the Soviet Union from gaining control of the key centers of industrial power that lay outside its grasp. Apart from the United States itself, these key centers were Western Europe and Japan.[28] More recently, the United States has added the goal of preserving Western access to oil from the Persian Gulf, because oil is a critical commodity for the United States and its industrial allies. Thus, the key elements of containment were deliberately finite in scope; it applied only to regions whose domination by the Soviet Union would allow it to assemble greater economic and military capacity than the United States and its remaining allies could assemble. After World War II, the Soviet Union was the only state that could hope to perform this feat, so it replaced Nazi Germany as the principal object of U.S. grand strategy. The point is crucial and bears repeating: the fundamental rationale for finite containment is the distribution of global power, defined in terms of military capability and industrial potential.[29]

Does Containment Still Make Sense?

In terms of the balance of power, four developments might justify abandoning containment. First, if the Soviet share of world power were to increase dramatically, the United States might be forced to take more aggressive measures in order to keep from falling too far behind. Such measures could include major increases in U.S. military spending or even a campaign to "roll back" the Soviet empire before it became too strong.[30] Second, if Soviet power declined substantially, then containment might be unnecessary (though the U.S. interest in keeping Eurasia divided would remain). Third, if the economic and military power of the United States were to erode significantly, maintaining its present commitments might become impossible. Finally, if the distribution of power in the rest of the world were to change, then the traditional locus of containment might become obsolete. Predictably, most analysts who advocate a new grand strategy invoke one or more of these arguments.[31] Let us consider the merits of these various claims.

The Myth of Soviet Geopolitical Momentum

First, do increases in Soviet power and global influence suggest that containment has failed? The answer is a resounding no. Not only do the United States and its major allies surpass the Soviet alliance network on the principal indices of national power but this favorable imbalance of power has remained roughly constant for the past four decades. The Western Alliance leads the Soviet bloc by nearly 3 to 1 in gross national product (GNP), by over 2 to 1 in population, and by roughly 20 percent in annual defense spending, and it has slightly more troops under arms.[32] The Western Alliance includes virtually all of the world's strategically significant states (most of them stable democracies), while the Soviet Union's main allies combine serious internal problems with widespread regional unpopularity.[33]

In addition, reports of "Soviet geopolitical momentum" are wildly exaggerated. Contrary to right-wing mythology, Soviet influence in the developing world has declined since the 1950s. Soviet gains in countries such as Ethiopia, Angola, or South Yemen are more than offset by their setbacks in Indonesia, China, Egypt, Somalia, Zimbabwe, Mozambique, and most recently, Afghanistan and Nicaragua.[34] Soviet ideology attracts a few converts, but most so-called radical states look primarily to the West for educational assistance and economic exchanges.[35] Indeed, of the more than 100 states that have gained independence since 1945, only a dozen or so can be considered close allies of the Soviet Union.[36] Most important of all, the United States has successfully prevented the Soviets from expanding into any of the "key centers" identified by Kennan four decades ago. In terms of the global balance of power, therefore, containment has worked quite well.

Why Containment Is Still Necessary

Second, do the internal difficulties currently afflicting the Soviet Empire (e.g., political reform in Eastern Europe, economic stagnation, resurgent nationalism, increasing ethnic tensions, declining health standards, etc.) mean that containment is no longer necessary? Such a conclusion is at best premature. The Soviet Union is still the world's second or third largest economy and possesses abundant economic potential. Its military capabilities are still formidable, especially its ground and air forces, and lie close to the key centers of industrial power. Although Mikhail Gorbachev has eschewed direct confrontations with the West and seems eager to resolve a number of regional conflicts, there is no guarantee that this restraint will not give way to adventurous policies in the future.[37] Indeed, if the United States abandoned containment, Soviet leaders might be tempted to address their internal problems through a more aggressive foreign policy, because the risks would be smaller and the prospects for success would be greater. Grand strategy must take both capabilities and intentions into account, and at present, reports of the Soviet Union's demise have been greatly exaggerated. However appealing the notion, we have not yet reached "the end of history." Thus, the basic rationale for containment remains intact.

Why Containment Is Still Possible

Third, has the relative decline of U.S. power left it too weak to bear the burdens of containment?[38] Once again, this conclusion is premature at best. Although the U.S. share of global power has shrunk over the past four decades, this "decline" is due to the United States' allies' postwar recovery rather than to a fundamental weakening of the U.S. economy. Moreover, the tendency to blame U.S. economic ills on "strategic overextension" (i.e., its overseas military commitments and defense spending) greatly oversimplifies the sources of U.S. economic problems.[39] For example, defense spending is not the sole (or even the most important) cause of the U.S. budget deficit; increased social services, the expansion of indexed entitlements, and a chronic unwillingness to levy adequate taxes are equally responsible.[40] Similarly, those who blame declining U.S. competitiveness on military expenditures tend to overlook the other factors that hinder U.S. productivity, such as the low rate of personal savings or the lack of a coherent industrial policy. The evidence that defense spending hurts economic performance is ambiguous at best; although excessive defense spending will hurt any economy, its ultimate effects depend heavily on specific macroeconomic circumstances. In any case, U.S. economic performance compares favorably with that of many of its allies (who spend less on defense), though not, of course, with that of all of them.[41]

Most important of all, even if excessive defense spending has weakened the U.S. economy, containment per se is not the real problem. The United States alone controls more industrial power than does the entire Warsaw Pact; with a proper strategy and adequate allied support, mounting an effective and credible defense of the key centers of industrial power is clearly not beyond its means. Instead, problems emerge when the United States adopts goals that have little to do with finite containment (as it did in Vietnam), or when it combines an extravagant defense buildup with fanciful fiscal policies such as Reaganomics. As always, the real question is not whether the United States is capable of maintaining its present commitments but whether the effort is still in the U.S. national interest. Although U.S. power has declined in relative terms, it is still in the United States' interest to ensure that several critical areas remain independent and at peace.[42] If a reduction in defense burdens is necessary, the logical approach is to liquidate peripheral commitments while maintaining essential ones. By confining U.S. strategic commitments to the key centers of industrial power, finite containment does exactly that.

Why Europe Is Still a Vital Interest

Finally, do changes in the distribution of power imply that the United States should reduce or redirect its overseas military commitments? Once again, the evidence suggests that such an approach would be unwise. Although Japan, Korea, and the Association of Southeast Asian Nations (ASEAN) have achieved impressive growth rates over the past two decades, Western Europe remains the largest economic prize. Western Europe produces approximately 22 percent of gross world product, while the Far East (including Japan but excluding China) produces only 12.5 percent.[43] Even more important, the nations of the Far East do not face as great a threat. The bulk of Soviet military power is directed at Western Europe, while roughly 20 percent of Soviet military assets are focused on China or the Far East.[44] As a result, the U.S. commitment there can remain relatively modest.

Furthermore, the relative decline of U.S. power suggests that the case for a U.S. commitment to Europe (and to a lesser extent, its allies in the Far East) may be even stronger today than it was immediately after World War II. Although the global balance of power greatly favors the West, U.S. allies play an increasingly important role in producing this favorable situation.[45] At the beginning of the cold war, the loss of Western Europe would have been serious but not disastrous; the United States controlled nearly 40 percent of gross world product in 1949, and Western Europe was just beginning its postwar recovery. Since then, however, the European contribution to NATO's economic and military strength has grown substantially, while the U.S. share has fallen.[46] If conquered and exploited, Europe's economic and military potential would increase Soviet war-making capabilities far more now than it would have several decades ago. Thus, while the Western Alliance retains an impressive lead over its main adversary, the United States is increasingly dependent upon allied contributions to achieve this favorable result. Both the neo-isolationists and the advocates of disengagement should consider how the world would look were these assets either absent from the equation or arrayed against the United States. The prospect is not comforting: Soviet control over Western Europe would provide the Soviet Union with an advantage of more that 2.5:1 over the United States in population and gross national product, to say nothing of direct military assets. In other words, as America's ability to defend Europe unilaterally has decreased, its interest in making sure that Europe remains independent has grown. Because Europe remains the largest concentration of economic and military power (apart from the two superpowers), and because the Soviet Union poses a larger threat there than in the Far East, the United States should continue to devote its main military effort to NATO.[47]

Why the Third World Doesn't Matter

By contrast, the case for a greater U.S. commitment in the Third World is extremely weak. Although several studies have recently proposed that the United States reduce its commitment to Europe in order to increase its capability to intervene in the Third World, there is little or no strategic justification for such a shift.[48] With the partial exception of oil from the Middle East, U.S. interests in the Third World are minor at best. The entire Third World produces less than 20 percent of gross world product, scattered over more than 100 countries. Africa has a combined GNP that is less than that of Great Britain alone, and all of Latin America has a combined GNP that is smaller than that of West Germany. Similarly, Nicaragua has one-third the population of New York City, and its annual GNP is roughly equal to the cost of one U.S. aircraft carrier (minus the planes). Because modern military power rests primarily upon industrial might, the strategic importance of the Third World remains paltry.[49]

Nor does the United States have important economic interests there. Trade is only 14 percent of U.S. GNP; nearly 65 percent of all U.S. trade is with our industrial allies in Western Europe, Canada, and Japan. In 1986, U.S. trade with the entire Third World (including the Organization of Petroleum Exporting Countries, or OPEC) was only 3.5 percent of GNP, divided among nearly 100 countries.[50] The same is true for overseas investment: U.S. direct investment abroad is a small fraction of total U.S. wealth, and most of it is in Europe and Canada.[51] In short, the United States has few economic interests to protect in the developing world.

Alarmists often point to alleged U.S. dependence on raw materials from the Third World. According to this view (which is popular with the U.S. Navy, the South African government, and representatives of mining and mineral interests), the U.S. economy requires reliable access to a wide variety of "critical strategic minerals" such as cobalt, chromium, the platinum group, or manganese. Together with South Africa, several Third World countries are among the leading exporters of these minerals, which raises fears of possible cutoff arising from Soviet penetration, leftist revolutions, or endemic political instability. Accordingly, some analysts argue that the United States must be prepared to intervene in order to preserve Western access to these raw materials and must also possess the capacity to defend the sea lines of communication (SLOC) between these countries and the United States. The need to support pro-Western mineral exporters (such as South Africa or the Mobutu government in Zaire) is often included as a further consequence of alleged U.S. dependence.[52]

Fortunately, these fears are wildly exaggerated. With the partial exception of oil, concern for "strategic raw materials" rests largely on propaganda. Although the United States imports a large percentage of its annual consumption of certain raw materials, it does so because foreign suppliers are the least expensive, not because they are the only alternative. The magnitude of a state's imports does not determine its dependence on others; what is important is the cost of replacing existing sources of supply or doing without them entirely.[53] As numerous studies have shown, the United States could employ a variety of options if its access to present suppliers were interrupted.[54] Moreover, a lengthy embargo is a remote possibility—why would a poor Third World country cut off its principal source of revenue?—and the United States can rely upon substitutes, alternative suppliers, and its own plentiful stockpiles.[55] An embargo might have some modest economic effects, but not much more than that. In short, the danger of a "resource war" is minuscule.

There is a final argument for a greater U.S. role in the Third World. Third World countries are said to be important for geopolitical reasons, because they occupy "strategic real estate."[56] The fear is that these countries might provide military facilities to the Soviet Union in time of war, thereby allowing the Soviets to threaten critical lines of communication. Even if these states lack meaningful capabilities of their own, therefore, their geographic position may give them some modest strategic value.

Once again, the importance of this factor is exaggerated. Given the low intrinsic value of the Third World, military bases there are important only if they can be used to affect events in areas that do matter. With the possible exception of Cuba (which might be able to delay, though not prevent, U.S. reinforcement of Europe), the Soviet Union's Third World clients could not affect the outcome of a major war. And because the Soviet Union cannot easily defend these regimes, they are likely to opt for neutrality, knowing that they would be among the first targets of a U.S. counterattack.[57] In short, although a few Third World states may have some modest strategic value, the overall strategic importance of the Third World remains small.[58] Those who would redirect U.S. military assets toward the Third World have got their priorities exactly backwards: they would weaken the U.S. position in the places that matter in order to stand guard in the places that do not.

To summarize: the basic rationale for finite containment rests upon an appraisal of the distribution of power, defined primarily in terms of economic and military capabilities. Although the global balance has changed somewhat since the late 1940s, these trends do not weaken significantly the case for finite containment.

THE OFFENSE/DEFENSE BALANCE: IS CONQUEST EASY OR DIFFICULT?

In recent years, a growing body of scholarship has suggested that the offense/defense balance plays a major role in the frequency and intensity of international conflict.[59] If offense is relatively easy (i.e., if states can expand at low cost), then states must worry more about their security and work harder to protect it. By contrast, when defense is easier (and when it is easy to distinguish between offensive and defensive capabilities), states can protect their territory with greater confidence at lower cost. The probability of war declines because potential aggressors will realize that they will pay a high price for relatively small gains.[60] As one would expect, therefore, competing assessments about the ease of offense or defense generally lead to different prescriptions for U.S. grand strategy.

In general, those who endorse strategies of rollback or global containment tend to believe that the United States and its allies are extremely vulnerable to attack by the Soviet Union or by other hostile forces, because they assume that offensive action is easy. At the same time, they also assume that the United States can score significant gains if it increases its military capabilities and employs them correctly. By contrast, those who favor isolationist strategies or limited versions of containment usually stress the relative advantages of defense. For these writers, even if the Soviet Union is extremely aggressive and U.S. interests are extensive, protecting them will still be a relatively easy task. By the same logic, these writers see inherent limits to what the United States can accomplish with its own military forces; although the United States can defend its own interests easily, efforts to expand U.S. influence through force or subversion (especially within the Soviet sphere) would be difficult and dangerous.

This general debate appears in many guises, corresponding to the different ways that states can threaten one another.[61] Throughout the cold war, for example, communist subversion has been seen as an offensive threat that justified an expanded U.S. commitment to distant regions.[62] Similarly, advocates of rollback have argued that the Soviet empire is vulnerable to subversion, propaganda, and other forms of "political warfare."[63] Taking this belief a step further, writers such as James Burnham claimed that rollback was necessary because the United States and the Soviet Union represented antithetical political values whose very existence threatened the other.[64] If both superpowers are vulnerable to political attack, then it is rational for the United States to try to topple its opponents before Soviet subversive efforts succeed.

In much the same way, advocates of global containment stress the offensive nature of Soviet military forces and suggest that it would be relatively easy for the Soviets to conquer vital areas such as Western Europe, the Persian Gulf, or the Middle East.[65] Furthermore, these writers tend to assume that contemporary politico-military conditions favor the attacker.[66] By contrast, those who downplay the danger of a Soviet assault generally believe that defenders enjoy a substantial advantage over attacking forces, at least when fighting from prepared positions.[67]

This dispute also reflects differing views on the significance of nuclear weapons. For example, advocates of global containment usually favor continued increases in U.S. counterforce capabilities. To justify this recommendation, they imply that nuclear weapons make conquest easier. In the 1970s, for example, Paul Nitze and others suggested that the "theoretical" vulnerability of U.S. land-based intercontinental ballistic missiles (ICBMs) would permit the Soviet Union to coerce the United States into major political concessions without firing a shot. By this logic, the alleged Soviet superiority in nuclear war-fighting capabilities would enable the Soviets to win major diplomatic victories.[68] Other writers go even further, arguing that an effective deterrent requires that the United States possess strategic superiority. In this view, threats to use nuclear weapons are not credible if the United States does not possess a superior war-fighting capability. If the United States does not possess such a capability, then the Soviet Union could use its conventional military assets and various subversive tools without fear of retaliation. In short, these writers believe that instead of making Soviet aggression riskier and more difficult, nuclear weapons give the Soviets a free hand. With nuclear weapons, in short, the requirements of deterrence become even more demanding.[69] In terms of U.S. strategy, those who endorse this view call for the United States to regain meaningful strategic superiority through increased counterforce capabilities and "defensive" weapons such as the Strategic Defense Initiative (SDI).[70]

By contrast, advocates of isolationist strategies or more limited forms of containment believe that nuclear weapons make defense easier. According to this view, the physical characteristics of nuclear explosives make it impossible for either superpower to escape the world of Mutual Assured Destruction.[71] Given the obvious costs of even a small nuclear exchange, both sides will be reluctant to threaten the other's vital interests. Because no political stakes would be worth a nuclear war, crises become contests of will; it is the balance of resolve, not the balance of forces, that determines the outcome. Because the side defending the status quo should possess greater resolve, nuclear weapons should aid defenders, irrespective of the precise balance of forces. In this view, therefore, the ability to defend vital interests is increased by the imposing deterrent effects of nuclear weapons.[72]

Finally, world order idealists adopt a somewhat different view on the question of the offense/defense balance. On the one hand, they agree that defensive strategies are desirable and feasible and therefore support a variety of schemes for territorial and "non-offensive" defense.[73] On the other hand, they reject reliance upon nuclear deterrence, arguing that the risks of a nuclear war outweigh the stabilizing effects of nuclear weapons. Instead, these writers favor continued disarmament efforts as a key component of a new world order, leading to the eventual banning of nuclear weapons.[74]

In short, competing appraisals of the offense/defense balance exert a significant influence on the choice of strategy and the assessment of military requirements. If offense is easy, then U.S. strategic requirements (broadly defined) increase significantly. Strategies of rollback or global containment become more attractive under these conditions. If expansion is hard, however, then U.S. leaders can take a more relaxed view of potential threats and adopt a less demanding grand strategy. The question, therefore, is which of these divergent views provides the best guidance for U.S. grand strategy and military policy today?

WHY DEFENSE HAS THE ADVANTAGE

The available evidence suggests that defense enjoys a major advantage in the contemporary world. This may not be true for all states in all circumstances, but in general, and especially with respect to key U.S. interests, conquest has become particularly difficult.

This condition results from four key developments. First, the spread of nationalism around the globe has increased the costs of expansion and foreign occupation. Nationalism aids defenders because they enjoy local knowledge and the support of the local population and because they care more about protecting their homeland than an aggressor will care about seizing it. The British experience in India, the French and American experience in Vietnam, the Soviet experience in Afghanistan, and Israel's occupation of Lebanon all support this conclusion: native populations are usually willing to bear greater costs than foreign invaders, which makes conquering and holding territory more expensive that it is often worth.[75] In addition, the growth of modern nationalism makes it likely that efforts to acquire global influence through subversion or penetration will backfire.[76]

This trend is enhanced by the increased availability of modern weapons, especially small arms. The expanding international arms market has made it easier for weak states to defend their territory against far more capable adversaries.[77] During the heyday of European expansion, colonial powers enjoyed near-total military supremacy over their opponents in Asia and Africa.[78] In the modern era, however, resistance movements can readily obtain the means of inflicting continued costs on a foreign invader. Together, the combination of nationalist beliefs and an active international arms market has created an impressive barrier to imperial expansion.[79]

Third, despite the creative efforts of some writers to plead the offensive implications of nuclear arms, they are an overwhelming addition to the defensive side. Not only do nuclear weapons make a direct attack on the United States virtually unthinkable but they have almost certainly played an important role in deterring threats to other interests as well. Although the historical record is not definitive, the evidence suggests that political leaders of all nuclear powers have been reluctant to challenge each other's vital interests in the face of even weak nuclear threats. We cannot prove that nuclear weapons have kept the peace and inhibited expansion, but the record of the past forty-five years is extremely suggestive.[80]

Fourth, U.S. security is enhanced by the fact that its vital interests are relatively easy to defend. In particular, the Central Front in Europe provides an ideal setting for a prepared forward defense against armored attack.[81] Defenders enjoy considerable advantages in this type of warfare, because they can fight from prepared positions and exact a favorable casualty-exchange ratio on the attacking forces. Similarly (and contrary to the views of many alarmists), a Soviet attempt to seize the Persian Gulf oil fields would be a risky and difficult operation. Not only is Iran likely to mount a fierce resistance but the oil fields lie roughly 1,000 kilometers from the Soviet border. The terrain is inhospitable, and road networks are primitive, which would greatly hinder a Soviet invasion. Moreover, Soviet armored forces would be vulnerable to air interdiction and would be forced to operate without significant air support. These obstacles do not guarantee that a Soviet attack would inevitably fail, but they suggest that deterring or defeating a Soviet attack is not beyond present U.S. capabilities.[82]

In sum, obstacles to aggression may be greater now than at any time in modern history.[83] This does not mean that expansion is impossible, but since World War II, successful examples have been few in number and have involved substantially greater costs than were originally anticipated.[84] Those who believe that offensive advantages render U.S. security especially precarious have yet to present strong evidence for their position. Indeed, the evidence strongly supports the opposite view.

Are these defensive advantages so great as to permit the United States to reduce its overseas commitments? Isolationist strategies tend to assume that nuclear weapons render the traditional focus on industrial power obsolete: in this view, even if the Soviet Union were able to seize Western Europe, it would be unable to exploit Europe's industrial potential and would still be deterred from attacking the United States directly by the threat of nuclear retaliation.[85] Similarly, analysts with great confidence in the credibility of extended deterrence have suggested that the United States could deploy a "trip-wire" force in Europe or the Persian Gulf and rely solely upon threats of escalation to deter an attack.[86] In either case, a belief in defense dominance can be used to justify the removal of U.S. forces.

These arguments are not without some basis, but the conclusion should be rejected for at least three reasons. First, the current condition of defense dominance is not independent of U.S. policy; its commitment to oppose Soviet expansion helps raise the existing obstacles to expansion.[87] Europe would still be difficult to conquer if the United States withdrew, but it would not be impossible. Thus, the U.S. commitment provides a valuable insurance policy against this remote but very important contingency.[88] Second, although the United States can easily maintain a robust second-strike capability today, an arms race with a Eurasian hegemon combining the technological and industrial assets of the Soviet Union, Western Europe, and Japan (possessing more than twice the U.S. GNP) would be a daunting prospect. Third, although nuclear weapons enhance the defender's advantage through deterrence, this advantage is not as great in protecting allies as it is when deterring direct attacks against one's homeland. Although a "trip-wire" strategy might work, in the absence of large U.S. conventional forces the Soviets could more easily convince themselves that the strategy was a bluff.[89] Maintaining a substantial conventional presence in Europe supplies a further margin of insurance, helps demonstrate Europe's importance to the United States, and provides a credible capacity to respond to a Soviet conventional assault. Given the costs and risks of any war in Europe and the fact that NATO is far wealthier than the Warsaw Pact, the continued deployment of U.S. ground and air forces is well worth it.[90]

All things considered, the prevailing state of defense dominance supports a strategy of finite containment. Preventing Soviet expansion is the central goal of this strategy; the fact that conquest is difficult makes it feasible and affordable. U.S. commitments in Europe and the Far East increase the obstacles to aggression and should be maintained for precisely this reason. Finally, defense dominance cuts both ways: the same factors that make it easy to defend U.S. interests would make a strategy that threatened key Soviet interests both costly and provocative. At present, therefore, arguments for a strategy of rollback or for the withdrawal of U.S. forces are not persuasive.

WHAT ARE SOVIET INTENTIONS?

The merits of alternative grand strategies are also influenced by one's image of the adversary. Obviously, states that are strongly motivated to alter the status quo pose a greater threat than those that seek only to defend their own territory. When facing a highly expansionist regime, other states will need greater military capabilities and more extensive alliance commitments in order to improve their chances of deterring or defeating an attack.

As one would expect, disagreements about U.S. grand strategy are shaped by differing appraisals of Soviet intentions.[91] Strategies of rollback or global containment usually rest on the assumption that the

Soviet Union is highly expansionist. Writers who favor these strategies tend to portray the Soviet Union as essentially equivalent to Nazi Germany; for them, it is a ruthless totalitarian power driven to relentless expansion by ideological convictions or domestic political requirements. Efforts at appeasement are doomed to fail; deterring Soviet expansion or reversing Soviet gains requires superior military power and unquestioned U.S. resolve.[92] By contrast, isolationist or idealist writers assume that the Soviet Union is a status quo power that is insecure and risk-averse. This view suggests that deterrence is unnecessary and that the United States should concentrate on alleviating Soviet insecurities through cooperative diplomacy.[93] Finally, those who favor more limited forms of containment tend to see Soviet foreign policy as driven both by insecurity and by ambition. They conclude that a combination of deterrent threats and positive inducements, corresponding to shifts in Soviet behavior, is the most promising way to preserve key U.S. interests.[94] Each of these positions is consistent with the analyst's assessment of Soviet intentions.[95]

At the onset of the cold war there was considerable uncertainty regarding both the scope and the urgency of Soviet aims. Forty years later, however, we have considerable historical experience upon which to base assessments of Soviet intentions. The evidence is not definitive, of course, because status quo powers and aggressors that have been successfully deterred tend to exhibit similar behavior. Nor does it provide a perfect guide to future conduct. Nonetheless, the experience of the past four decades should help narrow the range of disagreement.

First, although much of the literature on Soviet foreign policy remains relatively unsophisticated, the most careful analyses support an image of the Soviet Union as an ambitious but prudent state.[96] Unlike the great expansionist states of the past (revolutionary and Napoleonic France, Wilhelmine and Nazi Germany, Imperial Japan, etc.), the Soviet Union has yet to engage in a direct test of military strength with any of its major adversaries, and especially not with the United States. Soviet foreign policy has not been significantly more aggressive than that of the United States; Soviet interventions in Eastern Europe and support for Third World clients mirror the U.S. role in Latin America, the CIA's assorted covert action campaigns, and U.S. support for its own array of Third World allies. Furthermore, the Soviet Union's most aggressive postwar action—the invasion of Afghanistan in 1979—occurred in an area that the United States had long indicated was a minor interest at best. Even the deployment of missiles to Cuba in 1962 was a legitimate act of self-defense, given the strategic situation facing the Soviet Union at that time and the similarity between this action and the United States' own strategic policies in the early 1960s.[97] Finally, unlike irrational aggressors whose efforts to expand led to national destruction, the Soviet Union has shown a capacity to reverse course when costs and risks outweighed benefits. In this respect, the Soviet withdrawal from Afghanistan and the Soviets' declining interest in the Third World are instructive.[98] Although testing motivations is inherently difficult and the evidence is imperfect, an image of the Soviet Union as an ambitious but cautious great power is probably closest to the truth.

Do *glasnost* and *perestroika* suggest that this image no longer applies? In particular, does the "Gorbachev revolution" justify abandoning containment at this point? The answer is no. Although these reforms may eventually lead to a reduction in Soviet military capabilities (thereby reducing the requirements of containment), it would be unwise to alter U.S. strategy at this time. Gorbachev's efforts to "restructure" Soviet society have been only partially successful thus far, and they have yet to make a significant dent in Soviet military power. Even more important, the belief that *perestroika* and *glasnost* will reduce the Soviet threat rests on the widespread but as yet unproven hope that a more open Soviet society will be less interested in expansion.[99] To be sure, recent changes in the Soviet political process are heartening. Nonetheless, for the foreseeable future the Soviet Union will remain an authoritarian regime, and if *perestroika* succeeds in reinvigorating the Soviet economy and increasing the relative power of the Soviet Union, then the West might face a more formidable adversary in the future than it does at present. The United States should remain open to the possibility of a durable detente, both for its own sake and to prevent Gorbachev's diplomatic initiatives from undermining Western cohesion, but *glasnost* offers little reason to abandon containment at this point.[100]

These arguments carry several important implications. First, they suggest that deterring the Soviets does not require the extraordinary efforts proposed by advocates of rollback or global containment. The Soviet Union may exploit opportunities to make minor gains, but it has been reluctant to run significant risks even when the potential benefits were great. (Among other things, this tendency casts grave doubt on the hawkish view that Soviet leaders would blithely risk millions of their citizens' lives in a nuclear exchange.)[101] Second, the history of the cold war reminds us that the Soviet Union has its own security concerns. Thus, the degree to which the Soviets challenge U.S. interests is likely to reflect both the opportunities they foresee and the level of threat that they believe the United States poses to them. The first point highlights the continued need for deterrence; the second warns against excessive U.S. zeal. In terms of grand strategy, therefore, the image of Soviet intentions outlined here suggests that isolationism is dangerous because it might encourage Soviet expansion, but rollback and global containment are unwise because they could provoke Soviet responses that would not be in the U.S. interest. Given these constraints—and the United States' limited ability to influence Soviet domestic politics—finite containment remains the best alternative.

WHAT ARE THE CAUSES OF ALIGNMENT?

When formulating a grand strategy, national leaders must also consider the forces that will lead other states either to join forces with them or to unite in opposition. Because threatening configurations of power can arise either from a single state's growing too powerful or from a group of states' allying together, statesmen must weigh alternative strategies with an eye toward the likely responses of other significant states.

As one might expect, therefore, debates about foreign policy and grand strategy frequently turn on disputes about the causes of alignment.[102] In general, advocates of rollback and expanded containment argue that U.S. allies are likely to "bandwagon" with the Soviet Union should U.S. power or credibility begin to wane.[103] Throughout the cold war, this belief has been invoked repeatedly to justify military buildups or overseas intervention. When seeking support for the contras in Central America, for example, President Reagan predicted that "if we cannot win in Central America, our credibility will collapse and our alliances will crumble."[104] These writers also maintain that ideology is a powerful cause of alignment, which implies that leftist or Marxist states are strongly inclined to ally with the Soviet Union. If these hypotheses are true, the United States should act to prevent Marxist regimes from coming to power or take active measures to overthrow them if they do.[105]

By contrast, less ambitious strategies—such as finite containment—reflect precisely the opposite view. These strategies assume that states are more likely to balance against threats rather than bandwagon with them; as a result, Soviet efforts to expand will trigger increased opposition from other powerful states. Similarly, finite containment assumes that ideology is a rather weak force for alignment. Although U.S. leaders may prefer democracy on purely normative grounds, this view assumes that U.S. security is not endangered by a world of ideological diversity.[106]

Which of these competing beliefs is correct? The available evidence overwhelmingly supports the latter view. First, as I have argued at length elsewhere, balancing behavior predominates in international politics. This tendency defeated the various attempts to achieve hegemony in the European great power system, and the same tendency explains why the U.S. defeat in Indochina led to increased cooperation among the

ASEAN nations and accelerated the Sino-American rapprochement. These cases are hardly isolated examples; similar behavior has been documented in the Middle East and South Asia as well. Second, as the Soviet quarrels with Mao, Mugabe, Togliatti, Tito, Pol Pot, and Carillo reveal, Marxist ideology is a relatively weak cause of alignment. Indeed, centralized ideological movements (such as international communism or pan-Arabism) seem to be especially prone to ideological divisions, just as Kennan and others predicted.[107]

These results lay bare much of the justification for U.S. foreign policy since World War II. Contrary to the prescriptions of finite containment, the United States has consistently sought commitments beyond the defense of the key centers of industrial power and has occasionally tried to reverse communist gains in the Third World.[108] In other words, the United States has for the most part followed a strategy of global containment, with occasional efforts at rollback. These additional objectives were justified either by the fear that allies would bandwagon or by the belief that leftist forces in the Third World were inevitably drawn toward alignment with Moscow.[109]

In retrospect, however, neither fear was well-founded. Although a number of Third World countries have chosen to ally with Moscow, such action has been primarily because they faced serious internal and external threats (often including the United States) and could not obtain other powerful allies. Furthermore, the tendency for states to balance helps explain why the United States enjoys good relations with the industrial powers of Western Europe and the Far East, while its relations with much of the Third World have been poor. For most of the cold war, Soviet military power was confined to Eurasia, and the Soviet Union took a sympathetic approach to Third World nationalism. By contrast, the United States denounced neutralism as "immoral" and used its global military capabilities to intervene in a variety of developing countries. Thus, Soviet power threatened the developed world but not the former colonies; American power did just the opposite. Given this disparity, it is hardly surprising that the United States is closely allied with the industrial powers of Europe and Asia, while the Soviet Union has done relatively better in the Third World.[110]

We may draw several lessons from these results. The forces that create international alliances make finite containment relatively easy to accomplish. In particular, the United States does not need to intervene in peripheral areas in order to maintain the alliances that matter. The Soviet Union's geographic proximity and its impressive military power make it the main threat to Europe and Japan; because states tend to balance, virtually all of the world's strategically significant nations are strongly inclined to ally with the United States. By the same logic, strategies of rollback or global containment should be rejected as both unnecessary and provocative. Adopting these strategies would require the United States to use force more often and in more places, thereby making the United States appear more bellicose than the Soviet Union.[111]

Will U.S. Allies Balance if the U.S. Withdraws?

As noted earlier, those who favor a reduced U.S. role (either revised containment or neo-isolationism) tend to invoke the logic of balancing in order to justify this recommendation. After accusing U.S. allies of "free-riding," these writers argue that Europe and Japan would balance a U.S. withdrawal by greatly increasing their own defense efforts and that these states are fully capable of mounting an effective defense on their own. In short, instead of letting U.S. allies "free-ride," the United States should start "free-riding" on them.[112]

As just discussed, states do balance against threats, which means that a reduction in U.S. support is unlikely to trigger a stampede toward the Soviet bloc. Indeed, U.S. allies will probably do somewhat more if the United States does less. Yet the conclusion that is usually drawn from this tendency—that the United States can reduce its commitment to Europe substantially—should be rejected for at least four reasons.

First, the claim that a U.S. withdrawal is justified by allied "free-riding" greatly oversimplifies the issue of burden-sharing within the Western Alliance.[113] Although U.S. allies spend a smaller percentage of GNP on defense than the United States does (measured in terms of annual defense budgets), focusing solely on percentages of GNP ignores a host of important but intangible allied contributions.[114] Moreover, when spending figures are compared, U.S. defense costs are inflated by its reliance on an all-volunteer force as opposed to conscription.[115] Most important of all, the disproportionate burden borne by the United States may be due less to "free-riding" than to differing perceptions of the threat. Because U.S. allies do not believe that the Soviet Union is as dangerous as the United States believes it to be, and because they do not share the U.S. fear of leftist forces in the developing world, they do not spend as much to counter either threat. Thus the United States may spend more because U.S. leaders (and taxpayers) have accepted a more pessimistic view of the threat and have adopted more ambitious goals for dealing with it, not because U.S. allies are lazy or decadent.[116]

Second, advocates of withdrawal take the logic of balancing to an illogical extreme. The real question is not whether U.S. allies will do more if the United States withdraws but whether they will do enough. There are clearly grounds for concern. To compensate for the U.S. commitment, the rest of NATO would have to mobilize at least five hundred thousand more troops, along with the associated military hardware.[117] Given present demographic trends in Europe, that is an unlikely event.[118] Those who call for a U.S. withdrawal have yet to provide a detailed analysis of what an independent European force would look like, what it would cost, and how effectively it could fight or deter.[119] In this respect, the suggestion that the United States could withdraw within four or five years—as Melvyn Krauss and Christopher Layne have proposed—reveals a worrisome disregard of basic military realities.[120]

Furthermore, the logic of collective action would still exist following a U.S. withdrawal. Because security is a collective good, the separate European states would inevitably try to pass the burdens of deterring the Soviets onto each other. In the 1930s, for example, Britain and France tried to entice each other into taking the lead against Hitler, which crippled the effort to prevent German expansion. Even if Europe did balance after a U.S. withdrawal, the effort would still be substantially weaker than it is with the United States included.[121]

Third, advocates of withdrawal overlook the stabilizing effects of the U.S. presence in Europe and the Far East. The maintenance of regional peace is in the U.S. interest, and if its meddling in the developing world is often provocative, the U.S. commitment to NATO is not. America's global presence helps safeguard its allies from one another; as a result, they can concentrate on balancing the power of the Soviet Union because they need not worry about other threats. Moreover, although the Soviet Union would remain the principal adversary in the short term, rivalries within Europe would be more frequent and more intense if the United States withdrew. This conclusion may appear farfetched after forty years of peace, but not if one recalls the four centuries of conflict that preceded them.[122] The rapid reemergence of ethnic conflict in some of the nations of Eastern Europe in the aftermath of the overthrow of the Moscow-supported regimes is ample reminder of the political instability associated with the history of the region. This problem could be even more serious in the Far East, where a precipitous U.S. withdrawal could trigger renewed regional tensions.[123] Even if U.S. allies balanced after a U.S. withdrawal, they might do so in ways the United States would eventually regret. Such a step would encourage Britain and France to increase their nuclear capabilities, it would tempt a newly unified Germany to acquire a nuclear force of its own, and it could easily encourage a rapprochement between the Soviet Union and either China or Japan, depending on how regional relations in the Far East evolved. None of these developments would be especially desirable.

Finally, even if U.S. allies increased their defense efforts considerably, a U.S. withdrawal from Europe would still weaken deterrence. Although a war in Europe is improbable, its likelihood would increase if the Soviets believed they could wage war in Europe without the United States becoming involved. With the United States firmly committed, the Soviets face a coalition possessing vastly greater combined capabilities. But if the United States withdrew and demobilized (which would be necessary in order to save any money), then Soviet decisionmakers could more plausibly expect a blitzkrieg to succeed.[124] Students of history will recognize that this situation is similar to the deterrence failures that produced World Wars I and II.[125] The U.S. presence in Europe helps prevent a similar miscalculation today, because it provides a potent reminder that the Soviet Union cannot attack Western Europe without directly engaging the bulk of U.S. ground forces, backed by a formidable nuclear deterrent.

It is equally unwise to assume, as some isolationists do, that the United States could easily stay out of a major war on the Eurasian landmass.[126] Despite its isolationist traditions and modest military assets, the United States was eventually drawn into three of the last four European wars. As Stephen Van Evera has noted: "History warns that the U.S. gets into great European wars by staying out of Europe—not by being in."[127] An isolationist strategy increases the odds of war but cannot guarantee U.S. neutrality. Thus, the United States is better off with its present policy, which reduces the likelihood that it will be forced to fight any kind of war in Europe.

In short, although balancing is much more common than bandwagoning, this tendency does not mean that the United States would be better off leaving the defense of Eurasia to others. The neo-isolationists are correct to discount the danger of "Finlandization," but their confidence that Europe and Japan would fully compensate for a U.S. demobilization is too optimistic. Although the United States should continue to press for a more equitable distribution of Alliance burdens, it should not reduce its ground and air force presence in Western Europe and the Far East significantly, except as part of a joint NATO–Warsaw Pact agreement for conventional arms limitations. The Conventional Forces in Europe (CFE) negotiations are the appropriate mechanism for translating the political changes in Eastern Europe and the Soviet Union into beneficial and stabilizing reductions in force levels.

The Best Choice: Finite Containment

This analysis suggests that a strategy of "finite containment" remains the best choice for the United States. This conclusion rests on an assessment of the theoretical and factual disputes that underlie the current debate on U.S. grand strategy. The other strategies examined here all fail on one or more grounds; by contrast, finite containment is most consistent with the present state of the international system.[128] Of course, if further research were to reveal that my assessment of these different factors was wrong, then different conclusions might be in order. This possibility suggests that additional research on the four questions examined above should be part of further efforts to rethink U.S. grand strategy. Is defense, in fact, easier than offense? What measures would strengthen or weaken this condition? Are Soviet intentions becoming more benevolent? How can the United States reinforce this trend, and is it likely to be enduring? Under what conditions would U.S. allies be more inclined to bandwagon, and what events would lead states such as Japan to rearm or realign or both? As noted repeatedly in this chapter, issues such as these are fundamental to the success of U.S. strategy, and scholarly research has only begun to provide adequate answers.[129]

There is a final rationale for finite containment. In international politics, large changes are often destabilizing; statesmen are more likely to miscalculate when facing new and novel circumstances. After World War II, the United States and its allies devised a geopolitical formula for peace that has proven to be remarkably durable. Following the precept If it ain't broke, don't fix it, policymakers should be reluctant to discard arrangements that have worked so well thus far. Although circumstances do change and strategy must eventually adapt, the burden of proof should remain with those who now seek to abandon a winning strategy. They have yet to marshal an adequate case.

IMPLEMENTING FINITE CONTAINMENT

Properly conceived, the strategy of finite containment seeks to prevent Soviet expansion in the key centers of world power: Europe, the Far East, and the Persian Gulf. It rejects intervention in the Third World, because these areas are largely irrelevant to U.S. security. It also rejects efforts to overthrow leftist regimes, because these states pose little ideological or military threat to the United States. By returning to Kennan's original formula for containment, this strategy would be a significant departure from the more expansive form of containment that the United States has followed since 1950. As a result, implementing finite containment would entail a number of adjustments in U.S. foreign and defense policy. Although a detailed description of its implications is beyond the scope of this chapter, the broad outlines of the strategy can be sketched briefly.

Objectives and Capabilities

First, and most important, finite containment would maintain the United States' present commitment of ground and air forces in Western Europe and the Far East. These forces are the best symbol of the U.S. interest in preserving the independence of these regions, and because the main threat in Europe is the Soviet Union's powerful land army, U.S. forces are also the most valuable contribution that the United States can make to European defense in time of war. Moreover (and contrary to much of the conventional wisdom), the prospects for a successful defense in Europe are reasonably good provided that the United States does not withdraw its forces.[130] To improve its chances even more, NATO should spend less improving its offensive capabilities—such as deep-strike aircraft for so-called Follow-on Force Attacks (FOFAs)—and spend more on defensive measures designed to thwart a Soviet armored assault.[131] In the absence of negotiated reductions for both sides, however, finite containment implies little change in this aspect of U.S. military commitments and force posture.

Second, finite containment would drastically reduce U.S. preparations for intervention in the Third World. In addition to a major buildup in naval forces, the Reagan administration increased U.S. intervention capabilities by creating so-called light divisions in the Army, by increasing U.S. amphibious warfare and air- and sealift capacities, and by establishing a separate Special Operations Command responsible for low intensity conflict. Under finite containment, these programs would be eliminated. Of the twenty-one active army and marine divisions, only sixteen are assigned to missions in Europe, the Far East, or the Persian Gulf. The remaining divisions (including three light divisions and one marine division) should be viewed as intervention forces; among other things, these forces would be of little value against the Soviet army. Because the United States has few economic or strategic interests in the Third World, it can eliminate some or all of these units, along with most of its special forces and covert action capabilities.[132]

Third, although Third World intervention would be downplayed, finite containment would maintain the U.S. commitment to protect Western oil supplies in the Persian Gulf. Here again, pessimism about this mission is excessive: the impressive barriers to a Soviet invasion of the Gulf and the likelihood that regional powers would actively oppose Soviet aggression give the United States a good chance of deterring or defeating a Soviet attack.[133] Thus, finite containment would maintain the U.S. Central Command at roughly its present size.[134]

Fourth, because finite containment focuses U.S. commitments on the key centers of industrial power, the most obvious target for reductions is the U.S. Navy. In a major war, the navy's main mission would be to defend the SLOCs between the United States and its European and Far Eastern allies.[135] The main threats to the SLOCs are the Soviet Union's land-based aircraft and its fleet of attack submarines. The most effective defenses against these forces are NATO's own submarines, its antisubmarine warfare (ASW) ships and patrol aircraft, and land-based interceptors, employing a strategy of "defensive sea control."[136] Although U.S. aircraft carriers may play a role in SLOC defense, other forces will bear the brunt of this mission.[137] Aircraft carriers are useful primarily for "power projection" in the Third World, but except in the Persian Gulf, this mission is of minor importance. Moreover, in many cases, land-based aircraft can also perform the power projection mission more efficiently. Instead of the fifteen carrier battle groups currently deployed, a force of eight to ten carrier battle groups would easily fulfill the requirements of finite containment.[138] The United States should therefore abandon the Reagan administration's misguided Maritime Strategy (intended primarily to justify an expensive 600-ship fleet), because that strategy is infeasible, potentially destabilizing, and unnecessary for the defense of vital U.S. interests.[139] Under finite containment, the United States could begin a steady and substantial reduction in the surface navy, eventually eliminating five to seven carrier battle groups and a variety of other naval assets.

Fifth, finite containment would also permit reductions in U.S. strategic nuclear forces. Where rollback strategies require strategic superiority (i.e., a first-strike capability), containment requires only that the United States maintain a robust second-strike force. This requirement is easy to meet; according to one recent estimate, the United States would have at least four thousand warheads (totaling roughly 1,000 equivalent megatons) left after a successful Soviet first strike.[140] Much the same situation applies in reverse, of course, and because each superpower has a second-strike force that is far larger than it needs to destroy the other, both are deterred.[141] Recognizing the durable reality of Mutual Assured Destruction, finite containment would abandon the costly search for strategic superiority.[142] Specifically, the United States could cancel a number of current strategic programs (e.g., the B-2 bomber, the Trident D-5, the Midgetman and M-X missiles, and various schemes for land-mobile ICBMs) and still possess an overwhelming deterrent.[143] The U.S. strategic submarine fleet should be maintained and modernized, along with the current ICBM force and an expanding cruise missile arsenal (eventually incorporating Stealth technology). The Strategic Defense Initiative can be canceled for much the same reasons: the available evidence suggests that it will not work, and the United States would not want it even if it did. A modest research program should be continued as a hedge against future breakthroughs, but plans for the testing and deployment of strategic defenses should be abandoned.[144]

Sixth, finite containment does not require the United States to abandon its moral commitment to personal freedom and human rights. However, this strategy recognizes the inherent limits of an ideologically based foreign policy and adopts a realistic set of goals. Exporting political ideals is difficult and unpredictable, and U.S. leaders should realize that (1) efforts to "promote democracy" via military force will place the United States at odds with most of the world (including its major allies); (2) the "freedom fighters" that the United States now supports are unlikely to institute true democracy if they win; (3) the United States lacks an adequate theory explaining how states achieve stable democracy and thus cannot be confident about the U.S. ability to create democracy in unfamiliar settings; (4) the historical record of past efforts (in Panama, Nicaragua, Guatemala, Vietnam, Cuba, Lebanon) is not encouraging; (5) the rare successes (such as Germany and Japan after World War II) suggest that lengthy foreign occupation and radical social reform are necessary; and (6) crusades to "promote American values" usually require abandoning the very ideals that their promoters claim to be defending.[145] Because U.S. security interests do not require an aggressive campaign to export democracy, more modest but unambiguous objectives are appropriate.[146] In addition to publicly supporting the U.N. Declaration on Basic Human Rights, the United States should consistently oppose all regimes that engage in the systematic murder of unarmed opposition.[147] This criterion ignores what foreign leaders profess to believe and focuses on what they actually do. How the U.S. leaders respond to such regimes will vary on a case-by-case basis, but this general criterion is likely to command widespread support at home and abroad. Unlike the Reagan Doctrine (which has no place in finite containment), this standard does not commit the United States to ideological projects that it does not know how to perform and that violate the values it purports to defend.

Implications and Obstacles

Adopting the strategy of finite containment would go a long way toward alleviating the fiscal pressures that the United States will face in the 1990s. Furthermore, it would concentrate U.S. defense capabilities in the places that matter and reverse the policies that have undermined the U.S. position elsewhere in the world. It would also help correct the perception that Europe and Japan were "free-riding" on the United States. In effect, finite containment would bring U.S. grand strategy closer to its allies' perspective, which focuses on the main threat (the Soviet Union), and downplay both the Third World and the futile quest for strategic superiority. Finally, the reduction in U.S. naval forces implied by finite containment would encourage Japan to expand its responsibility for sea and air defense in the Far East (a trend that has already begun). As long as the United States maintains a tangible presence in East Asia (e.g., ground and air forces in Japan and Korea), increases in Japan's naval and air capabilities are less likely to destabilize political relations among the pro-Western powers in the region.[148]

Of course, there would be impressive domestic obstacles to the implementation of finite containment. Although there is a growing consensus that U.S. defense spending should be curtailed, the proposals outlined here would go well beyond the expedients that usually are used in lean budget periods.[149] Because finite containment would eliminate several traditional but unnecessary missions, service interests (especially the navy) and defense contractors are certain to resist its adoption.[150] We can expect a variety of arguments to be marshaled in support of more ambitious strategies, featuring many of the dubious assertions examined throughout this chapter. In order to succeed, therefore, a campaign to implement finite containment would require aggressive presidential leadership and a persistent and well-orchestrated effort to explain the rationale behind it. The foremost task of this campaign would be to educate the American public on the finite scope of U.S. security interests and the limited means that are necessary to protect them. In particular, U.S. citizens would have to be convinced that (1) U.S. security interests do not require that the United States control all international events; and (2) many alleged threats are in fact relatively unimportant.[151]

Because they do not have entrenched interests to defend, experts outside official circles—in universities, foundations, independent think tanks, and the media—must take a leading role in the war of ideas. By participating actively in the debate on U.S. grand strategy and, in particular, by performing rigorous and critical analysis of the assumptions that underlie competing proposals, independent analysts can provide the intellectual ammunition that meaningful reform will require. Without a lively and serious debate, the United States is likely to repeat past errors, postpone the necessary adjustments, or adopt misguided and excessive reforms. But if the debate on grand strategy attains reasonable standards of scholarship and rigor, then U.S. strategy in the 1990s is more likely to be consistent with U.S. national interests and better suited to the current international system.

CONCLUSION

After four decades, the changing patterns of world power have led many to question the central premises of U.S. grand strategy. By provoking a rigorous reassessment, the recent wave of writings on U.S. grand strategy has made a valuable contribution to this debate. Unfortunately, many of the solutions that have been proposed, particularly isolationism, are too extreme. Where reform is needed, these writers call for dissolution. Where adjustments should be made, they call for radical surgery. Yet if their predictions are wrong—and the weight of the evidence is against them—their prescriptions could have catastrophic results. Most important of all, the solution they propose is simply not necessary. Amputation will "cure" a skinned knee, but more refined treatments are preferable.

At the other extreme, those who believe that U.S. security can be enhanced by repeating past extravagances or by a renewed ideological offensive are equally misguided. A strategy of global containment will increase U.S. defense burdens in areas of little strategic value and will undermine the U.S. image in the eyes of the United States' principal allies. Similarly, an ideological crusade to export U.S. ideals is more likely to compromise these principles than to convert other nations to democracy. At best, these proposals will waste U.S. wealth and other peoples' lives. At worst, they will fan the flames of regional conflict and increase the danger of a larger war.

The essential elements of containment were identified four decades ago. They have never been implemented correctly, because America's dominant global position allowed it to indulge in a variety of excesses without incurring immediate penalties. By returning U.S. grand strategy to the original prescription for containment—by adopting finite containment—the United States can correct its present insolvency without jeopardizing its vital interests. The essential elements of containment have worked remarkably well thus far; its main failures have occurred when the United States tried to extend containment beyond its original sphere of application. The welcome prospects of democracy in Eastern Europe, an inward-looking Soviet Union, and reduced levels of forces in central Europe should serve to remind us of just how vital an interest Europe remains for the United States. The strategy of containment has brought forty years of great power peace, and the key ingredients of that recipe should not be casually discarded. Although amendments are now in order, this basic strategy remains America's best choice.

8

Realism Redux: Strategic Independence in a Multipolar World

CHRISTOPHER LAYNE

Notwithstanding often sharp disagreements about specific policies and tactics, since the late 1940s America's national strategy—usually described as cold war internationalism or containment—has been remarkably consistent in both its underlying assumptions and its objectives. Throughout the postwar era, America has sought not only to contain the expansion of Soviet power but also the creation, and institutionalization, of an ideologically congenial international milieu. The superstructures of postwar U.S. foreign policy—NATO, the multilateral free trade system, and the global network of bilateral American security commitments—have been familiar features of the international landscape for some forty-five years.

Initially, it was realism that shaped America's postwar switch from its traditional isolationism to active peacetime involvement in international security affairs. The postwar realists well understood that U.S. interests required a qualified, but not unlimited, engagement in world politics. They appreciated keenly that because America's finite capabilities imposed a limit on what it could accomplish in the international arena, it was imperative that U.S. foreign policy distinguish vital interests from peripheral ones. Realists posited that America's basic security interest was ensuring that the Soviet Union (or another similarly inclined power) did not gain global hegemony by dominating Eurasia's strategically and economically important regions.[1] America's postwar realists sought to achieve this goal by fostering the emergence (or reemergence) of independent power centers as counterbalances to the Soviet Union.

In the wake of World War II this task was not an easy one, because Europe's political collapse and Japan's crushing defeat shattered the pre-1939 balance of power. To reestablish a global balance, the United States provided material assistance to enable Western Europe and Japan to regain their political and economic stability. Because Western Europe and Japan were vulnerable to Soviet external pressure and communist-inspired internal subversion during their recovery periods, America undertook to ensure their security until the recuperative process was completed. Although this realist framework lay at the core of postwar U.S. foreign policy, by 1950 the cold war internationalists had transfigured America's national strategy significantly and embarked the United States on a far more ambitious course in world affairs.

Cold war internationalism rested on a markedly different set of assumptions from those undergirding postwar realism.[2] First, cold war internationalists believed that America's power was, for all practical purposes, boundless. At the time, such a belief was not without merit. The United States enjoyed a monopoly on nuclear weapons in the period immediately following World War II, and even after the Soviet Union acquired its own atomic and thermonuclear capabilities (in 1949 and 1952, respectively), the United States retained a decisive nuclear superiority that lasted well into the 1960s. Similarly, in 1945 the United States produced fully half of the world's manufacturing output, and in 1953 this figure stood at a still impressive 44.7 percent. Because of its immense industrial and financial advantages, it appeared that the United States could devote a substantial portion of its resources to defense, as well as to foreign economic and military assistance, without permanently damaging its economic base.

Second, true to their classical liberal antecedents, the cold war internationalists believed that international relations are governed by an underlying harmony of interests among states. When forced to confront the stubborn reality of persisting international conflict, cold war internationalists fell back on President Woodrow Wilson's corollary to the harmony of interests: the world will be peaceful and harmonious only if nondemocratic states (which are held to be inherently bellicose) become democracies (which are inherently pacific). Cold war internationalists accepted Wilson's dictum that democracies are responsible for imposing world order by transforming the domestic political structures of nondemocratic states. In embracing Wilsonianism, cold war internationalism sought to reshape the world in America's image by exporting its values and replicating its political and economic institutions throughout the world.

Finally, cold war internationalism rested on a series of interrelated geopolitical and psychological assumptions about world politics. Cold war internationalists believed that the postwar international system was both rigidly bipolar and extremely fragile. This conviction was reinforced by the ostensible "lessons" of Munich: that peace is indivisible; that aggression must be resisted everywhere; and, of course, that totalitarian states are insatiably expansionist. These presuppositions led to the globalization of U.S. strategic commitments because cold war internationalists felt compelled to counter every Soviet thrust. International politics came to be regarded as a zero-sum game, and U.S. policy was driven by the felt need to respond to threats rather than by an assessment of specific American interests.

Eventually, credibility itself came to be seen as a vital interest and was regarded as one of the few things worth fighting for. Thus, time and again the United States found itself defending "interests" that were viewed as symbolically important even though they were intrinsically worthless—Vietnam, for example. Although interventionism is no longer tolerated quite so readily by Congress and the American people, atavistic elements of cold war internationalism continue to lie at the heart of our national security strategy.

The purpose of this chapter is to argue for a return to true realism in our national security strategy by the adoption of a central paradigm of strategic independence for the 1990s. This analysis comprises three sections. First, I examine the question of U.S. interests and the constraints on and threats to those interests. Second, I examine the possible alternatives that might serve as the bases for U.S. national strategy in the 1990s. Finally, I propose the specific economic, diplomatic, and military tenets for a strategy of independence.

DEFINING INTERESTS, CONSTRAINTS, AND THREATS

The Central Role of the National Interest

The concept of national interest—realism's central tenet—is a starting point in policy formulation that focuses strategists' attention on the salient feature of world politics: "International relations continue to be a recurring struggle for wealth and power among independent powers in a state of anarchy."[3] Thus, in an anarchic international political system there is no fundamental harmony of interests, and each state's survival, and success, depends ultimately on its own efforts. Realists understand that the pursuit of power is of overriding importance because a nation cannot survive (and hence pursue its ethical or moral aspirations) without it. Cooperation with others is possible in world politics, but it is not rational for states to act altruistically or "for the good of the system" (unless the nation's selfish interests coincide with the system's). Unless they act irrationally, statesmen want their nations to survive by remaining independent. Therefore, nations form coalitions ("balance") against others that threaten them; nations seldom cast their lot with a threatening power (that is, they do not "bandwagon").[4]

Statesmen are not obligated to take account of realism's precepts, but nations that disregard the "rules of the game" risk paying a price for doing so. In this sense, states are a lot like individuals: their fates are shaped by the interaction of deterministic forces (i.e., systemic constraints) and free will (the foreign policy choices statesmen make voluntarily). The states (and individuals) that do best are the ones that make decisions not inconsonant with objective circumstances. Thus, as Henry Kissinger noted, the most skillful statesmen are those able to find the "margin between necessity and accident" and to avoid the twin perils of ignoring objective reality (on the one hand) and hiding behind historical inevitability (on the other).[5]

U.S. National Interests

The United States has enjoyed a significant advantage in its conduct of national security strategy: it has seldom been compelled to subordinate domestic concerns to foreign policy goals (though it has often chosen to do so), and it has enjoyed a robust and healthy political system. Because it has been relatively immune from external danger throughout its history, the United States has enjoyed an exceptional degree of freedom in defining its national interests. Nonetheless, those interests remain objectively rooted in traditional geopolitical factors: geography, economics, and domestic stability.

America's geographical isolation, in particular, has allowed her to stand conspicuously apart from other great powers in history. For them, the geographical proximity of threatening powers, a geopolitical reality in the cockpit of European power politics, necessarily defined security as their overriding purpose and compelled them to subordinate domestic objectives to the imperative of safety from external attack. Thus, geography—buttressed by the European balance of power, the Royal Navy, and the absence of powerful nations on U.S. borders—protected America's physical security.

Although it is generally unappreciated, in the nuclear age geography counts for more than ever. Today, the prospects of a Eurasian hegemon invading the United States are too remote to be a factor in planning national strategy. As Robert Tucker observed, "Whereas in the 1940s it was still entirely possible, if not plausible, to imagine an imbalance of military power that would threaten the physical security of America, today this contingency is no longer a meaningful possibility."[6] If one assumes that America's strategic forces assure her safety from a direct nuclear attack on her homeland, then, ironically, the only real danger to America's physical security today stems from its decision to extend nuclear deterrence to protect U.S. allies overseas. Nonetheless, America retains an interest in preventing any hostile power from achieving hegemony in Eurasia, as well as in ensuring that no threat to her borders emerges within the Western Hemisphere.

The maintenance of a strong domestic economy is America's second major interest. America's economic position—in particular her natural resources, an educated citizenry, and her industrial base—certainly provides her with significant advantages here. Her dominant position in the world economy in the aftermath of World War II allowed her to serve as the systemic hegemon, establishing a new economic order based on liberal trade relationships and fixed exchange rates tied to the dollar. While America's strong economy continues to give her significant freedom of action, unfortunately, as we shall see, the United States is more constrained in this dimension of her interests than her policies would suggest.

Yet America's very status as a superpower gives her an extra degree of latitude in choosing the national interests that makes her economic constraints more difficult to observe. This point is not at all understood by cold war internationalists, because like Charles Krauthammer, they believe that "a great power is practically defined by its having interests beyond the security of its borders. Therefore, if it decides nonetheless to take national interest to mean only national security, it essentially renounces its position as a great power."[7] The cold war internationalists are simply wrong on this point. Serious students of international politics know that great powers are defined by their capabilities in relation to those of other states, that is, their ranking in the categories of size of territory and population, resource endowment, economic and technological capabilities, military strength, political stability and competence.

Despite this tremendous freedom to choose her interests, it is a mistake to believe that this freedom is complete. Today, America must come to terms with a significant constraint on her ability to choose her interests: her relative decline in power in the military and, especially, the economic spheres.

Confronting the Reality of Relative Decline

Changes in the international environment in the late 1980s precipitated the debate about the relative decline of U.S. power and its implications for America's national strategy.[8] Predictably, cold war internationalists have reacted harshly to the suggestion that America's military and economic power has diminished; indeed, they have attempted to turn *decline* into a dirty word.

Cold war internationalists argue, for example, that the notion of American decline is a myth; America hasn't gotten weaker, they say, others have gotten stronger.[9] (To which one responds: "Yes, but that's what relative decline is all about.") Another avenue of attack (notwithstanding that few "anti-declinists" are trained economists) is to question the validity of the economic data generally cited as evidence of U.S. decline.[10] A related argument is that any purported symptoms of decline—the U.S. trade and budget deficits, for example—are traceable solely to the alleged folly of Reaganomics; thus, it is claimed, any harm that was done during the Reagan years can be undone by following more sensible policies in the future.[11] Cold war internationalists also dismiss the notion that U.S. defense burdens are the primary cause of America's lagging competitiveness; if the United States is not investing enough to shore up its economic base, it is because Americans spend their wealth instead of saving it.[12] Moreover, as cold war internationalists see it, even if America's global strategic burdens were undermining U.S. prosperity, the United States could not afford to abandon its overseas commitments. According to cold war internationalists, if the United States scaled back its international obligations, baleful consequences would ensue: America's allies would be vulnerable, the Soviet Union would be emboldened, global instability would increase, and world order would be imperiled.[13]

Relative decline is not an epithet, it is a fact: by any measure, U.S. military and economic strength in relation to that of other major nations has declined from its postwar apogee. This slippage was inevitable because America's commanding postwar position rested more on other nations' temporary weakness than on its own innate power. In the military sphere, for example, it was perfectly predictable that the Soviet Union would seek to match the nuclear and global power projection capabilities of its rival superpower. After all, because international politics is a competitive realm, states tend to imitate the military strategies and technologies of their rivals. Similarly, in the economic sphere, America's overwhelming predominance reflected the simple fact that in 1945 the United States was unscathed, while Western Europe and Japan were in ruins. Once the West Europeans and Japanese got back on their feet, it was a foregone conclusion that they would close the economic gap with the United States.

The United States is not exempt from the forces of history; the relative decline of American power is not a unique phenomenon. As Robert Gilpin and Paul Kennedy have explained, the relative rise and decline of great powers is a recurring pattern in international politics.[14] As they have observed, a nation's power ultimately rests on its economic base. However, for a variety of political, economic, and technological reasons, the power positions of states change at differential, not parallel, rates. Thus, the relative power standing of states changes because some are gaining (or losing) power faster than others. Therefore, although the prevailing international distribution of wealth and power, and the hierarchy of prestige among states, reflects the influence of the dominant (hegemonic) power, international politics is not static. Over time, power and wealth are diffused throughout the international system (a process often paradoxically stimulated by the hegemon's policies), and the hegemon will experience a relative power decline.

Sooner or later the hegemon's international primacy will be challenged. It then faces a dilemma because the costs of maintaining its position tend to rise as its ability to afford them decreases. This happens because the hegemon must devote an increasing share of its resources to defense, foreign aid, support of allies, and the like, at the same time that its economic growth rate is slowing because public and private consumption have displaced investment in productive capability. As its commitments abroad outstrip the resources available to support them, the hegemon experiences (in Paul Kennedy's phrase) the strategic crisis of "imperial overstretch." Ironically, by trying to sustain its international position, the hegemon weakens its economy even further and thus actually hastens its relative decline (and also risks absolute decline unless it redresses the gap between power and commitments). As Gilpin explains:

> If the productive base of the economy erodes, it becomes more difficult to meet the rising demands of protection [i.e., national security] and consumption without further cutbacks in investment, thus further weakening the future economic health of the society. The society enters a downward spiral of rising consumption and declining investment that undermines the economic, military and political foundations of the state's international position.[15]

The United States today is caught in the type of downward spiral that Gilpin describes. Unless economic growth and productivity are spurred, the United States can maintain current levels of defense expenditure only by diverting an increasing amount of resources (capital, labor, and technology) from civilian to military purposes. Yet such a shift would undercut the already lagging growth of productivity in the civilian economy. If historical rates of growth in defense spending are sustained, the deterioration in future economic growth and productivity will be exacerbated. Such an approach, in turn, would mean even poorer future quantitative and qualitative resources available for national defense.

Threats in an Era of Relative Decline

Since America has a relatively high degree of freedom to choose her interests, logically she can also control, in part, the threats to which she must be prepared to respond. But where those threats do exist objectively, the United States must respond—remembering that threats are only relevant when they are considered in light of some real interest.

The logic of the relative decline school suggests that the interest threatened most directly is America's economic position, and the threat is made ever greater by a continuing strategy of cold war internationalism. Wasteful military spending is not only unnecessary, it is counterproductive.

Geopolitically, recent events suggest that there is little evidence that the Soviet Union (or any other power) threatens to gain hegemony over the Eurasian landmass in the near future. Several trends are reassuring in this regard. First, the Soviet Union appears to be both less capable and less intent on gaining hegemony over Western Europe and other strategically significant areas of Eurasia. The collapse of the Iron Curtain, the ousting of communist governments throughout Eastern Europe, and the beginnings of multiparty political processes in the Soviet Union itself are ample evidence of the dramatically reduced Soviet threat. General Secretary Mikhail Gorbachev's intent to pare down both the size of the Soviet military machine and its budget suggests that coexistence is the watchword for the foreseeable future. At the same time, the greater political integration of Western Europe promised by events of 1992 suggests that the Western allies are especially well prepared to deter (and, if necessary, defeat) any renewed Soviet threat to the West.

Within the Western Hemisphere, there is little evidence that the nature of the threat posed by the states to the south is military in nature. Certainly, political instability—brought on by economic stagnation and inequality, as well as a massive debt burden—should be a concern. But American political and military tinkering can only ameliorate a situation that is already bad. Indeed, high U.S. interest rates—brought on by the huge deficits that accompanied the Reagan defense buildup, among other factors—have been a principal cause of our neighbors' problems.

Given the nature of the interests and threats that should stand as the basis of our national security strategy, one can only conclude that the era of cold war internationalism has long passed. It is time that America, as well as the Soviet Union, became engaged in some new thinking.

THE STRATEGIC DEBATE OF THE 1990S

The 1990s will be a watershed decade for American foreign policy. The political, military, and economic balance of world forces is shifting dramatically, and a comprehensive review of U.S. foreign policy is long overdue. The threshold question facing American policymakers is whether America's postwar national strategy has outlived its usefulness. If so, the next, more difficult question is, What will replace it? Broadly speaking, there are three alternatives to a cold war internationalist strategy: (a) reform; (b) liberal multilateralism; and (c) strategic independence.

The debate about U.S. national strategy revolves around the comparative merits of these four approaches to national security strategy. In reality, however, this debate, while nominally quadrilateral, is really a contest between cold war internationalism and strategic independence. While not without their useful insights, reform and liberal multilateralism are deeply flawed national security strategy approaches.

Strategic Reform

Strategic reformers have adopted almost verbatim, usually without acknowledgment, most of the successor generation realists' critique of cold war internationalism.[16] Thus reformers and realists share the belief that changes in the international system require the rethinking of existing U.S. foreign policy. Reformers and realists alike recognize that the relative decline of U.S. economic power must be arrested, and both desire, in William Hyland's words, "to concentrate on America's own problems even at the expense of international obligations and commitments."[17] Finally, reformers and realists have in common the conviction that real breakthroughs in U.S.-Soviet relations are possible.

However, when it comes to actual policies, realists and reformers part company on some critical issues. Although claiming that America needs a new national strategy, reformers want incremental—not bold—changes that would leave the superstructure of the old policy intact (including U.S. alliances). Notwithstanding their belief that the United States is strategically overstretched, reformers strive only for marginal burden-sharing adjustments that would secure a "fairer" distribution of security costs between the United States and its allies. And while they acknowledge that the postwar era of U.S. preeminence has ended, reformers are notably reluctant to yield the hegemonial prerogatives of that bygone period.

In contrast to the reformers, successor generation realists are interested in a real devolution of security responsibilities—burden-shifting,

not burden-sharing. Moreover, realists believe that the postwar structures to which the reformers are so reflexively attached are part of
America's foreign policy problem, not part of the solution. From the
realist perspective, the reformers are the victims of cognitive dissonance.
They say that the world has changed greatly since 1945, but their policy
recommendations suggest that in fact America's international position
differs very little from what it was during the postwar era. This belief
is especially evident in the realm of nuclear strategy. Although the SALT
I treaty (1972) ratified strategic nuclear parity between the superpowers,
strategic reformers still have not truly come to grips with the momentous
implications of their acquiescence in this change in the U.S.-Soviet nuclear balance.

At best, strategic reformers offer a "Michelob Light" foreign policy
("You can have it all") that strives for cut-rate hegemony. All the while,
however, the reformers duck the really hard choices imbedded in their
analysis of geopolitical trends. The strategic reformers are far too intelligent not to see the causes and consequences of America's foreign
policy problems, but they are too much a part of the postwar system,
and too burdened by the dead weight of inertia, to break with the past
and give America a new national strategy that accommodates the United
States to a changing world.

Liberal Multilateralism

The liberal multilateralist and cold war internationalist approaches to
U.S. national strategy both trace their roots to the same source: nineteenth-century liberalism. Indeed, the postwar liberal internationalist
foreign policy consensus that lasted until Vietnam resulted from the
fusion of these two outlooks. But this marriage was always a rocky
one. Cold war internationalists were security-oriented and concerned
primarily with organizing resistance to Soviet and communist aggression. Liberal multilateralists, on the other hand, were equity-oriented
and more universalistic. They sought to use international law, and
organizations such as the United Nations, to promote peaceful coexistence among all states. At the same time, they called for international
cooperation to promote economic and social justice worldwide. As
Carnegie Endowment president Thomas Hughes has written, American
internationalism's security and equity perspectives pulled in opposite
directions; inevitably, the simultaneous pursuit of liberal multilateralism
and cold war internationalism produced tension and acrimony.[18]
Vietnam fractured liberal internationalism into warring liberal multilateralist and cold war internationalist camps.

Liberal multilateralists believe that the world has entered an era of "complex interdependence" in which the usefulness of military power has been substantially devalued and the utility of economic power and diplomacy has been correspondingly upgraded. Some prominent liberal multilateralists have stated that force is not a legitimate or necessary instrument of the U.S. policy arsenal. In their view, U.S. military power should not be used until a decision to do so has been subjected to an international review process resulting in a consensus approving U.S. action. Liberal multilateralists believe that America's alliances should be true partnerships in which decision-making power is equally shared. In the Third World, multilateralism requires the United States to defer to the wishes and interests of local nations. Liberal multilateralists claim that these Third World countries are better equipped than the United States to resolve regional conflicts. Because they believe that complex interdependence circumscribes the scope for independent American actions, multilateralists believe that the United States must act with other states, preferably through established international institutions, to address a broad range of international problems. The multilateralist agenda stresses respect for international law, arms control and disarmament, nuclear nonproliferation, human rights, and a more equitable distribution of the world's wealth, both among nations and within them.

Multilateralism is not an appropriate basis for U.S. national strategy. Indeed, multilateralists utterly fail to understand that effective strategies are holistic, interweaving military power, economic strength, and diplomacy into a single integrated design. Multilateralists do not understand that in the competitive, anarchic realm of world politics, force remains the *ultima ratio* among nations. Although multilateralists vastly exaggerate the objective constraints on U.S. policy, they would impose stringent artificial limitations on America's external relations. Liberal multilateralists forget, however, that the United States has national interests that cannot always, or even often, be subordinated to the requirements of multilateral diplomacy. Thus, while the United States should always welcome overseas support for its foreign policy initiatives, it should never make its actions conditional upon such backing. To suggest otherwise is to ignore the elementary maxim of statecraft that in the final analysis, great powers are responsible for protecting their own interests and security. Finally, as Charles Krauthammer has observed, multilateralism collapses of its own weight.[19] There is a striking disparity between multilateralism's ambition to advance U.S. world order aspirations by exporting American values, on the one hand, and its proscription against using the very instruments of national power needed to make these objectives realizable, on the other.

Strategic Independence versus Cold War Internationalism

Strategic independence builds upon the realist tradition in American foreign policy exemplified in the early postwar years by scholar-diplomat George F. Kennan, commentator-analyst Walter Lippmann, political scientist Hans Morgenthau, and political figures such as President Dwight Eisenhower, Secretary of State George C. Marshall, and Ohio Republican Senator Robert A. Taft.

Like their predecessors, today's successor generation realists understand that American power is finite and that the world is not infinitely malleable. Now, as then, realists believe that the purpose of foreign policy is, in Lippmann's now familiar formulation, to bring "into balance with a comfortable surplus of power in reserve, the nation's commitments and the nation's power."[20] Now, as then, realists believe that an ideologically driven policy of containing communism and promoting U.S. liberal democratic values worldwide will lead to the open-ended expansion of U.S. commitments abroad, thereby straining America's economy and its domestic political institutions. Now, as then, realists eschew a foreign policy that defines U.S. interests in terms of world order aspirations in favor of a strategy that delineates U.S. interests within the traditional realpolitik framework of the balance of power. Now, as then, realists believe that this approach best reconciles the twin imperatives of protecting America from external threats to its security and simultaneously preserving the strength and vitality of its economy and domestic political system.

Successor generation realists believe that America's cold war internationalist strategy no longer is the best vehicle for pursuing U.S. interests. On the contrary, as the postwar realists predicted would be the case, in crucial respects cold war internationalism has undermined U.S. interests instead of promoting them. This condition has been especially true in the economic realm. The causes of America's deepening economic predicament are manifold and complex, but two stand out: (1) the United States has been overstretched by its worldwide strategic commitments, and (2) it has been disadvantaged by sticking to free trade in a world that is increasingly mercantilistic.

It is painfully apparent that America's external and domestic aspirations have outstripped the nation's ability—or willingness—to pay for them. Because the economy is the very foundation of both the nation's geopolitical power and its internal well-being, successor generation realists believe that America's relative decline poses the principal long-term peril to its external security and its domestic stability.[21] The gap between America's overseas commitments and its needs and wants at home, on the one hand, and the nation's resources, on the other hand, must be closed. If it is not, the United States runs the risk that as in the case of Britain earlier in this century, a predictable and normal relative decline may become a far more serious absolute decline.

When assessing America's world role in the 1990s and beyond, successor generation realists are struck by a paradox. In some respects, U.S. national strategy will be far more constrained in coming years than it was during the postwar years. Relative economic decline has underscored the limits of American power. It is no longer possible, as it seemed to be forty-five years ago, for the United States to pursue all of its domestic and international objectives without immediate sacrifice or harmful long-term consequences. The flip side of U.S. economic decline is the corresponding rise of Japan, the reemergence of the unified German economy, the West European Economic Community (which will become a single integrated market in 1992), and the newly industrializing countries. Clearly, "geoeconomics" is increasing in salience to all major nations as policymakers come to comprehend more fully the vital role of economic power in national strategy.

Militarily, the United States also finds itself circumscribed by shifts in the strategic balance and by the worldwide spread of advanced weaponry. Rather belatedly, it has become apparent that strategic nuclear parity and extended deterrence do not mix. With the loss of U.S. nuclear superiority, the difficulties of extending the protective mantle of American power to foil attacks on overseas allies have multiplied dramatically.[22] This fact has especially weighty implications for future U.S.–West European relations. On both sides of the Atlantic policymakers are rethinking long-held political and military assumptions as it becomes clear that NATO's cost/benefit matrix has been altered significantly. Meanwhile, in the Third World the diffusion of military technology has made outside powers' intervention in regional conflicts increasingly costly and problematic.

Yet, although these factors constrict the United States, there are other trends in international politics that, if taken advantage of, could actually enhance U.S. foreign policy options. First, the politico-military bipolarity of the postwar era is giving way to a multipolar system of four or five great powers (the United States, the Soviet Union, Japan, China, and perhaps Western Europe).[23] Second, the world has become ideologically far more pluralistic than it was thought to be at the cold war's height. Nationalism, nonalignment, and religious fundamentalism have proved to be of more transcendent importance in the Third World than communism and Marxism.[24] Indeed, more often than not these indigenous factors have proved to be more effective bulwarks against Soviet expansionism than U.S. intervention has been. Finally, the superpower relationship is being transformed profoundly. The Soviet Union's absorption with the formidable task of economic restructuring is bound to be long-term. In all likelihood, the Soviet Union's internal difficulties will have a restraining effect on its foreign policy. Influenced by Mikhail Gorbachev's "new thinking," Soviet diplomacy itself is changing. The importance of ideology in Soviet foreign policy is diminishing. The Soviet Union has conceded its empire in Eastern Europe. Moscow is scaling back its Third World commitments. The Kremlin is seeking new ways of lessening the burdens of the strategic competition with the United States in order to free up the inputs of capital and technology that are needed to rebuild the Soviet Union's civilian economy.

Unfolding international conditions are thus conducive to American strategic independence. In the bipolar postwar world, American foreign policy was inevitably preoccupied with, and defined by, the essentially conflictive relationship with the Soviet Union (and vice versa). However, in a multipolar world, neither superpower will focus so exclusively on its relationship with the other. Moreover, it will become increasingly apparent that the United States and Soviet Union are engaged in a traditional great power rivalry and are not engaged (if they ever truly were) in a Manichean ideological struggle between good and evil. Thus, as multipolarity takes deeper root, there are likely to be greater opportunities for meaningful political accommodation between the two superpowers. For the United States, multipolarity is particularly attractive because it means that there are (or will be) other great powers available to act as the primary counterweights to the Soviet Union (or any other future potential hegemon). Multipolarity means that many of America's burdensome strategic obligations can be shifted to others. As long as the United States is careful to play the regulating role of balancer, it can rely primarily on the emerging multipolar balance to safeguard its vital overseas interests. Similarly, because pluralism has blurred ideological bipolarity, and because the Soviet Union has decided for its own reasons that its vital interests are not engaged in the Third World, the United States can afford to take a less dogmatic view of regional turmoil.

STRATEGIC INDEPENDENCE: A NATIONAL STRATEGY FOR THE 1990S

The main objective of American national strategy in the 1990s should be the restoration of the nation's solvency and the revitalization of its resource base. For too long American policymakers have been seduced by an illusion of limitless possibilities into thinking that the United States could do all it wanted externally and domestically. Only a nation long shielded from resource constraints could be shocked to discover that even superpowers are not omnipotent. In the real world, resources are always scarce in comparison with desired objectives at home and abroad. Invariably, policymakers must set priorities among external security interests and then balance the state's strategic goals against its internal and economic ones. In so doing, "policy-makers must decide," Arnold Wolfers said, "whether a specific increment of security is worth the specific additional deprivations which its attainment through power requires."[25] This process is the essence of strategy making; a state that could fulfill all its needs and wants internationally and domestically would not need a strategy.

With this strategic imperative in mind, U.S. national interests in the 1990s are easily stated. First, the nation's core security (national survival, independence, and territorial integrity) must be maintained. This goal means that the United States must be able to deter (and perhaps defend against) a nuclear attack on the American homeland; ensure that no hostile power achieves hegemony over Eurasia; and uphold its geostrategic interests in the Western Hemisphere. Second, for both strategic and domestic reasons, the United States needs to shore up its declining economic position. Third, the social and political fabric of American society must be preserved intact. The specific strategic policies needed to further these interests are described in the following sections.

Economic Strategy

America's economic decline has three principal causes: (a) the U.S. commitment to multilateral free trade; (b) the persistent and worsening budget deficits of the past twenty years; and (c) America's strategic overextension. The economic component of a sound U.S. national strategy, therefore, must redress these problems.

First, U.S. trade policy should be tailored to deal bilaterally with America's trade partners on the same terms as those on which they deal with the United States. Free traders subscribe to the classical liberal belief that politics and economics are discrete activities that do not impinge on one another. They argue that an open international economy promotes efficiency and growth and enhances consumer welfare. Under free trade, they say, everyone gains something. Free traders are not concerned, however, with how the gains are distributed among the players in the game. And indeed, sometimes, as between 1945 and 1970, free trade works so well that even the players themselves put distributive issues on the back burner.

Free trade is an attractive theory, but the real world is fundamentally mercantilistic. In E. H. Carr's words, "the science of economics presupposes a given political order, and cannot be profitably studied in isolation from politics."[26] Unlike free traders (who are happy if everyone becomes wealthier in absolute terms), strategists are concerned with the relative power relations among states. Strategically, the key question about international economic policy is not, Will everyone gain something? but, Who will gain the most? Because economic power ultimately translates into politico-military strength, a nation that does relatively worse than others in the former sphere will see its overall international power standing decline in relation to its rivals.

In a mercantilist world, free trade stops at water's edge. It certainly does for America's economic rivals, who have capitalized on U.S. free trade policies and turned the postwar multilateral free trade system to America's disadvantage. As economists Pat Choate and Juyne Linger point out, "Others compete in the world marketplace with vastly different economic assumptions serving vastly different ends than America's."[27] Japan, Western Europe, and the newly industrialized countries have mixed economies in which the government sets goals and channels resources with the explicit aim of enhancing the state's relative international power position. While enjoying more or less unfettered access to the U.S. market, America's competitors employ mercantilism's standard tools: national industrial policy, tariff and nontariff trade barriers (the latter are especially important), subsidies to exporters, and controls over the outflow of capital and technology. Today, some 75 percent of the world's commerce is conducted by nations with economic systems that reject free trade in favor of a strategic approach to international trade.[28] With 1992 approaching in Western Europe, and Japan quietly formulating plans to create a yen trading bloc in the Pacific, the likelihood is that the world will become even more mercantilistic in the 1990s and that the West Europeans and Japanese will become even more formidable competitors than they are at present.

Second, while autarky is neither possible nor desirable, the United States should jealously guard its economic sovereignty. This approach is obvious with respect to industries and technologies with critical national security implications. While free traders extol interdependence and hail, as an example, the emergence of an integrated Japanese-American ("Nichibei") economy, strategists are less sanguine. The logic of interdependence (which makes states economically vulnerable to decisions made by others) clashes with the international political imperative that nations in a self-help system should pursue policies of independence and insulation. The need to protect U.S. economic sovereignty should be obvious as well with respect to the key tools of macroeconomic policy—taxation, exchange rates, and interest rates. Already, America's dependence on foreign capital to finance the deficit has given West German and Japanese central bankers real leverage over U.S. economic policy.

Moreover, private foreign investment also is troublesome. Therefore, the third component of U.S. economic strategy should be the formulation of guidelines for private foreign investment in the United States, and such investments should be closely monitored. Even when it adds to America's productive capabilities, private foreign investment still has downside effects.[29] For example, America sinks more deeply into international debtor status, and an increasing share of the nation's wealth is siphoned off (in the form of profits, dividends, and rents repatriated abroad). Thus, whether such investment ultimately is beneficial depends on how much of this repatriated wealth is reinvested in the United States. Moreover, as Martin Tolchin and Susan Tolchin point out in *Buying Into America,* "There is persuasive evidence that some foreign investors, notably the Japanese, have purchased U.S. companies to acquire their technology and ultimately eliminate U.S. competition in key industries" (11).

Fourth, trade should occur within a framework that advances basic national economic and security interests. America cannot and should not cease trading with the rest of the world, but its approach to international economic policy must change. Instead of giving primacy to efficiency or consumer welfare considerations, the thrust of U.S. economic policy should be to enhance America's relative power. Foremost among these interests is the need to preserve America's industrial manufacturing base. In his *Report on Manufactures* (1791), Alexander Hamilton observed that "not only the wealth but the independence and security of the country appear to be materially connected with the prosperity of manufactures."

Today, the United States needs to rediscover this indigenous tradition of strategic trade. Great powers are just as constrained to emulate the strategies of their rivals in the economic sphere as they are in the domain of military affairs. As Clyde Prestowitz, among others, has pointed out, the fact that Japan views industrial and financial primacy as an integral part of national security strategy—and that the United States does not—is the primary reason why the United States is losing the contest for world economic leadership.[30]

Additionally, as Stephen C. Cohen and John Zysman have shown, manufacturing matters more than ever.[31] First, America's defense capability is driven largely by commercial development (not the reverse), especially in leading-edge industries such as semiconductors, computers, and telecommunications. Absent dynamic private sector producers of these (and other) goods, the military would be forced to develop and maintain on its own a technological and productive capability superior to that of America's rivals. This requirement would be costly and perhaps impossible (24–27). Second, and perhaps more important, America's wealth—that is, the ability to generate the resources to build a strong and prosperous society—depends upon strength in manufacturing. The United States cannot simply shift out of manufacturing and into services; on the contrary, there are tight developmental linkages between the highest value–added service sectors and manufacturing industries. If America's manufacturing industrial base erodes, the United States will lose its leadership in the very service industries that are critical to its economic future (chaps. 1–2). Similarly, the ongoing erosion of U.S. leadership in leading-edge service sectors, particularly in financial services, will adversely affect such American industries as telecommunications and computers.[32] America's rivals understand the importance of manufacturing. Rather than allow their industries to wither away, they modernize and automate them (74–76). If the United States does not follow suit and protect its own manufacturing base, it will impair its security, its economic health, and perhaps its very social fabric.

Finally, if it is to work, American economic strategy must synchronize all aspects of U.S. economic policies, both foreign and domestic. First, trade policies must be complemented by macro- policies that create comparative advantages for the United States in the key factors of production.[33] Comparative advantage is dynamic, not static and immutable as free traders believe. The United States is handicapped by a deteriorating infrastructure and is losing out to its rivals because it is falling behind in capital formation and savings, technology, work force educational and skill levels, and research and development. Policymakers need to think more broadly about the components of overall national strategy than they heretofore have done. America's leaders would do well, for example, to remember that at the turn of the century the struggle for world economic (and hence geopolitical) leadership was largely, in military historian Corelli Barnett's words, "lost in the school yards and quadrangles of Britain."[34]

To create U.S. comparative advantages, the United States needs to invest in rebuilding its economy. Therefore, U.S. macro-policies must be driven by the imperative to reduce the federal budget deficit. The budget deficit absorbs more than half of America's national savings. The deficit also hinders domestic investment by driving interest rates up (making capital more expensive) and causing the rate of capital accumulation to decline (because government borrowing "crowds out" private savings). The deficit also has been the main culprit in America's emergence as the world's largest debtor—a fact which, in turn, helped contribute to the trade deficit. During the 1980s, huge inflows of foreign capital masked America's relative economic decline and made it possible for Washington to cut taxes while simultaneously increasing defense spending. In the long term, however, U.S. reliance on foreign capital will accelerate America's economic decline. As Gilpin points out, the United States is trapped in a vicious cycle:

> On the one hand, it requires foreign capital to finance its deficit. On the other hand the availability of foreign capital causes a greatly over-valued dollar that decreases the competitiveness of the American economy and industrial base. A weakened economy in turn increases the need for foreign capital, and the drain of interest payments further undermines the competitiveness of the economy. The most serious threat in this situation is that the competitiveness and industrial base of the American economy may erode to such a point that the process cannot be reversed.[35]

Therefore, an attempt to reduce the budget deficit through adjustments in fiscal policy must be synchronized with a monetary policy designed to reduce the value of the dollar in international markets. The decline in the dollar's value (and the concomitant U.S. export surge) during the late 1980s really does not change this analysis. A lower dollar and lower interest rates contain built-in inflationary pressures. As long as the budget deficit remains uncontrolled, the need for foreign capital to finance it, and the need to squelch a renewed bout of inflation (which would wreck America's economic prospects), eventually will force Washington to raise interest rates, which of course will strengthen the dollar. At this point, the vicious cycle will begin anew as imports, interest rates, and the dollar rise while U.S. exports decline.

Reducing the federal budget deficit, though crucial, seems like a herculean task: tax increases are economically unsound and politically unpopular; social security and national debt service are untouchable; and further domestic spending cuts are unrealistic politically.[36] Unless the United States is prepared to risk recession (from higher taxes), increased social and political tensions at home (by cutting domestic programs and entitlements), or lower standards of living (by consuming less), there is only one way to really cut the deficit: slashing military spending by reducing America's strategic commitments abroad. These commitments are a serious drain on the American economy. The U.S. commitment to NATO, for example, accounts for between 40 percent and 60 percent of the defense budget; defense analyst Earl Ravenal estimates that in fiscal 1985 America spent between $130 billion and $150 billion just on NATO.[37]

Moreover, America's military commitments abroad have serious hidden costs that place the United States at a real disadvantage in the global economy. While U.S. capital and technology are diverted from the private sector to the military sector, Western Europe and Japan take advantage of U.S. security guarantees by enhancing their economic competitiveness with resources they otherwise would spend on defense. Unsurprisingly, there is a negative correlation between high military spending and national productivity gains. For example, in 1983 Japan devoted a mere 1 percent of its GNP to defense (a figure that had not changed by 1990); between 1973 and 1983 its national economic productivity improved by 2.8 percent. The comparable figures for West Germany were 3.4 percent and 2.3 percent, and for France, 4.3 percent and 2.2 percent. The United States, which spent 6.9 percent of its GNP on defense, realized a minuscule 0.3 percent gain in national economic productivity.[38]

Diplomatic Strategy

America's diplomatic strategy in the 1990s must complement her economic strategy in order to restore the balance between means and ends. Toward this end, the paramount objective of U.S. diplomacy in the next decade should be to promote the transition of the strategic environment from bipolarity to multipolarity. Bipolarity imposes enormous security costs on superpowers but, by definition, forecloses any significant shifting of strategic burdens to others. Thus, after World War II the United States was not merely the organizer of an antihegemonic coalition seeking to maintain the global balance of power; it was, in effect, one side of the balance. However, as Kennan realized as early as 1947, the enormous national security costs of bipolarity would ultimately prove to be beyond America's resources.[39]

From the end of World War II until the Korean War, an influential (though not dominant) realist segment of the American foreign policy community preferred a multipolar postwar world to a bipolar one. In 1947, Secretary of State George C. Marshall said that America's objective should be to restore a balance of power in Europe and Asia, and Kennan observed that "it should be a cardinal point of our policy to see to it that other elements of independent power are developed on the Eurasian landmass as quickly as possible in order to take off our shoulders some of the burden of 'bipolarity.' "[40] Multipolarity's postwar proponents questioned whether America's economy and domestic political system could withstand the long-term stress of dominating large parts of the world for the purpose of denying them to the Soviets. They were also concerned that a long-term U.S. commitment to Europe would sap the Europeans' will to defend themselves and cause the Old World to become an American strategic appendage rather than an autonomous power center.

The Marshall Plan aimed to reestablish Western Europe's strategic capabilities by restoring political stability and economic vitality to the Continent. To put Western Europe on its feet, the United States opened its market while allowing the Europeans to protect their recovering industries with the Common Market trade bloc and other barriers. A similar policy was followed with respect to Japan. U.S. policy made it inevitable that these countries would become richer at America's expense. This structural disadvantage was judged an acceptable price because Washington expected that the diffusion of world economic power would lead to a parallel diffusion of military power to Western Europe and Japan, thus relieving America of many of global containment's burdens. This, of course, did not happen.

Today the time has come for Western Europe to play an independent strategic role commensurate with its military potential. Western Europe's GNP is twice as large as the Soviet Union's, it is far ahead of the Soviets technologically, and its population is one and one-half times as great. During the 1990s, the United States should devolve to Western Europe full responsibility for its own defense.[41] The logic of devolution is compelling. First, because NATO is America's most expensive and most extensive overseas obligation, a substantial reduction in the U.S. presence in Europe is the sine qua non of a policy that aims to close the gap between commitments and resources through strategic adjustment. Europe presents Washington with its most favorable opportunity to capitalize on the trends toward multipolarity. Second, disengagement is the only way the United States can escape from the dangers of extended deterrence.[42]

Although cold war internationalists and reformers recoil at the prospect of U.S. withdrawal from Western Europe, their arguments are unconvincing because NATO's importance to the United States has declined markedly. Western Europe is no longer needed as a base for U.S. strategic forces, it often refuses to serve as a platform for projecting U.S. power into the Third World, and it is being supplanted in relative economic importance by the Pacific basin. At the same time, fears that the Soviet Union would gain direct military control over Western Europe, or indirect political control (through Western Europe's "Finlandization"), were vastly overdrawn and certainly have no basis in the aftermath of the dramatic events in Eastern Europe.[43]

In the 1990s, U.S.-Soviet relations should enter into a new and more positive phase. Therefore, the second major component of U.S. diplomacy should focus on taking advantage of these improved relations to promote U.S. interests while simultaneously decreasing America's strategic overstretch. Both superpowers are experiencing relative decline, albeit for very different reasons. America's troubles result primarily from its persistence in a foreign policy that has outlived its usefulness. The Soviet Union, on the other hand, confronts a deep systemic crisis of efficiency that, if it is not resolved, could turn into a crisis of survival.

Measured in terms of immediate post–World War II objectives of the postwar realists, America's Soviet policy has been remarkably successful over the past forty-five years. The Soviet Union has not upset the global balance of power and probably is incapable of doing so. Indeed, to speak of "balance" is misleading: the combined military and economic resources of the United States, Western Europe, Japan, and China—all of which Moscow must reckon as potential foes—dwarf those of the Soviet Union. The Soviet Union is also disadvantaged because it no longer is an attractive ideological or cultural model for other nations. Finally, by any reasonable test, the "mellowing" of Soviet power that Kennan and other postwar realists sought to bring about through containment has been achieved.[44] The Soviet Union has evolved considerably from Stalinism. Instead of the stereotypical monolith, it has become a complex and highly nuanced society. Regardless of Mikhail Gorbachev's personal fate, or the degree of relative success his reforms attain, there is a growing consensus that glasnost and perestroika have changed the Soviet Union importantly and permanently in many key respects.

The climate of superpower relations is improving for a number of reasons. Both the United States and the Soviet Union are coming to realize that in the Third World, the game of great power competition is not worth the candle. Moscow has concluded that its Third World allies are subtracting from Soviet strength rather than adding to it. In the strategic area, Soviet new thinking about mutual security and defensive sufficiency are encouraging developments. Unilateral Soviet force reductions and Soviet proposals at the Conventional Forces in Europe arms control negotiations are indicative of these changes. Finally, Soviet views of international relations are changing, too, and Moscow appears to be putting behind it the belief that world politics is a struggle between classes or social systems.[45]

In some respects, however, Gorbachev's new thinking will make life more difficult for U.S. policymakers. Moscow's ability to present a less threatening image will increase the strains on U.S. alliances, particularly with Western Europe. Nevertheless, transformation in the transatlantic relationship should not be regarded as unexpected or unnatural. As Kenneth Waltz observes, "Alliances are made by states that have some but not all of their interests in common. The common interest is ordinarily a negative one: fear of other states."[46] In any alliance, fragmentation occurs when the common threat to the partners' security is perceived to diminish. As former CIA official Graham Fuller notes, a less threatening Soviet Union has implications for both the United States and its allies: "When you have a hostile Soviet Union, it's clear what is the basis of U.S. alliances. But what if the threat isn't present any longer? What's the premise of U.S. alliances, and what's the role for U.S. power?"[47] Indeed, Gorbachev's nimble diplomacy demonstrates that he has a leg up on his U.S. counterparts in understanding what constitutes effective foreign policy in a multipolar world. Soviet initiatives toward Western Europe and China (and ultimately, one expects, Japan) serve a double purpose: they help break the Soviet Union's encirclement while simultaneously weakening the geostrategic links between those countries and the United States.

Nevertheless, as the world moves steadily toward multipolarity, the outlook for U.S.-Soviet relations should brighten even further for several reasons. First, in a multipolar world there are peripheries, and international politics is not a zero-sum game. In part, this is because multipolarity increases the number of possible great power relationships. These relationships are likely to contain a more balanced mix of cooperation and conflict than heretofore have obtained in the Soviet-American relationship. As Karl Deutsch and J. David Singer observed, "As possible trade-offs increase, the greater the possibility for compensatory and stabilizing interactions to occur."[48] In a world where great powers have common as well as antithetical interests, the salience of ideology would be reduced. This decrease would drain great power rivalries of much of their venom and improve the prospects of political accommodation. The relatively moderate U.S. response to the repression in China in the aftermath of the political unrest in 1989 shows that U.S. policy is already heading in the right direction. Moreover, in a multipolar world, "as the number of independent actors in a system increases, the share of its attention that any one nation can devote to any other must of necessity diminish" (319). Although such an international system does not guarantee the absence of tension, nations are less likely to devote to one another the threshold degree of attention required to trigger a conflict. In this respect, the history of U.S. relations with czarist Russia and the Soviet Union is suggestive. Despite deep American ideological antipathy for both regimes, in a multipolar world the two nations paid little attention to each other, because the geostrategic conflicts between them were minimal. Essentially, it was the historical accident of bipolarity (a consequence of World War II) that locked the United States and Soviet Union into a seeming perpetual and globally pervasive confrontation. In a multipolar world U.S.-Soviet relations might look a lot more like they did during the previous multipolar era and be a lot less like they have been during the past forty-odd years. Moreover, in a multipolar world statesmen will have to relearn Lord

Palmerston's famous dictum that nations have permanent interests, not permanent allies or enemies. Thus, it is conceivable that the emergence of new great powers—Japan or China or Germany, for example—could give rise to U.S.-Soviet strategic and diplomatic cooperation by the early twenty-first century.

To develop a new relationship with the Soviet Union, American leaders will have to break free of their paradoxical tendency to view the Soviet Union, in the words of Walter Lippmann, "as both a cadaver and worldwide menace."[49] This viewpoint, which portrays a malevolent Soviet Union determined to break America's power and yet simultaneously so unstable as to be on the verge of possible collapse, distorts America's policy by making its prime goal the alteration of the Soviet Union's domestic political system. Although this view normally is associated with the neo-conservative Right, it is embraced across the political spectrum.

It is doubtful that America has the means to shape internal developments in the Soviet Union to any great degree. Therefore, the goal of transforming Soviet society should give way to a more important, and attainable, U.S. foreign policy objective: using diplomacy to channel Moscow's external behavior into more acceptable directions and securing agreements that enhance both superpowers' interests and security. In this respect, heretofore unimagined opportunities may now exist for agreements on regional conflicts and arms control. It would be tragic if the United States failed to explore these possibilities because it clung to the view that ideological or political differences make it impossible to negotiate with the Soviet Union. As Walter Lippmann said, "The history of diplomacy is the history of relations among rival powers, which did not enjoy political intimacy. . . . Nevertheless there have been political settlements. . . . For a diplomat to think that rival and unfriendly powers cannot be brought to settlement is to forget what diplomacy is all about."[50]

Military Strategy

U.S. military strategy in the 1990s should be linked much more closely to U.S. diplomatic policy. In a multipolar world the United States would no longer be on the front lines of every international flash point. Instead, in the first instance, the United States would rely on the independent strategic capabilities of the other power centers to maintain the global balance. This approach would act to frustrate a potential hegemon, because it would be in the other major powers' interests to do so. However, strategic independence would not be isolationism; the United States would be prepared, if necessary, to backstop the efforts of other great powers by entering into temporary and informal defensive commitments. Like Britain in the eighteenth and nineteenth centuries, America would be the "holder" of the global balance. Assuming that America acts wisely to arrest its relative decline, her weight would be decisive when added to the power of any antihegemonic nation or coalition. Because the paramount U.S. geopolitical objective is the negative one of preventing another state from achieving hegemonic preponderance, the United States would have the diplomatic flexibility to play the balancer's role. In this context, the objectives of strategic independence and America's geopolitical position dictate the following defense priorities for the United States in the 1990s: (1) strategic forces; (2) maritime forces; (3) tactical air forces and airlift capabilities; and (4) ground forces.

American nuclear strategy should switch from extended deterrence to residual deterrence. This shift in strategy requires a commensurate shift in the U.S. nuclear force structure. First, for strategic and diplomatic reasons, the United States should no longer deploy short-range nuclear weapons systems abroad. The present forward deployment of U.S. tactical and intermediate-range nuclear weapons to "couple" America to other nations' security is unacceptably dangerous. If deterrence failed, the automaticity of escalation upon which extended deterrence rests would almost certainly lead to the American homeland's destruction. Moreover, the presence of U.S. tactical nuclear weapons on foreign territory serves to fuel serious tensions between Washington and the host country. Indeed, in U.S.–West German relations, theater nuclear weapons have become a source of poison.

A new residual deterrence policy—based on the recognition that deterrence is in part existential and in part a function of U.S. strategic capabilities—would, however, enable the United States to extend a considerable measure of protection to Western Europe (and other key regions) without the risks of its present strategy. A residual deterrence strategy would give the United States the option of selectively using nuclear weapons in Europe's defense but would not irrevocably commit the United States to doing so. Deterrence can be effective even without the explicit understandings and formal symbols of an alliance. This approach was demonstrated in the late 1960s when America used its deterrent threat to dissuade Moscow from launching a preemptive war on China—a nation with which the United States did not even have formal diplomatic relations.[51]

A change in emphasis would also be required for U.S. strategic nuclear forces. Residual deterrence would rest on the enhancement of several strategic capabilities. First, the United States needs to ensure that it acquires adequate survivable counterforce and first-strike capabilities.

This posture entails continued development and deployment of the rail-launched MX missile and Trident II submarine with the D-5 missile. Second, selective and limited targeting options must be refined. This requirement entails not only an improvement in U.S. nuclear planning but an improvement in strategic command and control systems as well. Third, research on (and, if feasible, deployment of) strategic defenses should be accelerated. Finally, the United States should develop and deploy highly accurate U.S.-based air- and sea-launched cruise missiles that could be used in a theater support role.

Although some West European defense planners might argue that this new strategy would degrade the effectiveness of deterrence, such an argument would not be convincing. Regardless of whether U.S. troops and tactical nuclear weapons were deployed there, the Soviet Union would still realize that America would remain interested in Europe's fate. The mere fact that the United States has nuclear weapons and might use them on Western Europe's behalf almost certainly would be enough to dissuade the Soviets from attacking. Moreover, the credibility of deterrence would be enhanced, because a residual deterrence force posture would give the United States the capability of using nuclear weapons to defend Western Europe without destroying itself in the process. Whether used or not, this capability is a factor that the Soviets would have to take into account.

During the 1990s, in addition to deterring a direct attack on the United States, residual deterrence would offset the Soviet Union's conventional superiority. As long as the Soviet Union posed a significant threat to Western Europe's security, the United States would maintain intact the strategic nuclear capabilities needed to implement a residual deterrence strategy. Nevertheless, the purpose of adopting a residual deterrence strategy would not be to seek nuclear superiority or escalate the arms race. Rather, it would be to make explicit the nuclear/conventional nexus and to serve as a lever to persuade the Soviets to continue the comprehensive discussions encompassing the full range of European security issues.[52]

Strategic independence would alter the U.S. conventional force posture, too. Although reductions from present levels would be possible and desirable, strategic independence would require the United States to maintain strong naval and air forces and the airlift capability to move ground units quickly to threatened regions. Because of their mobility, naval and air forces could be deployed rapidly to overseas trouble spots in the event that U.S. intervention was necessary. Naval and air forces are also important because they can be used for diplomatic and crisis management purposes. However, emphasis within both the air force and the navy needs to be placed on improving fast sealift and heavy airlift capabilities.

In addition, strategic independence would result in U.S. ground forces being reduced to approximately one-third of their current strength. This policy would entail both a reduction of army units from eighteen to seven active divisions and a reorganization of the remaining forces. American troops would be withdrawn gradually from Western Europe and South Korea, and the bulk of these forces would be demobilized. For crisis management purposes, the United States would retain a limited capability to reinsert its forces by leaving prepositioned equipment for two armored divisions in Europe and for one heavy infantry division in South Korea. These three divisions, and their airlift, would be based in the United States. At the same time, because the United States has few concrete interests in the Third World (with the clear exception of Central America), American involvement in the Third World stems mostly from intangible ideological, not balance-of-power, concerns. By jettisoning cold war internationalism's ideological baggage, and by cutting U.S. reliance on Third World markets and raw materials, strategic independence would enable the United States to reduce to four light divisions its Third World contingency forces.

IMPLICATIONS OF STRATEGIC INDEPENDENCE

Strategic independence would actually enhance U.S. influence in the world. Strategic independence would be a flexible, dynamic policy that would enable the United States to respond as needed to the shifting correlation of forces. Downplaying formal commitments, and defining vital U.S. interests abroad only in general balance-of-power terms, strategic independence is a policy that would avoid falling into the trap of foreign policy rigidity that has plagued cold war internationalism during the past four decades. By following this "free hand" policy—an interest-rather than threat-based strategy—America would let others know that its support could no longer be taken for granted. This strategy would spur other nations to assume the primary responsibility for their own defense and would rectify one of the worst effects of America's current unconditional security guarantees: the incentive that recipients of U.S. protection have to free-ride on the back of the United States.

By relying on the demonstrable propensity of nations to balance against threats, and by ignoring events in peripheral regions, the United States would no longer have to adopt a supplicant psychology of begging other nations to allow it to defend them. However, at the same time, America's power would make it an attractive potential ally for other nations, and because of its insularity and the narrow scope of its vital interests in a multipolar world, the United States would seldom be perceived as the primary threat to their security. In a multipolar world the United States would be able to extract meaningful quid pro quos for its commitments—something it is not well placed to do with its present cold war internationalist policy.

Strategic independence would prove similarly beneficial in the economic realm. "Interdependence" is commonly used to mean that the international economy is so tightly integrated that all nations are mutually and equally vulnerable to others' actions. Contrary to the conventional wisdom, however, the United States, while involved in the global economy, is not in a condition of interdependence. Precisely because of its leading great power status, America is relatively unaffected by others' actions, while they tend to be very heavily dependent on the United States. The United States is less involved in the international economy than are other nations (among great powers, only the Soviet Union is more autarkic than the United States) and less reliant on overseas raw materials. Thus, the United States enjoys a relatively greater, though not unrestricted, freedom of action than do others. The international economic component of strategic independence would maximize U.S. self-sufficiency, which, because it increases America's ability to act unilaterally to advance its national interests, is an intrinsic good. The United States cannot cut itself off from international economic intercourse, and it should not forgo the efficiency and consumer welfare benefits that come from free trade. However, strategic independence would give first priority to national interests and would give a greater weight to self-sufficiency than to free trade gains.

In the final analysis, the disagreement between successor generation realists and cold war internationalists is as much (perhaps more) about values as it is about strategy. Cold war internationalism represents one of the two paradigmatic visions of this country's role in world politics that has persisted throughout American history: the belief that liberty and affluence at home are promoted by actively pursuing greatness abroad.[53] Cold war internationalists believe that realists are obsessed with the national interest but blind to the promotion abroad of American values such as freedom and democracy. It is this vision of America's mission that leads them to reject any kind of strategic retrenchment and to argue that regardless of the cost, the United States must maintain a favorable international environment. As former Defense Secretary James Schlesinger told the Senate Foreign Relations Committee in February 1985: "The United States, as a great power, has essentially taken on the task of sustaining the world order. And any abandonment of major commitments is difficult to reconcile with that task."[54]

Successor generation realists represent the other major tradition in American foreign policy: a belief that America's political institutions and domestic well-being are best safeguarded by a policy of restraint in foreign affairs. Remaking the world is a noble aspiration, but realists know that policies must be judged by their consequences, not by the intentions underlying them. Realists ask not only what kind of world is desirable but what kind of world is practically attainable, and at what cost to America's well-being.

Successor generation realists are at least as motivated by moral values and ideals as are cold war internationalists; unlike the latter, however, they have as their first concern the vigor and solidity of America itself. In this respect, the United States has been injured by cold war internationalism. A foreign policy that is open-ended, threat-based, and ideologically driven places extraordinary demands on a nation's social, economic, and psychological resources. Vietnam, Watergate, and the Iran-contra affair are reminders that a foreign policy that seeks to transform the world may have the unwanted effect of transforming America instead.[55] The relative decline of U.S. economic power is a reminder that balancing resources and commitments is a moral as well as strategic imperative, because states that tolerate a persistent imbalance between the ends and means of policy run the risk of ruin.

Cold war internationalists have adopted a chillingly perverse view of the relationship between U.S. foreign policy and domestic politics. Many seem to believe that America's citizens, resources, and, indeed, its political institutions have justifiable utility only as assets to support cold war internationalism's overseas pretensions. This view became evident during the Iran-contra scandal when some cold war internationalists claimed that America's democratic system prevented the United States from discharging effectively its superpower responsibilities. More recently, in a different context, Samuel P. Huntington asserted that America's worldwide military commitments are not weakening the U.S. economically. If the United States falters economically, he proclaims, it will be because Americans "overindulge[d] themselves in the comforts of the good life. Consumerism not militarism is the threat to American strength."[56]

Cold war internationalists need to go back to school and retake courses in basic civics and American history. They are so fixated on the purported threats to their chimerical goal of a U.S.-imposed world order that they are endangering America's most basic vital interests. American foreign policy has a single overriding purpose: to protect the nation's permanent interest in preserving the values and structures that lie at the heart of its domestic system. In this country the purpose of foreign policy is to ensure the nation's safety precisely so that its citizens can enjoy the good life: individual freedom of choice, the fruits of a free and dynamic economy, and the ordered liberty of democratic government. One of America's wisest twentieth-century statesmen, President Dwight Eisenhower, warned that Americans must be careful that their foreign policy objectives do not become so ambitious that their pursuit ends up destroying what they seek to defend, namely, the vitality and strength of America's political and economic institutions.[57] Cold war internationalists have forgotten this lesson—if indeed they ever learned it.

In the past, the proponents of restraint have usually lost America's periodic foreign policy "great debates." Too often realists have allowed themselves to be depicted as amoral (or even immoral) practitioners of a realpolitik devoid of moral content. As the late Robert E. Osgood observed, the struggle between the advocates of restraint and the proponents of activism has been a battle for control of the symbolic spigots of popular idealism. Successor generation realists should not hesitate to fight on this terrain. This time, they are well placed to prevail, because they can demonstrate that a balance-of-power policy of strategic independence is consistent with America's external interests and with its domestic needs and values.

9

Liberalism and the Formulation
of U.S. Strategy

MICHAEL W. DOYLE

The fundamental problem of national strategy rests in the definition of national interests. These interests should reflect the values for which the state stands and for which it is willing to expend national resources. The fundamental values of the state are shaped by domestic political, economic, and social factors, as well as by the nature of the external environment. Therefore, the sources of national interests are both domestic and external.

The influences of these internal and external factors in the formulation of U.S. national interests are not always in concert. Realists would argue that geopolitical balance of power considerations should dominate national strategy. States that threaten the international balance should be opposed, and allies sought, regardless of ideology. Liberals, on the other hand, would argue that stable and peaceful international relations are dependent upon the nature of the states involved in the system. In practice, American liberalism has taken two distinct forms: an isolationist liberalism, predicated on the believe that the best way to promote democracy abroad is to focus internally, to make the United States exemplary of democratic ideals; and a liberal internationalism, predicated on the belief that the United States should actively intervene in the affairs of other states to help promote democratic political structures.

The history of U.S. national strategy in the cold war period has been the clash of these different views; yet, neither vision has dominated the formulation of national interests. However, in cases where liberal ideological considerations have entered the strategic calculus, two trends appear relevant. First, liberal internationalism has dominated the isolationist approach to the transformation of the international system. Second, liberal ideas frequently have been abused or applied in an arrogant manner. They have been used as justifications for the pursuit of geopolitical or economic interests rather than as a separate interest reflective of the values upon which the United States was founded. Consequently, the concept of liberalism as a basis for American action has been denigrated. Yet liberalism is at the heart of America's values and should provide the basis for the formulation of U.S. national interests and, hence, for the foundation of U.S. national strategy in the future.

In order to defend these views, in this essay I address three fundamental questions. First, what is *liberalism*? Second, why is a conception of national interest and national strategy based on liberalism a sound course of action for a state to follow? Third, what should U.S. national interests and national strategy based on liberalism be?

In the first section of this essay I examine the concept of liberalism and develop the political and economic premises that are derived from it. As will be shown, liberalism is a distinct ideology and set of institutions that has shaped the perceptions of and capacities for foreign relations of political societies that range from social-welfare or social-democratic to laissez-faire.

Liberalism, however, is not inherently "peace-loving"; nor is it consistently restrained or peaceful in intent. Furthermore, liberal practice may reduce the probability that states will successfully exercise the consistent restraint and peaceful intentions that a world peace may well require in the nuclear age. Yet the peaceful intent and restraint that liberalism manifests in limited aspects of its foreign affairs announce the possibility of a world peace. Such intent and restraint have strengthened the prospects for a world peace established by the steady expansion of a separate peace among liberal societies. In the second section of this essay I examine both the positive aspects and the limitations of using liberal principles as a basis for formulating national interests.

In the third section I show how the United States, by following liberal principles, can identify national interests in the 1990s. This discussion is followed by a section that develops a set of criteria for classifying the nature of states, thereby defining the actions necessary to promote the establishment of a "pacific union." The final section is a discussion of the implications of a U.S. national strategy based on liberal principles, as well as the opportunities and risks in the future should the United States truly adopt such a national strategy.

DEFINING LIBERALISM

Liberalism can best be identified by an essential principle: the importance of the freedom of the individual. Above all, this is a belief in the importance of moral freedom, of the right to be treated, and a duty to treat others, as ethical subjects, not as objects or means only. A commitment to this principle has generated rights and institutions.

A threefold set of rights forms the foundation of liberalism. Liberalism calls for freedom from arbitrary authority, "negative freedom," which includes freedom of conscience, a free press and free speech, equality under the law, and the right to hold and exchange property without fear of arbitrary seizure. Liberalism also calls for the "positive freedoms" that are necessary to protect and promote the capacity to exercise free choice, which include equality of opportunity in education and access to health care and employment. A third liberal right, democratic participation or representation, is necessary to guarantee the other two. To ensure that morally autonomous individuals remain free in those areas of social action where public authority is needed, public legislation has to express the will of the citizens making laws for their own community.

Liberalism is thus marked by a shared commitment to four essential institutions. First, citizens possess juridical equality and other fundamental civic rights such as freedom of religion and the press. Second, the effective sovereigns of the state are representative legislatures deriving their authority from the consent of the electorate and exercising their authority free from all restraint apart from the requirement that basic civic rights be preserved. Most pertinently for the impact of liberalism on national strategy, the state is subject to neither the external authority of other states nor the internal authority of special prerogatives held, for example, by monarchs or bureaucracies over foreign policy. Third, the economy rests on a recognition of the rights of private property, including the ownership of means of production. Property is justified by individual acquisition (for example, by labor) or by social agreement or social utility. This excludes state socialism or state capitalism, but it need not exclude market socialism or various forms of the mixed economy. Fourth, economic decisions are predominantly shaped by the forces of supply and demand, domestically and internationally, and are free from direct state control.

These principles and institutions have shaped two high roads to liberal governance.[1] In order to protect the opportunity of the citizen to exercise freedom, laissez-faire liberalism has leaned toward a highly constrained role for the state and a much wider role for private property and the market. In order to promote the opportunity of the citizen to exercise freedom, welfare liberalism has expanded the role of the state and constricted the role of the market. Both, nevertheless, accept the four institutional requirements and contrast markedly with the colonies, monarchical regimes, military dictatorships, and Communist party dictatorships with which they have shared the political governance of the modern world.

BASING NATIONAL INTERESTS ON LIBERALISM

The principal rationale for basing national interests on liberalism is the finding that liberal states tend to create a separate peace among themselves. This separate peace advances the fundamental interests of the state—security and prosperity—and realizes the fundamental principles of free citizens. However, in addition to this positive effect, there are two negative effects that liberal principles and institutions have had on the foreign affairs of liberal states. An understanding of the role that liberalism can play in the formulation of U.S. interests, both positive and negative, calls for an examination of these three effects of liberal institutions and principles on the foreign affairs of liberal states.

The Pacific Union

The positive effect of liberalism on the ability of states to accomplish their national interests is the establishment of a peace among liberal states.[2] Beginning in the eighteenth century and slowly growing since then, a zone of peace, which Immanuel Kant called the "pacific federation" or "pacific union," began to be established among liberal societies.[3]

During the nineteenth century, the United States and Great Britain engaged in nearly continual strife. But after the Reform Act of 1832 defined actual representation as the formal source of the sovereignty of the British parliament, Britain and the United States negotiated their disputes despite, for example, British grievances against the Northern blockade of the South, with which Britain had close economic ties. Despite severe Anglo-French colonial rivalry, liberal France and liberal Britain formed an entente against illiberal Germany before World War I. In 1914–15, Italy, the liberal member of the Triple Alliance with Germany and Austria, chose not to fulfill its treaty obligations under the Triple Alliance to support its allies. Instead, Italy joined in an alliance with Britain and France, which prevented it from having to fight other liberal states, and then declared war on Germany and Austria. Despite generations of Anglo-American trade with Germany, the United States leaned toward Britain and France from 1914 to 1917, before entering World War I on their side. Nowhere was this special peace among liberal states more clearly proclaimed than in President Woodrow Wilson's war message of 2 April 1917: "Our object now, as then, is to vindicate the principles of peace and justice in the life of the world as against selfish and autocratic power and to set up amongst the really free and self-governed people of the world such a concert of purpose and of action as will henceforth ensure the observance of those principles."[4]

The apparent absence of war between liberal states, whether adjacent or not, for almost two hundred years is significant. What is perhaps more significant is that when states are forced to decide on which side of an impending world war they will fight, liberal states wind up all on the same side, despite the complexity of the paths that take them there. And we should recall that medieval and early modern Europe were the warring cockpits of states, wherein France and England and the Low Countries engaged in nearly constant strife. Then in the late eighteenth century there began to emerge liberal regimes. At first hesitant and confused, and later clear and confident as liberal regimes gained deeper domestic foundations and longer international experience, a pacific union of these liberal states became established. These characteristics do not prove that the peace among liberals is statistically significant, nor that liberalism is the peace's sole valid explanation.[5] But they do suggest that we consider the possibility that liberals have indeed established a separate peace, but only among themselves.

The peace appears to be attributable to liberalism itself. Neither specific regional characteristics nor historic alliances or friendships describe the wide reach of the liberal peace. The peace extends as far as, and no further than, the relations among liberal states, not including nonliberal states in a predominantly liberal region (such as the north Atlantic in the 1930s) nor excluding liberal states in a nonliberal region (such as Central America or Africa).

And relations among any group of states with similar social structures or with compatible values are not similarly peaceful.[6] Feudal warfare was frequent and very much a sport of the monarchs and nobility. There have not been enough truly totalitarian, fascist powers (nor have they lasted long enough) to test fairly their pacific compatibility, but fascist powers in the wider sense of nationalist, capitalist, military dictatorships fought each other in the 1930s. Communist powers have engaged in wars more recently in East Asia. And we have not had enough democratic socialist societies to consider the relevance of socialist pacification. The more abstract category of pluralism does not suffice. Certainly Germany was pluralist when it engaged in war with liberal states in 1914; Japan as well in 1941. But they were not liberal. Peace among liberals thus appears to be a special characteristic.

Liberal principles and institutions also promise a distinctively attractive prospect for the future. The decline of U.S. hegemonic leadership in the 1990s may pose a danger for the liberal world. This danger is not that today's liberal states will permit their economic competition to spiral into war but that the need for coordination has decisively increased. In the early postwar period the United States provided leadership, funds, and institutional innovation in helping to sustain liberal domestic orders in the face of mounting economic crises. No single liberal state appears to have a position equivalent to the position the United States held then.

Yet liberals may have escaped from the single, greatest, traditional danger of international change—the transition from one hegemonic leader to another. Historically, when one great power began to lose its preeminence and to slip into mere equality, a warlike resolution of the international pecking order became exceptionally likely. New power challenges old prestige, excessive commitments face new demands; so Sparta felt compelled to attack Athens, France warred Spain, England and Holland fought with France (and with each other), and Germany and England struggled for the mastery of Europe in World War I.[7] But here liberals may again be an exception, for despite the fact that the United States constituted Britain's greatest potential challenger along all the dimensions most central to the British maritime hegemony, Britain and the United States accommodated their differences. After the defeat of Germany, Britain eventually, though not without regret, accepted its replacement by the United States as the commercial and maritime hegemon of the liberal world.

Two factors thus can help moderate economic and political rivalries among the liberal states of Europe, Japan, and the United States. One is the promise of a peaceable transition to the next liberal hegemon. The other is that longer promise—the Kantian promise of a world peace.

Liberalism also seems to carry with it two other effects: what the British philosopher David Hume called "imprudent vehemence" and "supine complaisance."[8] These two effects limit the ability to effectively base national interests solely on liberalism. We should, therefore, assess the impact that these effects have had on the foreign affairs of liberal states.

Imprudent Vehemence

Peaceful restraint only seems to work in the liberals' relations with other liberals. Liberal states have fought numerous wars with nonliberal states. This fact is the basis of Hume's assertion of "imprudent vehemence." But proneness to war is not a measure of imprudent aggression. Many wars are defensive, and thus prudent by necessity. Liberal states have been attacked and threatened by nonliberal states that do not exercise any special restraint in their dealings with liberal states. Authoritarian rulers both stimulate and respond to an international political environment in which conflicts of prestige, of interest, and of pure fear of what other states might do all lead states toward war. War and conquest have thus characterized the careers of many authoritarian rulers and ruling parties. Yet, we cannot blame warfare simply on the authoritarians or totalitarians, as many of our more enthusiastic politicians would have us do.[9] Both liberal and nonliberal states have acted as initiators in interstate wars.

Although liberal initiation of wars suggests some basis for Hume's assertion, it does not resolve the claim he made. Initiation or response may reflect either aggressive or defensive policy, in that an aggressive policy may provoke a rival to initiate a war and a defensive policy may require preemption. Hume appears to have been suggesting that liberal policy has a tendency to be unnecessarily aggressive. In order to assess his assertion, we need to take into account the specific circumstances, a historical understanding of time and place. Liberal states' relations with nonliberals appear complicated, neither always aggressive nor always nonaggressive. Consequently, it may be possible only to illustrate imprudent vehemence on the part of liberal states.

Most wars seem to arise out of calculations and miscalculations of interest, misunderstandings, and mutual suspicions, such as those that characterized the origins of World War I. But we can find expressions of aggressive intent and apparently unnecessary vehemence by the liberal state characterizing a large number of wars.[10]

In relations with powerful nonliberal states, liberal states have missed opportunities to pursue the negotiation of arms reduction and arms control when it was in the mutual strategic interest and have failed to construct wider schemes of accommodation needed to supplement arms control. For example, there is evidence that a deeply ingrained suspicion characterizes U.S. diplomacy toward the Soviet Union. In the postwar period, and particularly following the outbreak of the Korean War, U.S. diplomacy equated the "international communist movement" (all communist states and parties) with "communist imperialism" and with a domestic tyranny in the Soviet Union that required a cold war contest and international subversion as means of legitimizing its own police state. John Foster Dulles expressed this conviction most clearly when he declared: "We shall never have a secure peace or a happy world so long as Soviet communism dominates one third of all the peoples that there are, and is in the process of trying at least to extend its rule to many others."[11]

Opportunities for splitting the Communist bloc along cleavages of strategic national interest were delayed. Burdened with the war in Vietnam, the United States took ten years to appreciate and exploit the strategic opportunity of the Sino-Soviet split, which emerged in 1960. Even the defection of Yugoslavia from the Soviet bloc did not receive the wholehearted welcome that a strategic assessment of its importance would have warranted.[12] Both relationships, with Yugoslavia and China, become subject to alternating, largely ideologically derived moods: visions of exceptionalness (they were "less ruthless," more organic to the indigenous, traditional culture) sparred with bouts of liberal soul-searching ("We cannot associate ourselves with a totalitarian state").

Imprudent vehemence is also associated with liberal foreign policy toward weak, nonliberal states; no greater spirit of accommodation or tolerance informs liberal policy toward the many weak, nonliberal states in the Third World. For example, during the postwar period, when the U.S. cold war internationalism sought to protect liberals in the Third World from the "communist threat," the consequences of liberal foreign policy on the nonliberal society often became far removed from the promotion of individual rights or of national security. In Vietnam and elsewhere, intervening against "armed minorities" and "enemies of free enterprise" meant intervening for other armed minorities, some sustaining and sustained by oligarchies, others resting on little more than U.S. foreign aid and troops. Indigenous liberals simply had too narrow a base of domestic support. These interventions did not advance liberal rights, and to the extent that they were driven by ideological motives they were not necessary for national security.

To the conservative liberals, the alternatives are starkly cast: Third World authoritarians with allegiance to the liberal, capitalist West or "communists" subject to the totalitarian East (or leftist nationalists, who even if elected are but a slippery stepping stone to totalitarianism).[13]

Conservative liberals are prepared to support the allied authoritarians. The communists attack property in addition to liberty, thereby provoking conservative liberals to covert or overt intervention, or "dollar-diplomacy" imperialism. The interventions against Mossadegh in Iran, Arbenz in Guatemala, Allende in Chile, and the Sandinistas in Nicaragua appear to fall into this pattern.[14]

To the social-welfare liberals, the choice is never so clear. The large number of conservative oligarchs or military bureaucracies with whom the conservative liberal is well at home are not so congenial to the social welfare liberal; yet the communists are still seen as enemies of liberty. They justify more extensive intervention first to discover, then to sustain, Third World social democracy in a political environment that is either barely participatory or highly polarized. Thus Arthur Schlesinger recalls President Kennedy musing shortly after the assassination of Trujillo (former dictator of the Dominican Republic): "There are three possibilities in descending order of preference, a decent democratic regime, a continuation of the Trujillo regime [by his followers] or a Castro regime. We ought to aim at the first, but we can't really renounce the second until we are sure we can avoid the third."[15]

The record of liberalism in the nonliberal world is not solely a catalogue of oppression or imprudence. The North American West and the settlement colonies—Australia and New Zealand—represent a successful transplant of liberal institutions, albeit in the special circumstances of a temperate, sparsely populated environment and at the cost of Indian and Aborigine rights. Similarly, the twentieth-century expansion of liberalism into less powerful nonliberal areas has also had some striking successes. The forcible liberalization of Germany and Japan following World War II and the long covert financing of liberal parties in Italy are the more significant instances of successful transplant. Covert financing of liberalism in Chile and occasional diplomatic demarches to nudge aside military threats to noncommunist democratic parties (as in Peru in 1962, South Korea in 1963, and the Dominican Republic in 1965 and again in 1978)[16] illustrate policies that, though less successful, were directed toward liberal goals. These particular postwar liberal successes also are the product of special circumstances: the existence of a potential liberal majority, temporarily suppressed, that could be readily reestablished by outside aid or unusually weak oligarchic, military, or communist opponents.[17]

Supine Complaisance

The final effect apparent in the international relations of liberal states is Hume's second assertion: "supine complaisance." This effect takes two forms: failure to support allies and failure to oppose enemies; both represent failures to adequately "balance" against threats.

Liberal internationalism among liberal states has been shortsighted in preserving its basic preconditions under changing international circumstances, and particularly in supporting the liberal character of its constituent states. The liberal community of nations has failed on occasion, as it did in regard to Germany in the 1920s, to provide international economic support for liberal regimes whose market foundations were in crisis. It failed in the 1930s to provide military aid or political mediation to Spain, which was challenged by an armed minority, or to Czechoslovakia, which was caught in a dilemma of preserving national security or acknowledging the claims (fostered by Hitler's Germany) of the Sudeten minority to self-determination. Farsighted and constitutive measures seem to have been provided by the liberal international order only when one liberal state stood preeminent among the rest, prepared and able to take measures, as did the United States following World War II, to sustain economically and politically the foundations of liberal society beyond its borders. Then measures such as the British Loan, the Marshall Plan, the North Atlantic Treaty Organization (NATO), the General Agreement on Tariffs and Trade

(GATT), the International Monetary Fund (IMF), and the liberalization of Germany and Japan helped construct buttresses for the international liberal order.[18]

Ideologically based policies can also be self-indulgent. Oligarchic or authoritarian allies in the Third World do not find consistent support in a liberal policy that stresses human rights. Contemporary conservative critics claim that the security needs of these states are neglected, that they fail to obtain military aid or more direct support when they need it (the Shah's Iran, Humberto Romero's El Salvador, Somoza's Nicaragua, and South Africa). Equally disturbing from this point of view, communist regimes are shunned even when a detente with them could further U.S. strategic interests (Cuba, Angola). Welfare liberals particularly shun the first group, while laissez-faire liberals balk at close dealings with the second. In both cases U.S. economic interests or strategic interests can be slighted.[19]

A second manifestation of complaisance lies in a reaction to the excesses of interventionism, causing a shift toward liberal isolationism. A mood of frustrated withdrawal affects policy toward strategically and economically important countries. Just as interventionism seems to be the typical failing of the liberal great power, so complaisance characterizes declined or not quite risen liberal states.[20] Especially following the exhaustion of wars, representative legislatures may become reluctant to undertake international commitments or to fund the military establishment needed to play a geopolitical role. Purely domestic concerns seem to take priority, as they did in the United States in the 1920s. Rational incentives for "free-riding" on the extended defense commitments of the leader of the liberal alliance also induce this form of complaisance. During much of the nineteenth century the United States informally relied upon the British fleet for many of its security needs. Today, the Europeans and the Japanese, according to some American strategic analysts, fail to bear their "fair" share of alliance burdens.

Liberalism thus carries with it three connected legacies—peace among liberals, imprudent vehemence toward nonliberals, and complaisance toward the future. The first appears to be a special feature associated with liberalism, and it can be demonstrated statistically. The latter two cannot be shown to be special to liberalism, though their effects can be illustrated historically in liberal foreign policy.

In his essay "Perpetual Peace," Kant showed how the peace among republics is produced by liberal principles and institutions and how that liberal peace would, unfortunately, be compatible with war and imprudent policy toward nonliberal states. First, representative government and a separation of powers protect the freedom of the individual and provide a constitutional guarantee that the aggressive instincts of rulers will be tamed by the requirement that the interests of the citizenry be represented in the decision to go to war. Since the citizens would bear the costs of war, "caution" would replace the "caprice" authoritarian rulers have traditionally been capable of exercising at the expense of their subjects. But "caution," he noted, would not end wars (as so many liberal theorists have assumed it would); it would merely ensure that wars would be fought only for popular purposes. Popular wars fought to promote freedom, to protect private property, or to support liberal allies against threats from nonliberal enemies were fully within the liberal legacy (and Kant warned liberals of their susceptibility to these wars).

Second, an international guarantee of respect prevents wars specifically among liberal states. International liberal respect, or trust, comes from the same source from which citizens of liberal states derive respect for their own government. The liberal state derives its authority from the consent of the governed. Themselves domestically just and based upon consent, liberal states presume that foreign liberal states, which also rest on consent, are also just and therefore deserving of accommodation. At the same time, they assume that nonliberal states, which do not rest on free consent, are not just. And since they are in a state of aggression with their own people, nonliberal governments become deeply suspect in their foreign relations.

Third, international trade and personal contacts between the citizens of liberal societies add material incentives to moral commitments. Extensive trade can produce mutual economic benefits. Having a variety of contacts ensures that no single conflict sours an entire relationship. Ties of interdependence rely upon the expectation that the next transaction will also be based on exchange rather than coercion. A sense of suspicion (such as that characterizing relations between liberals and nonliberals) can lead to restrictions on the range of contact between societies, increasing the prospect that one conflict will determine a relationship.

The survival and growth in the number of liberal states suggests that imprudent vehemence and complaisance have not overwhelmed liberalism's efficacy as a form of governance. Therefore, the formulation of national interests based on liberal principles appears to improve the prospect for creating an international milieu conducive not only to the promotion of world freedom but to the promotion of national security as well, as long as the effects of imprudent aggression and complaisance can be mitigated.

A LIBERAL GRAND STRATEGY FOR THE 1990S

Identifying National Interests

If the United States seeks to promote world freedom, then it must abandon the calculus of the geopolitical balance of power in formulating national interests and substitute guidelines for dealing with the liberal and nonliberal world based on general liberal principles. Liberal policies must attempt to secure personal and civil rights, to foster democratic government, and to expand the scope and effectiveness of the world market economy, as well as to meet those basic human needs that make the exercise of human rights possible. Powerful and weak nonliberal states must be treated according to the same standards. There can be no special geopolitical clients, no geopolitical enemies. The interests of the United States must be consistent with its principles. The United States must have no liberal enemies and no unconditional alliances with nonliberal states.

In order to avoid the extremist possibilities of liberal imprudence or complaisance, U.S. national interests should be further constrained by a realistic assessment of the external environment. While liberal democracy can identify U.S. natural allies abroad, the United States must let its enemies identify themselves.

One reason for this approach is that the United States cannot embark upon an indiscriminate crusade for democracy. In a world armed with nuclear weapons, crusading is suicidal. In a world where changes in regional balances of power could be extremely destabilizing for the United States and its allies, indiscriminate provocations of hostility (such as against the People's Republic of China) could create increased insecurity (for Japan and the United States). The United States simply does not have the excess strength that would free it from a need to economize on dangers.

A second reason why the United States should let its enemies identify themselves is that U.S. liberal values require that it should reject indiscriminate crusading. If Americans seek to promote democracy because it reflects the rights of all to be treated with equal respect—irrespective of race, religion, class, or nationality—then equal respect must guide both their aims and their means. Strategies of geopolitical superiority and liberal imperialism, for example, have required increased arms expenditures and international subversion and have had little (or, more accurately, a retrogressive) effect on human rights in the countries that were U.S. targets.

Criteria for Classifying States

The paramount national interest is the support of liberal democracies; therefore, U.S. policies toward specific states must be consistent with the degree to which a state is founded upon liberal institutions and adheres to liberal principles. A new calculus of security thus provides a benchmark of survival and prudence from which a liberal strategy that recognizes national security as a liberal right can navigate. This benchmark consists of prudent policies toward the most significant threat to the liberal world and indeed the only strategic threat the United States faces—the Soviet Union. Once a prudent policy toward the Soviet Union has been set, more supportive and interdependent policies toward those countries more liberal than the Soviet Union, and more constraining and more containing policies toward countries less liberal, can be defined. Both these measures can change over time. Indeed, the differences in treatment might serve as an indirect incentive for the liberalizing reform of nonliberal countries.

The Components of a Liberal Strategy

There is no reason to expect a simple formula for a national strategy. Specific and changing circumstances clearly prevent such simplicity. But as an example of how a liberal grand strategy could be formulated, I suggest the following.

President Gorbachev's reforms are especially significant for liberal grand strategy. They have begun to create a marked reduction in the overall threat to the pacific union of liberal states. Recent Soviet actions, such as unilateral force reductions, arms control proposals, the apparent shift in Soviet military doctrine toward "defensive sufficiency," and support for democratization in Eastern Europe, may indicate a fundamental shift in Soviet policy.

What is just as important, the greatly widened scope for free expression of dissent and for fair representation of differing views in the Supreme Soviet suggest the possibility of the beginning of a transformation toward a genuine socialist democratic republic based on "universal human values"; such a republic would confirm pacific policies. Although the hegemony of the Communist party has been abandoned, the Soviet Union is not yet a democratic state by liberal criteria, and until the institutional reforms are complete Gorbachev is vulnerable to upheavals or coups within the Soviet Union.

Calculating against a potential Soviet threat is still prudent. The United States needs, on the one hand, to maintain a capacity to deter against a Soviet attack on itself or its allies and, on the other hand, to frankly accept that it can do little to accelerate Soviet reform. The best the United States can do is to promote mutually beneficial arrangements to the extent they do not violate liberal principles or favor long-run Soviet interests over the long-run interests of the United States and the liberal world.[21] Arms control would be central to this policy, as would the expansion of civilian trade.

In relations with the People's Republic of China, liberal principles suggest appropriately constrained treatment, not geopolitical favoritism. Liberal principles permit trade to a state no more restrictive of its subjects' liberty than is the Soviet Union. The imposition of restrictions on arms sales and strategic trade to the People's Republic as a result of the regime's repressive response to political unrest are consistent with this criterion. As events have shown, strategic temptations toward a further alliance should be curbed. Such an alliance would backfire, perhaps disastrously, when liberal publics confronted policymakers with the Chinese shadows of antiliberal rule, exhibited in the emergence of a hardline regime and the harsh backlash against prodemocracy protesters in June 1989. However, if the People's Republic moderates its behavior in the future, U.S. policy should be adjusted accordingly.

According to a liberal model of national strategy, arms control, trade, and accommodation toward nonliberal Third World nations must first be measured against a prudent policy toward the Soviet Union and then reflect the relative degrees of liberal principle that their domestic and foreign policies incorporate. Although U.S. policy should be directed by liberal principles, it should free itself from the pretension that by acts of will and material benevolence the United States can replicate itself in the Third World. The liberal alliance should be prepared to have diplomatic and commercial relations such as those it has with the Soviet Union with every state that is no more repressive of liberal rights than is the Soviet Union, including, for example, North Korea, Mozambique, and Vietnam. Being one of the few states that deny even the formal legal equality of its subjects, South Africa should be treated as Amin's Uganda and Pol Pot's Khmer Republic should have been, in a more containing fashion than is the Soviet Union. No arms should be traded, investment should be restricted with a view to its impact on human rights, and trade should be limited to humanitarian items that do not contribute to the longevity of apartheid.

Elsewhere, the United States should be prepared to engage in regular trade and investment with all Third World states less restrictive of liberty than is the People's Republic, and this could include the sale of arms not sensitive to the actual defense of the liberal world. Furthermore, the United States should take additional measures of aid to favor Third World states attempting to address the basic needs of their own populations and seeking to preserve and expand the roles of the market and democratic participation. Much of the potential success of this policy rests on an ability to preserve a liberal market for Third World growth, for the market is the most substantial source of Third World accommodation with a liberal world whose past record includes imperial oppression. The market should be supplemented with mutually beneficial measures designed to improve Third World economic performance. Export earnings insurance, international debt management assistance, export diversification assistance, and technical aid are among such measures. In the case of the truly desperate poor, such as in some of the populations of Africa, more direct measures of international aid and famine relief are required.

In addition, the United States should persevere in attempts to keep the world economy free from destabilizing, protectionist intrusions. Although intense economic interdependence generates conflicts, it also can sustain the material well-being underpinning liberal societies and promise avenues of development to Third World states with markets currently limited by low income. Discovering ways to manage interdependence when rapid economic development has led to industrial crowding (at the same time as it retains massive numbers of the world's population in poverty) will call for difficult economic adjustments at home and institutional innovations in the world economy. These innovations may even require more rather than less explicit regulation of the domestic economy and more rather than less planned disintegration of the international economy. Under these circumstances, the United States will need to ensure that those suffering losses, such as from market disruption or restriction, do not suffer a permanent loss of income or exclusion from world markets. Furthermore, to prevent these emergency measures from escalating into a spiral of isolationism, the United States should undertake these innovations only by international negotiation and only when the resulting agreements are subject to a regular review by all the parties.[22]

Above all, a liberal grand strategy should strive to preserve the pacific union of similarly liberal societies. It is not only currently of immense strategic value (being the political foundation of both NATO and the Japanese alliance); it is also the single best hope for the evolution of a peaceful world. The United States should be prepared, therefore, to defend and formally ally with authentically liberal, democratic states that are subject to threats or actual instances of external attack or internal subversion.

The United States has underestimated the importance of the democratic alliance. U.S. alliances in NATO and with Japan are not only crucial to the United States' present security, they are its best hopes for long-term peace and the realization of U.S. ideals. They deserve the United States' careful investment. Spending $200 million to improve the prospects of President Corazon Aquino's efforts to achieve a transition to stable democracy in the Philippines cannot be considered too large an investment. Placing a special priority on helping the Argentinians and Mexicans manage their international debts is a valuable form of discrimination, if we take into account that financial decompression in those countries might undermine their democratic governance. Protecting the United States' relationship with New Zealand from a spillover of the dispute on nuclear basing warrants similar attention. But much of the United States' success in alliance management has to be achieved on a multilateral basis. Much of its success will rest on shoring up its economic supports. Reducing the U.S. budget and trade deficits will especially require multilateral solutions. Some unilateral solutions (exchange rate depreciation, increased taxation) are necessary but not sufficient, and others (protectionism) are neither. To avoid a costly economic recession calls for trade liberalization and the expansion of demand abroad to match the contraction of governmental and private spending in the United States. Finally, the creation of a diplomatic atmosphere conducive to multilateral problem solving will in its turn probably require an increased responsiveness from the United States on noneconomic issues such as arms control and restraint in violent interventions abroad.

IMPLICATIONS OF A LIBERAL NATIONAL STRATEGY

No country lives strictly according to its political ideology, and few liberal states are as hegemonically liberal as the United States.[23] Even in the United States certain interests and domestic actors derive their sense of legitimacy from sources other than liberalism. The country's national security bureaucracy has often reflected an approach to politics among nations that focused solely on the balance of power. Its policies correspondingly tend to fall into the geopolitical frame of reference. Certain of the West European states and Japan have more syncretic and organic sources of a "real" national interest. But in the United States, and in other liberal states to a lesser degree, public policy derives its legitimacy from its concordance with liberal principles. Policies not rooted in liberal principles generally fail to sustain long-term public support.

These principles are a firm anchor of the most successful zone of international peace yet established; but they are also a source of conflicted and confused foreign policy toward the nonliberal world. Strategists of the balance of power are likely to judge this liberal foreign policy to be either too much of a commitment or too little. They argue that through a careful reading of the past we can interpret in a clear fashion a ranked array of present strategic and economic interests. Strategically beneficial allies, whatever their domestic system, should be supported. The purposes of U.S. power must be to maximize present U.S. power. Global ecologists and world reformers claim an ability to foresee future disasters that we should be preparing for now by radical institutional reforms.

But liberals have always doubted the ability to interpret the past or predict the future accurately and without bias. Liberalism has been an optimistic ideology of a peculiarly skeptical kind. Liberals assume individuals to be both self-interested and rationally capable of accommodating their conflicting interests. They have held that principles that follow from mutual accommodation among rational, self-interested people—such as rule under law, majority rule, and the protection of private property—are the best guide to present policy. These principles preclude taking advantage of every opportunity of the present. They also discount what might turn out to have been farsighted reform. The implicit hope of liberals is that the principles of the present will engender accommodating behavior that avoids the conflicts of the past and reduces the threats of the future. The gamble has not always paid off in the past. It certainly is not guaranteed to work in the future. But liberalism cannot politically sustain nonliberal policies. Liberal policies rest upon a different premise. They are policies that can be accepted by a liberal world in good faith and sustained by the electorates of liberal democracies.

In responding to the demands of their electorates, liberal states must also ascribe responsibility for their policies to their citizenry. The major costs of a liberal national strategy are borne at home. Not merely are its military costs at the taxpayers' expense, but a liberal strategy requires adjustment to a less controlled international political environment, a rejection of the status quo. The home front becomes the front line of liberal strategy. Tolerating more foreign change requires a greater acceptance of domestic change. Not maintaining an imperial presence in the Persian Gulf calls for a reduction of energy dependence. Accepting the economic growth of the Third World may require trade and industrial adjustment. The choice is one between preserving liberalism's material legacy of the current world order at the cost of liberal principles and finding ways of adjusting to a changing world order that protect liberal principles.

Notes

Introduction

1. Paul Kennedy, *The Rise and Fall of the Great Powers: Economic Change and Military Conflict from 1500 to 2000* (New York: Random House, 1987), 521.

2. Morton Kondracke, "Blind Men's Bluff," *New Republic,* 6 March 1989, 20.

3. Francis Fukuyama, "The End of History," *National Interest,* Summer 1989, 3–18.

4. Basil H. Liddel Hart, *Strategy,* 2d rev. ed. (1967; reprint ed., New York: Signet, 1974), 322.

5. See, in particular, Nicholas Spykman, *The Geography of the Peace* (New York: Harcourt, Brace, 1944); and idem, *America's Strategy in World Politics: The United States and the Balance of Power* (New York: Harcourt, Brace, 1942).

6. Paraphrased from a speech by Alcibiades in response to Nicias's warnings, in Thucydides *The Peloponnesian War* 6.8–14. For a discussion of the Sicilian adventure see bks. 6 and 7.

7. For a discussion of Roman strategy see Edward N. Luttwak, *The Grand Strategy of the Roman Empire: From the First Century A.D. to the Third* (Baltimore: Johns Hopkins University Press, 1976).

8. For a discussion of Britain's economic situation see Kennedy, *Rise and Fall of the Great Powers,* esp. 151–69, 198–248; E. J. Hobsbawm, *Industry and Empire* (London: Weidenfeld & Nicolson, 1968); and A. H. Imlah, *Economic Elements in Pax Britannica* (Cambridge: Harvard University Press, 1958).

9. For a discussion of technological developments of the time see William McNeill, *The Pursuit of Power* (Chicago: University of Chicago Press, 1982), esp. chap. 8. Paul Kennedy discusses the impact of these developments on British strategic position in *The Rise and Fall of British Naval Mastery* (London: Macmillan, 1976), esp. pt. 3, "Fall"; and idem, *Strategy and Diplomacy, 1870–1945* (London: Allen & Unwin, 1983), esp. chaps. 7 and 8.

10. S. B. Saul, *Studies in British Overseas Trade, 1870–1914* (Liverpool: Liverpool University Press, 1960), 45.

11. For a general discussion of these actions see Michael Howard, *The Continental Commitment* (London: Temple South, 1972); and Kennedy, *Rise and Fall of British Naval Mastery,* esp. chap. 8.

12. See Aaron L. Friedberg, *The Weary Titan: Britain and the Experience of*

Relative Decline, 1895–1905 (Princeton: Princeton University Press, 1988), esp. chaps. 6 and 7.

Chapter 1. The Evolution of U.S. National Strategy

1. See, e.g., U.S. Congress, House, Committee on Armed Services, *National Security Policy,* 100th Cong., 1st sess. (Washington, D.C.: USGPO, 1987); and U.S. Congress, Senate, Committee on Armed Services, *National Security Strategy,* 100th Cong., 1st sess. (Washington, D.C.: USGPO, 1987). See also the report of the Commission on Integrated Long-Term Strategy, *Discriminate Deterrence* (Washington, D.C.: USGPO, January 1988), as well as the congressionally mandated *National Security Strategy Report* (Washington, D.C.: USGPO, January 1988).

2. These often conflicting definitions are discussed in Edward N. Luttwak, *Strategy: The Logic of War and Peace* (Cambridge: Harvard University Press, 1987), app. 1, "Definitions of Strategy."

3. Karl von Clausewitz defined military strategy as "the use of engagements for the object of war" (see *On War,* edited by Michael Howard and Peter Paret [Princeton: Princeton University Press, 1976], 128). His definition is not inconsistent with mine if one remembers his thesis that the "object" of war is always the political objective of the state and that war must, by definition, involve action taken against some other group of people.

4. Defined by Basil H. Liddel Hart as efforts to "take account of and apply the power of financial pressure, of diplomatic pressure, of commercial pressure, and not least of ethical pressure to weaken the opponent's will" (*Strategy* [1967; reprint ed., New York: Signet, 1974], 322).

5. For the text of NSC-68 see *Naval War College Review* 27 (May–June 1975): 51–108. See also Samuel F. Wells, "Sounding the Tocsin: NSC-68 and the Soviet Threat," *International Security* 4, no. 2 (Fall 1979): 116–48; and John L. Gaddis, *Strategies of Containment* (New York: Oxford University Press, 1982), chap. 4.

6. For a general review and analysis of U.S. strategic planning efforts see Aaron L. Friedberg, "History of U.S. Strategic Planning Efforts," in Future Security Environment Working Group, Commission on Integrated Long-Term Strategy, *Sources of Change in the Future Security Environment* (Washington, D.C.: USGPO, 1988), 164–84.

7. Amos A. Jordan, "U.S. National Strategy for the 1990's," *Washington Quarterly* 10 (Summer 1987): 15–24.

8. Friedberg, "History of U.S. Strategic Planning Efforts," 172–73.

9. On budget-strategy cycles see Gaddis, *Strategies of Containment,* chap. 11; Samuel P. Huntington, "The Defense Policy of the Reagan Administration, 1981–1982," in *The Reagan Presidency: An Early Assessment,* edited by Fred I. Greenstein (Baltimore: Johns Hopkins University Press, 1983), 82–116; and idem, "Radicalism and Conservatism in National Defense Policy," *Journal of International Affairs* 13, no. 2 (1954): 206–22.

10. See James R. Schlesinger, "Flexible Strategic Options," extracted from the Annual Defense Department Report of FY 1975 in *American Defense Policy,* edited by John Endicott and Roy Stafford, Jr. (Baltimore: Johns Hopkins University Press, 1977), 82–88. For a discussion of the history of limited nuclear options see Lawrence Freedman, *The Evolution of Nuclear Strategy* (New York: St. Martin's, 1983), chap. 25.

11. This conservatism on the use of force is most vividly expressed in former

Secretary of Defense Caspar Weinberger's six prerequisites to the use of force. See Caspar Weinberger, "The Uses of Military Power," address to National Press Club, Washington, D.C., 28 December 1984; and idem, *Annual Report to the Congress: Fiscal Year 1987* (Washington, D.C.: USGPO, 1987), 77–81.

12. See Samuel P. Huntington, "U.S. Defense Strategy: The Strategic Innovation of the Reagan Years," in *American Defense Annual, 1987–1988,* edited by Joseph Kruzel (Lexington, Mass.: Lexington Books, 1987), 23–43.

13. Strategy Commission, *Discriminate Deterrence,* 5–39.

14. I am referring, of course, to Paul Kennedy's thesis advanced in his controversial book, *The Rise and Fall of the Great Powers: Economic Change and Military Conflict from 1500 to 2000* (New York: Random House, 1987). For responses to Kennedy see Richard N. Haass, "The Use (and Mainly Misuse) of History," *Orbis* 32, no. 3 (1988): 411–19; and Samuel P. Huntington, "The U.S.—Decline or Renewal?" *Foreign Affairs* 67, no. 2 (1988/89): 76–96.

15. David C. Jones, "What's Wrong With the Defense Establishment," in *The Defense Reform Debate,* edited by Asa A. Clark et al. (Baltimore: Johns Hopkins University Press, 1984), esp. 275.

16. For some of the reasons why, see Samuel P. Huntington, *American Military Strategy,* Policy Papers in International Affairs, no. 28 (Berkeley: Institute of International Studies, 1986), 28–30.

Chapter 2. Military Threats to U.S. National Interests in the 1990s

1. See, e.g., the discussion in Future Security Environment Working Group, Commission on Integrated Long-Term Strategy, *Sources of Change in the Future Security Environment* (Washington, D.C.: USGPO, 1988), 17.

2. Army General A. D. Lizichev, "October and the Leninist Teaching on the Defense of the Revolution" (in Russian), *Kommunist,* no. 3, February 1987.

3. N. V. Ogarkov, *Vsegda v gotovnosti k zashchite otechestva* [Always in readiness for defense of the homeland] (Moscow: Voyenizdat, 1982), 31.

4. Col. Gen. M. A. Gareyev, *M. V. Frunze—Voyenney teoretik. Vzglady M. V. Frunze i sovremennaya voyennaya teoriya* [M. V. Frunze—military theoretician: The views of M. V. Frunze and contemporary military theory] (Moscow: Voyenizdat, 1985), 425.

5. Col. Gen. V. A. Merimskiy, *Takicheskaya podgotovka motostrelkovykh i tankovykh podrazdelnyy* [Tactical preparation of motorized rifle and tank subunits] (Moscow: Voyenizdat, 1984), 8.

6. Col. Gen. I. Golushko, "The Rear in Conditions of the Use by the Enemy of High-accuracy Weapons" (in Russian), *Tyl' i snabzheniye* [Rear services and supply], no. 7, July 1984, 18.

7. Col. Stanislaw Kozeiz, "Anticipated Directions for Change in Tactics of Ground Troops" (in Polish), *Przeglad wojsk Ladowych* [Polish ground forces review], September 1986.

Chapter 3. Nontraditional Challenges

1. For a useful treatment of the strategist's penchant for ethnocentric and superficial perspectives on the Third World see Ken Booth, *Strategy and Ethnocentrism* (New York: Holmes & Meier, 1979).

2. Edward A. Kolodziej, "Superpower Competition in a Divided and Decentralized International System," in *The Limits of Soviet Power in the Developing*

Nations: Thermidor in the Revolutionary Struggle in the Third World, edited by Roger Kanet and Edward A. Kolodziej (Baltimore: Johns Hopkins University Press, 1989), 29.

3. Charles William Maynes, "America's Third World Hang-ups," *Foreign Policy,* no. 71, Summer 1988, 121.

4. An overview of trends in global population growth may be found in Gregory D. Foster et al., "Global Demographic Trends to the Year 2010: Implications for U.S. Security," *Washington Quarterly* 12 (Spring 1989): 5–24.

5. For an excellent analytical review of the scholarly literature see Leonard Binder, "The Natural History of Development Theory," *Comparative Studies in Society and History* 28, no. 1 (1986): 3–33.

6. See Paul St. Cassia, "Patterns of Covert Politics in Post-Independence Cyprus," *Archives Européenes de Sociologie* 24, no. 2 (1983): 115–35.

7. See the seminal essay by Clifford Geertz, "The Integrative Revolution: Primordial Sentiments and Civil Politics in the New States," in *Old Societies and New States: The Quest for Modernity in Asia and Africa,* edited by Clifford Geertz (New York: Free Press, 1963), 105–57.

8. Hanna Batatu, "Iraq's Shi'a: Their Political Role, and the Process of Their Integration into Society," in *The Islamic Impulse,* edited by Barbara Freyer Stowasser (London: Croom Helm in association with the Center for Contemporary Arab Studies, Georgetown University, 1987), 204–13; the quotation comes from p. 204. See also Augustus Richard Norton, *Amal and the Shi'a: Struggle for the Soul of Lebanon* (Austin: University of Texas Press, 1987).

9. See Clifford Geertz, "The Judging of Nations: Some Comments on the Assessment of Regimes in the New States," *Archives Européenes de Sociologie* 18, no. 2 (1977): 245–61, esp. 250. Jerrold D. Green and the author are developing this argument in their forthcoming book, *Culture and Politics in the Middle East* (New York: Harcourt, Brace, Jovanovich, forthcoming).

10. The term was coined by Jerrold Green.

11. Cf. the fourth of the five principles for success, apparently developed by the Army–Air Force Center for Low Intensity Conflict, as cited in Commission on Integrated Long-Term Strategy, *Supporting U.S. Strategy for Third World Conflict* (Washington, D.C.: USGPO, June 1988), 21.

12. Ali Banuazizi, "Social-Psychological Approaches to Political Development," in *Understanding Political Development,* edited by Myron Weiner and Samuel P. Huntington (Boston: Little, Brown, 1987), 281–316; the quotation is from 306.

13. Leonard Binder, *Islamic Liberalism* (Chicago: University of Chicago Press, 1988).

14. This section draws, in part, on the richly informed analysis of Christos P. Ioannides in his unpublished 1987 paper, "Religion and Politics in Iran and Cyprus."

15. Robert Bianchi, "Interest Group Politics in the Third World," *Third World Quarterly* 8 (April 1986): 507–39; see esp. 527–28.

16. The author wishes to thank the Carnegie Council for permission to use the following material, which is adapted from the author's "Drawing the Line on Opprobrious Violence," *Ethics and International Affairs* 4 (1990): 123–33.

17. Raymond Aron, *Peace and War: A Theory of International Relations* (Garden City: Anchor Books, 1973), 153.

18. Adam Roberts, "Ethics, Terrorism and Counter-Terrorism," *Journal of Terrorism and Political Violence* 1, no. 1 (1989): 62.

19. See John Murphy, *State Support of International Terrorism: Legal, Political, and Economic Dimensions* (Boulder: Westview Press, 1989), 3.

20. Deputy Secretary of State John C. Whitehead, in an address before the Brookings Institution Conference on Terrorism, Washington, D.C., 10 December 1986.

21. Stanley Hoffmann, *The Political Ethics of International Relations,* Seventh Morgenthau Memorial Lecture on Ethics and Foreign Policy (New York: Carnegie Council on Ethics and International Affairs, 1988), 17.

22. See, e.g., the *Public Report of the Vice President's Task Force on Combatting Terrorism* (Washington, D.C.: USGPO, February 1986), 1, where it is argued that terrorism is the "*unlawful use* or threat of violence against persons or property to further political or social objectives. It is generally intended to intimidate or coerce a government, individuals or groups to modify their behavior or policies" (emphasis added).

23. Paul Wilkinson, *Terrorism and the Liberal State* (New York: John Wiley & Sons, 1977). See also Oleg Zinam, "Terrorism and Violence in the Light of Discontent and Frustration," in *International Terrorism in the Contemporary World,* edited by Marius H. Livingston (Westport, Conn.: Greenwood Press, 1978), 240–65.

24. U.S. Department of State, *Patterns of International Terrorism, 1982* (Washington, D.C.: USGPO, 1983).

25. This perspective, though developed independently, is close to that of Michael Walzer, who argues that terrorism's method is "the random murder of innocent people. Randomness is the crucial feature of terrorist activity" (*Just and Unjust Wars: A Moral Argument with Historical Illustrations* [New York: Basic Books, 1977], 197).

Chapter 4. The Political Economy of U.S. National Security Policy

I am grateful to Rebecca Blank, Michael Doyle, David Epstein, Robert Gilpin, Fred Greenstein, James Hines, Jane Katz, Klaus Knorr, Andrew Marshall, Irving Sirken, and Nicholas Zeigler for their comments on various drafts and to Michael Gilligan for research assistance.

1. David Calleo, *The Atlantic Fantasy: The U.S., NATO, and Europe* (Baltimore: Johns Hopkins Press, 1970).

2. David P. Calleo, *Beyond American Hegemony: The Future of the Atlantic Alliance* (New York: Basic Books, 1987), 41.

3. For a more detailed discussion of these developments see David P. Calleo, *The Imperious Economy* (Cambridge: Harvard University Press, 1982).

4. David P. Calleo, "Inflation and American Power," *Foreign Affairs* 59, no. 4 (1981): 784.

5. Calleo, *Beyond American Hegemony,* 83.

6. As Calleo describes it: "American monetary and fiscal policies were sucking capital from Europe, and the consequences were blighting Europe's domestic prosperity" (101).

7. Keith M. Carlson, "Trends in Federal Revenues: 1955–1986," *Federal Reserve Bank of St. Louis Review* 63, no. 5 (1981): 34.

8. Peter G. Peterson, "The Morning After," *Atlantic Monthly* 260 (October 1987): 44. The real significance of even these larger deficits was (and is) a subject of debate among economists. One authority has recently argued that conventional methods of calculating the magnitude of the deficit without correcting for inflation are seriously

misleading. Properly adjusted, the deficits of the inflationary late seventies actually appear as real surpluses (see Robert Eisner, *How Real Is the Deficit?* [New York: Free Press, 1986]). For a review of changing expert opinion on the significance of budget deficits see Peter G. Peterson, "The New Politics of Deficits," *Political Science Quarterly* 100, no. 4 (1985–86), 575–601.

9. James L. Clayton, "The Fiscal Limits of the Warfare-Welfare State: Defense and Welfare Spending in the United States since 1900," *Western Political Quarterly* 29 (September 1976): 364–83.

10. As Calleo acknowledges, "The unbalanced fiscal policy of the 1960s could not, of course, be blamed on military and space spending alone." And of the 1970s he points out that "while U.S. military expenditures did fall in the wake of Vietnam, the rapid growth of domestic social services more than offset that decline" (Calleo, *Beyond American Hegemony*, 87, 91).

11. Figures calculated from tables in Office of Management and Budget (OMB), *The United States Budget in Brief, FY 1989* (Washington, D.C.: USGPO, 1988), 102, 116. For a review of spending on the various components of the budget during the Reagan years see ibid., 49–90.

12. According to one projection, if there had been no change in tax policy, by 1986 federal budget receipts would have equaled 24 percent of GNP (Carlson, "Trends in Federal Revenues," 37). As things turned out, at that point revenues had fallen to around 18 percent of GNP, while expenditures had risen to around 23 percent (Office of Management and Budget, *Economic Report of the President, 1988* [Washington, D.C.: USGPO, 1988], 31).

13. M. Ishaq Nadiri, "Increase in Defense Expenditure and Its Impact on the U.S. Economy," in *Constraints on Strategy: The Economics of Western Security,* edited by David Denoon (New York: Pergamon-Brassey's, 1986), 33–34.

14. Deficits averaged $157 billion for the years 1980–87 and reached a peak of $221 billion in 1986 (OMB, *Economic Report of the President,* 337). In 1986 the deficit equaled a full 4.9 percent of GNP (Peterson, "The Morning After," 44). Interest payments went from 8.8 percent of outlays and 1.9 percent of GNP in 1980 to 13.8 percent and 3.1 percent, respectively, in 1987 (OMB, *U.S. Budget in Brief,* 102, 116).

15. During the Korean War, for example, defense budgets grew from under 5 percent of GNP to over 13 percent in four years (as compared with a less than 2 percent increase over the course of seven years). While the war was going on, however, taxes were increased, civilian spending was permitted to fall as a percentage of GNP, and as a result deficits increased only slightly (Robert W. DeGrasse, Jr., *Military Expansion, Economic Decline* [New York: Council of Economic Priorities, 1983], 135–37). For a comparison of the Korea, Vietnam, and Reagan buildups see also Lester Thurow, "How to Wreck the Economy," *New York Review of Books,* 14 May 1981, 3–8.

16. Whether the aim of government policy ought to be the total, automatic elimination of yearly deficits is, of course, another question. For the case against reflexive budget balancing see Eisner, *How Real Is the Deficit?* 145–64. For a history of the balanced budget as a potent political symbol see James D. Savage, *Balanced Budgets and American Politics* (Ithaca: Cornell University Press, 1988).

17. For a range of estimates see "Rosy Scenario Rides Again," *The Economist,* 20 February 1988, 25–26.

18. Calleo, *Beyond American Hegemony,* 269.

19. "The Pentagon Is Learning to Live with Less," *New York Times*, 3 April 1988, E5.

20. William Kaufmann has suggested a variety of other reductions (especially in strategic nuclear and naval forces) that could save close to $370 billion over the next five years without requiring a withdrawal of U.S. ground forces from Europe (David P. Calleo, Harold van B. Cleveland, and Leonard Silk, "The Dollar and the Defense of the West," *Foreign Affairs* 66, no. 4 [1988]: 854–55). For an analysis of how even more significant cuts in defense spending could be made see William W. Kaufmann, *Glasnost, Perestroika, and U.S. Defense Spending* (Washington, D.C.: Brookings Institution, 1990).

21. By one estimate, increasing the top marginal income tax rate from 28 percent to 30 percent could generate $76 billion in additional revenues over the next five years. Adding a 33 percent bracket would affect only a relatively small number of taxpayers but could yield almost $30 billion over the same period. Higher taxes on beer, wine, distilled spirits, and cigarettes could bring in over $43 billion between 1989 and 1993 (see Congressional Budget Office [CBO], *Reducing the Deficit: Spending and Revenue Options* [Washington, D.C.: USGPO, 1988], 285–88, 351–53).

A flat 5 percent value-added tax (VAT) would yield almost $460 billion over the next five years. Even if items such as food, housing, and medical care were excluded (to reduce what might otherwise be a disproportionate burden on people with lower incomes), a national VAT would still bring in over $260 billion during the same period (ibid., 342–45). For an analysis of possible taxes on consumption see Charles E. Walker and Mark A. Bloomfield, eds., *The Consumption Tax: A Better Alternative?* (Cambridge: Ballinger, 1987). For a variety of other tax proposals see "Doing the Unthinkable: Six Recipes for Raising Federal Taxes," *New York Times*, 16 October 1988, F2. See also Herbert Stein, "Tax the Rich, They Consume Too Much," ibid., 23 October 1988, F2.

A $5 per barrel fee on domestic and imported oil would bring in $106 billion over five years. An oil import fee alone would yield $41 billion. A $0.12 per gallon increase in the tax on motor fuel would raise $57 billion. Imposing a charge on sulfur dioxide and nitrogen oxide emissions and on the production of hazardous wastes could bring in almost $12 billion in five years (CBO, *Reducing the Deficit*, 351–56).

22. Canceling a planned NASA space station would eliminate $13 billion in expenditures between 1989 and 1993. Eliminating the controversial Superconducting Super Collider particle accelerator would save over $2 billion during the same period (ibid., 184–85, 188–89). Establishing a 2 percent annual cap on pay increases for government employees might save as much as $21 billion over the next five years (259–61).

23. In 1986 the federal government paid $455 billion to individuals, with the great majority going to non-means-tested programs such as Social Security and Medicare ($271 billion), civil service and military retirement benefits ($47 billion), and agricultural subsidies ($26 billion). By contrast, unemployment compensation amounted to only $18 billion (Peterson, "The Morning After," 61).

24. Former Secretary of Commerce Peter Peterson estimates that if retirement ages are gradually increased, initial benefits are lowered to those in upper income brackets, and taxes are imposed on benefits that exceed contributions, the federal government could save over $50 billion annually by the year 2000 (ibid., 69).

25. One proposal calls for limiting cost-of-living adjustments on Social Security, railroad retirement, and other non-means-tested programs to 66 percent (instead of 100 percent) of any increase in the consumer price index over the next five years. Offsetting increases could be provided to the recipients of means-tested programs and Medicare benefits. This approach could save over $62 billion, but assuming continued moderate inflation, it would leave beneficiaries 7 percent worse off in 1993 than they would have been under full price indexing (CBO, *Reducing the Deficit*, 145–49). For additional discussion of the entitlements issue see Murray Weidenbaum, *Rendezvous with Reality: The American Economy after Reagan* (New York: Basic Books, 1988), 33–37. See also Peter G. Peterson and Neil Howe, *On Borrowed Time: How the Growth in Entitlement Spending Threatens America's Future* (San Francisco: Institute for Contemporary Studies Press, 1988).

26. The idea that uneven economic development is an important underlying cause of international conflict dates back to Thucydides, although it was reintroduced in this century by Lenin (see the discussion in Robert Gilpin, *The Political Economy of International Relations* [Princeton: Princeton University Press, 1987], 54–56).

27. Paul Kennedy, *The Rise and Fall of the Great Powers: Economic Change and Military Conflict from 1500 to 2000* (New York: Random House, 1987), xv–xvi. Kennedy suggests elsewhere that "the speed of . . . global economic change has not been a uniform one, simply because growth is itself irregular, conditioned by the circumstance of the individual inventor and entrepreneur as well as by climate, disease, wars, geography, the social framework, and so on" (439). Scholars from a variety of disciplines have all tried to explain why it is that growth rates are uneven across countries and why, in any one state, they tend to diminish over time (see Carlo Cipolla, ed., *The Economic Decline of Empires* [London: Methuen, 1970]; Mancur Olson, *The Rise and Decline of Nations* [New Haven: Yale University Press, 1982]; and Robert Gilpin, *War and Change in World Politics* [New York: Cambridge University Press, 1981]).

28. For a review of early modern thinking on this subject see Gordon H. Mc-Cormick, "Strategic Considerations in the Development of Economic Thought," in *Strategic Dimensions of Economic Behavior,* edited by Gordon H. McCormick and Richard E. Bissell (New York: Praeger, 1984), 3–25.

29. Kennedy, *Rise and Fall of the Great Powers,* xxiii.

30. Steve Chan, "The Impact of Defense Spending on Economic Performance: A Survey of Evidence and Problems," *Orbis* 29, no. 2 (1985): 409. For a small sampling of the available literature see: James L. Clayton, ed., *The Economic Impact of the Cold War* (New York: Harcourt Brace, 1970); Lloyd J. Dumas, *The Over-burdened Economy* (Berkeley: University of California Press, 1986); Mary Kaldor, *The Baroque Arsenal* (New York: Hill & Wang, 1981); Gavin Kennedy, *The Economics of Defence* (London: Faber & Faber, 1975); Kurt W. Rothschild, "Military Expenditure, Exports and Growth," *Kyklos* 26, no. 4 (1973): 804–14; Bruce Russett, "Defense Expenditures and National Well-Being," *American Political Science Review* 76, no. 4 (1982): 767–77; Dan Smith and Ronald P. Smith, *The Economics of Militarism* (London: Pluto Press, 1983); Harvey Starr et al., "The Relationship between Defense Spending and Inflation," *Journal of Conflict Resolution* 28, no. 1 (1984): 103–22; *Report of the U.S. President's Committee on the Economic Impact of Defense and Disarmament* (Washington, D.C.: USGPO, 1965).

31. For an overview of the debate see Chan, "Impact of Defense Spending," 405–

10. See also David K. Whynes, *The Economics of Third World Military Expenditure* (Austin: University of Texas Press, 1979).

32. One recent study finds, for example, that "if there can be any single conclusion about the effects of military expenditure on the economy, it must be that it depends on the nature of the expenditure, the prevailing circumstances, and the concurrent government policies" (Ronald P. Smith and George Georgiou, "Assessing the Effect of Military Expenditure on OECD Economies: A Survey," *Arms Control* 4 [May 1983]: 15).

33. See, e.g., an analysis of the likely macroeconomic impact of the Reagan buildup in Congressional Budget Office, *Defense Spending and the Economy* (Washington, D.C.: USGPO, 1983), 9–36.

34. The claim that defense hurts investment is supported, for example, by a comparison of the fourteen Organization for Economic Cooperation and Development (OECD) countries between 1954 and 1973 (Ronald P. Smith, "Military Expenditure and Investment in OECD Countries, 1954–1973," *Journal of Comparative Economics* 4 [1980]: 19–32). Another similar study of 17 industrialized countries from 1960 to 1980 found that "nations with a larger military burden tended to invest less," but it concluded also that there was only "weak evidence that higher military spending correlates with lower real economic growth" (DeGrasse, *Military Expansion, Economic Decline,* 67–68).

See the critique of Smith and DeGrasse in Gordon Adams and David Gold, *Defense Spending and the Economy: Does the Defense Dollar Make a Difference?* (Washington, D.C.: Defense Budget Project, 1987), 14–19. For a brief critical overview of the literature on this question see David Greenwood, "Note on the Impact of Military Expenditure on Economic Growth and Performance," in *The Economics of Military Expenditures,* edited by Christian Schmidt (New York: St. Martin's, 1987), 98–103. After reviewing the performance of Britain, France, Germany, Japan, and the United States during the nineteenth and twentieth centuries, two researchers recently concluded: "It seems that the defense-investment substitution effect is not quite as prevalent as many think" (Karen Rasler and William R. Thompson, "Defense Burdens, Capital Formation, and Economic Growth," *Journal of Conflict Resolution* 32, no. 1 [1988]: 81).

35. Kennedy, *Rise and Fall of the Great Powers,* 609.

36. While Kennedy's work raises both of these questions, it does not provide a definitive answer to either one. Although he has sometimes been criticized for doing so, Kennedy does not in fact maintain that postwar military expenditures caused America's economic decline. Indeed, his book contains no direct assessment of what the cumulative impact of that spending has been. As to whether defense spending at existing levels will be sustainable in the future, Kennedy strongly implies that it may not be, but he cannot be said to rule out the possibility altogether.

37. Some authors have suggested, however, that the U.S. decline is not as severe as the usual indicators would seem to suggest (see Samuel P. Huntington, "The U.S.—Decline or Renewal?" *Foreign Affairs* 67, no. 2 [1988/89]: 76–96. See also Susan Strange, "The Persistent Myth of Lost Hegemony," *International Organization* 41, no. 4 [1987]: 551–74; and Bruce Russett, "The Mysterious Case of Vanishing Hegemony; or, Is Mark Twain Really Dead?" ibid. 39, no. 2 [1985]: 207–31).

38. The U.S. share of gross world product was down from 25.9 percent in 1960 to 21.5 percent in 1980 (Kennedy, *Rise and Fall of the Great Powers,* 436). But as

Huntington points out, between 1970 and 1987 the U.S. share varied between 22 percent and 25 percent. In 1987 the figure was 23 percent (Huntington, "The U.S.—Decline or Renewal?" 82).

The U.S. share of world trade was down from 18.4 percent in 1950 to 13.4 percent in 1977 (Robert O. Keohane, *After Hegemony* [Princeton: Princeton University Press, 1984], 36). The U.S. share of production of industrial manufactured goods was down from around 50 percent in 1945 to 44.7 percent in 1953 to 31.5 percent in 1980 (Kennedy, *Rise and Fall of the Great Powers,* 432).

39. In this sense, as one observer has pointed out, "the relative decline in American global economic preeminence occurred not in spite of America but because of America" (Zbigniew Brzezinski, "America's New Geostrategy," *Foreign Affairs* 66, no. 4 [1988]: 693). For a similar argument see Joseph S. Nye, Jr., "America's Decline: A Myth," *New York Times,* 10 April 1988, 31.

40. Kennedy, *Rise and Fall of the Great Powers,* 432.

41. By the seventies, U.S. and average European Community GNP growth rates were about the same, with the U.S. GNP growing somewhat faster in the eighties. U.S. and EEC per capita GNP growth rates converged in the seventies and remained roughly equal in the eighties. After lagging throughout the sixties and seventies, American manufacturing productivity seems finally to be increasing slightly faster than that in France and Germany (for figures see the Central Intelligence Agency's *Handbook of Economic Statistics, 1987* [Washington, D.C.: USGPO, 1987], 39, 40, 43; see also Huntington, "The U.S.—Decline or Renewal?" 82–83).

42. Lester Thurow, "Budget Deficits," in *The Deficits: How Big? How Long? How Dangerous?* by Daniel Bell and Lester Thurow (New York: New York University Press, 1985), 122–24. Kennedy advances a variant of this argument when he suggests that declining world powers tend to "allocate more and more of their resources into the military sector, which in turn squeezes out productive investment and, over time, leads to the downward spiral of slower growth . . ." (*Rise and Fall of the Great Powers,* 533).

43. This relationship is usually presented as an equation:

$$Y = C + I + G + (X - M)$$

where: Y national income; C consumption; I investment; G government expenditures; X exports; M imports.

44. According to one calculation, between 1960 and 1979, 7.4 percent of U.S. gross domestic product (GDP) went to military spending. The figures for Britain, West Germany, and Japan were 5.4 percent, 3.9 percent, and 0.9 percent, respectively (see Kenneth A. Oye, "International Systems Structure and American Foreign Policy," in *Eagle Defiant,* edited by Kenneth A. Oye, Robert J. Lieber, and Donald Rothchild [Boston: Little, Brown, 1983], 10).

45. Fixed capital formation made up 17.6 percent of U.S. GDP during the sixties and seventies as compared with 18.4 percent for Britain, 24.1 percent for West Germany, and 32.7 percent for Japan (ibid.).

46. For the period 1960–79, private consumption made up 63 percent of U.S. GDP, compared with 62.8 percent in Britain, 55.6 percent in West Germany, and 55.4 percent in Japan (ibid.).

47. Thurow, "Budget Deficits," 123. In fact, several comparisons of the composition of U.S. GNP before and after World War II suggest that the level of gross private domestic investment did not change very much (standing, according to one calculation, at around 14–15 percent in 1930, 1940, 1953, and 1957). The increase

in peacetime military expenditures after 1945 seems to have been made up for by a drop in the share of GNP devoted to personal consumption (for the first calculation see Kenneth E. Boulding, "The Impact of the Defense Industry on the Structure of the American Economy," in *The Economic Consequences of Reduced Military Spending*, edited by Bernard Udis [Lexington: D. C. Heath, 1973], 225–52. For the second see Charles J. Hitch and Roland M. McKean, *The Economics of Defense in the Nuclear Age* [Cambridge: Harvard University Press, 1963], 39).

48. The case for cuts in consumption is made in Peterson, "The Morning After." For an opposing view that favors reducing defense and increasing "public investment" see Jeff Faux, "America's Economic Future," *World Policy Journal* 5, no. 3 (1988): 367–414. See also Robert Eisner, "To Raise the Savings Rate, Try Spending," *New York Times*, 29 August 1988, A19.

49. For an analysis of the various ways in which private and overall national savings might be increased see Lawrence Summers and Chris Carroll, "Why Is U.S. National Savings So Low?" *Brookings Papers on Economic Activity* 2, 1987.

50. Charles L. Schultze, "Economic Effects of the Defense Budget," *Brookings Bulletin* 18, no. 2 (1981): 2. In the end, Thurow acknowledges this point by saying: "It is technically feasible for America to spend more on defense than Japan and still have a world-class economy if we are willing to pay for it by raising taxes to cut civilian consumption." (Thurow, "Budget Deficits," 124).

51. In Thurow's words, "defense spending is a form of consumption" (ibid., 122). In 1987, however, the federal government spent over $40 billion, or almost 14 percent, of the military budget on defense research and development (R&D) (National Science Foundation [NSF], *National Patterns of Science and Technology Resources: 1987*, NSF 88-305 [Washington, D.C., 1988], 15).

52. Lester Thurow, "America Among Equals," in *Estrangement*, edited by Sanford Ungar (New York: Oxford University Press, 1985), 175. Again, Kennedy makes a similar argument: "If the Pentagon's spending drains off the majority of the country's scientists and engineers from the design and production of goods for the world market while similar personnel in other countries are primarily engaged in bringing out better products for the civilian consumer, then it seems inevitable that the American share of world manufacturing will steadily decline, and also likely that its economic growth rates will be slower than in those countries dedicated to the marketplace" (*Rise and Fall of the Great Powers*, 532).

53. It is possible, however, that the effects of such a drain might be subtle, lagged, and hard to measure. Some experts have suggested that the competition for scarce research talent may, in the past, have bid up the cost of R&D and reduced the feasibility of some civilian projects (see Harvey Brooks, "The Strategic Defense Initiative as Science Policy," *International Security* 11, no. 2 [1986]: 184). This possibility deserves further study.

54. After dipping in the seventies, the number of students receiving degrees of all sorts in science and engineering has increased steadily since the early eighties. The growth in doctoral degrees has, however, been due largely to an influx of foreign graduate students to American universities. The long-term implications of this trend for the U.S. economy are unclear and will depend in part on how many foreign students eventually settle and work in the United States (NSF, *National Patterns*, 28–30).

55. A 1978 National Science Foundation survey found that 16.2 percent of scientists and engineers worked primarily on defense projects, with another 3.8

percent concentrating most heavily on work connected with the space program (DeGrasse, *Military Expansion, Economic Decline,* 102). Other analysts put the figure at close to 50 percent. For a range of estimates see Adams and Gold, *Defense Spending and the Economy,* 50–51. For a 1981 breakdown by specialty of skilled personnel involved in defense work see John P. Holdren and F. Bailey Green, "Military Spending, the SDI and Government Support of Research and Development: Effects on the Economy and the Health of American Science," *Journal of the Federation of American Scientists* 39, no. 7 (1986): 7.

Drawing on NSF survey data, a National Research Council (NRC) report finds that between 1972 and 1984 the fraction of scientists and engineers with bachelor's degrees working on Defense Department–sponsored projects fell from 18.6 percent to 15.5 percent. The figures for researchers with master's and doctoral degrees went from 23.8 percent to 19.9 percent and from 10.5 percent to 8.5 percent, respectively (NRC, *The Impact of Defense Spending on Nondefense Engineering Labor Markets: A Report to the National Academy of Engineering* [Washington, D.C.: National Academy Press, 1986], 74–76).

56. NRC, *Impact of Defense Spending,* 9–10, 91.

57. For example, a 1987 report by the Defense Science Board found that mean salaries at one government laboratory were $14,000 less than at a facility operated by private contractors. The best researchers at the government lab could be paid no more than $72,000 a year, while their private-sector counterparts sometimes made over twice as much (Defense Science Board, *Technology Base Management* [Washington, D.C.: USGPO, December 1987], 16–17).

58. For recommendations along these lines aimed at satisfying "both national security and commercial needs" see U.S. Congress, Office of Technology Assessment, *The Defense Technology Base: Introduction and Overview—A Special Report,* OTA-ISC-374 (Washington, D.C.: USGPO, March 1988), 18.

59. Total U.S. R&D expenditures now equal 2.7 percent of GNP, around the same as in West Germany and Japan. When defense-related R&D is excluded, however, the U.S. total falls to 1.8 percent of GNP, while in Japan and West Germany less than 10 percent of research is defense-related. Although the amounts spent are smaller, these two countries have been devoting more of their GNP to civilian research than the United States for over fifteen years (NSF, *National Patterns,* 19–20).

60. OMB, *Economic Report of the President,* 179–80.

61. One author asserts, for example, that "the much vaunted 'spinoff' or 'spillover' argument that military-oriented technological development produces massive improvements in areas of civilian application and thus does not retard civilian technological progress makes very little conceptual sense and, more to the point, is massively contradicted by straightforward empirical observation" (Lloyd J. Dumas, "Military Spending and Economic Decay," in *The Political Economy of Arms Reduction,* edited by Lloyd J. Dumas [Boulder: Westview Press, 1982], 13). For the opposite viewpoint see Hitch and McKean, *Economics of Defense,* 82–83.

62. Kennedy points out that there are "technical spinoffs from weapons research," but he does not consider them sufficient to offset the other, negative consequences of defense spending (*Rise and Fall of the Great Powers,* 532). According to one proponent of considerable cuts in defense spending, however: "Clearly, military research has yielded a large number of commercially viable products—including many of the breakthroughs in electronics, recombinant DNA, jet engines, fiberglass and other composite materials, and a major portion of communications technologies.

Indeed, many of the inventions that have most altered the postwar world economy have evolved from military-related research" (Ann Markusen, "The Militarized Economy," *World Policy Journal* 3, no. 3 [1986]: 503). For a useful survey of the military's role in the development of American technology see Meritt Roe Smith, ed., *Military Enterprise and Technological Change* (Cambridge: MIT Press, 1987).

63. Brooks, "The Strategic Defense Initiative as Science Policy," 183.

64. For these reasons, Harvey Brooks concluded in 1986 that "any viable U.S. industrial policy is likely to derive from military policy for many years to come if only because of the traditional reluctance of Americans to accept government intervention in the market economy" (ibid.). There is now some evidence of movement in precisely this direction (see "Bigger Role Urged for Defense Department in Economic Policy," *New York Times*, 19 October 1988, A1).

65. Measures of this sort could include changes in the tax laws and selective relaxations in antitrust restrictions prohibiting collaboration by major producers in the same industrial sector (see a report to the Secretary of Defense by the Under Secretary of Defense [Acquisition], *Bolstering Defense Industrial Competitiveness* [Washington, D.C.: Department of Defense, July 1988], 16–18).

66. Jacques Gansler has suggested, for example, that the Defense Department could invest more heavily in developing certain kinds of manufacturing technology instead of focusing its R&D efforts so heavily on particular full-scale weapons systems. According to Gansler: "These manufacturing technologies could contribute significantly to the nation's ability to produce high-quality, low- cost military equipment, in addition to contributing to the long- term competitiveness of the nation's industrial base" (Jacques S. Gansler, "Needed: A U.S. Defense Industrial Strategy," *International Security* 12, no. 2 [1987]: 55–56).

67. The list of suspects includes, but is by no means limited to, the following: systematically misguided management practices, poor labor-management relations, insufficient incentives for productive domestic investment, fluctuating government macroeconomic policies, a poorly designed tax code, a perpetually overvalued dollar, and spreading government regulations. For entry into the vast literature on these subjects see Bruce R. Scott, "U.S. Competitiveness: Concepts, Performance, and Implications," in *U.S. Competitiveness in the World Economy*, edited by Bruce R. Scott and George C. Lodge (Boston: Harvard Business School Press, 1985), 13–70; Otto Eckstein et al., *The DRI Report on U.S. Manufacturing Industries* (New York: McGraw Hill, 1984); and Seymour Zucker et al., *The Reindustrialization of America* (New York: McGraw Hill, 1982).

68. Calleo, Cleveland and Silk, "The Dollar and the Defense of the West," 862.

69. For the argument that arms control is, in fact, a superior substitute for burden-sharing see Jack Beatty, " 'Burden-Sharing,' Jolted," *New York Times*, 3 April 1988, E17. For discussions see James B. Steinberg, "Rethinking the Debate on Burden-sharing," *Survival* 29, no. 1 (1987): 56–78; James Chace, "Ike Was Right," *Atlantic Monthly* 260 (August 1987): 39–41; "The High Cost of NATO," *Newsweek*, 7 March 1988, 54–55; Pat Schroeder, "The Burden-Sharing Numbers Racket," *New York Times*, 5 April 1988, A23; and "Fiscal Squeeze Renews Debate on Arms Burden," ibid., 20 May 1987, A14.

70. For the argument that the Europeans are now doing more than they are usually given credit for see Klaus Knorr, "Burden-Sharing in NATO: Aspects of U.S. Policy," *Orbis* 29, no. 3 (1985): 517–36. See also "The False Promise of Burden-Sharing," *New York Times*, 1 May 1988, E26.

71. As Samuel Huntington has warned, even if the allies raise their military expenditures in the wake of a U.S. pullback, "such increased efforts . . . are unlikely to fill the gap left by the U.S. reductions, and the collective impact of the increases by individual countries is likely to be limited by the absence of effective coordination among them. The Soviet Union could end up benefiting both from a reduced total effort and from less integration and more intensified antagonisms among the allies" (Samuel P. Huntington, "Coping with the Lippmann Gap," *Foreign Affairs* 66, no. 3 [1987/88]: 471). The case for a total U.S. withdrawal from Europe is made in Melvyn Krauss, *How NATO Weakens the West* (New York: Simon & Schuster, 1986).

Chapter 5. Congress and National Strategy

1. See Edward N. Luttwak, *Strategy: The Logic of War and Peace* (Cambridge: Harvard University Press, 1987), 239–41, for a discussion of definitions of strategy.

2. 299 U.S. 304.

3. *Schecter Corp. v. United States*, 295 U.S. 495; *Panama Refining Co. v. Ryan*, 293 U.S. 388 (1935).

4. See Louis Fisher, *Constitutional Conflicts between Congress and the President* (Princeton: Princeton University Press, 1985), 109, and sources cited therein.

5. *Youngstown Sheet and Tube Co. v. Sawyer*, 343 U.S. 579, 636 n. 2 (1952).

6. *American International Group v. Islamic Republic of Iran*, 657 F.2d 430 (D.C. Cir. 1981).

7. Richard E. Neustadt and Ernest R. May, *Thinking in Time: The Uses of History for Decision Makers* (New York: Free Press, 1986), 258–59.

8. Ralph G. Carter, "Presidential Effectiveness in Congressional Foreign Policymaking: A Reconsideration," in *The American Presidency: A Policy Perspective from Readings and Documents,* edited by David C. Kozak and Kenneth N. Ciboski (Chicago: Nelson Hall, 1985), 311–25.

9. Eugene Wittkopf and James M. McCormick, "Was There Ever a Foreign Policy Consensus?" (Paper presented at the annual meeting of the American Political Science Association, Washington, D.C., September 1988).

10. On the apparent increase in congressional assertiveness see, e.g., Ronald C. Moe and Steven C. Teel, "Congress as Policy-Maker: A Necessary Reappraisal," in *Congress and the President,* edited by Ronald C. Moe (Pacific Palisades, Calif.: Goodyear, 1971); John F. Manley, "The Rise of Congress's Foreign Policy-Making," *Annals of the American Academy of Political and Social Science* 337 (1971): 60–70; Edward A. Kolodziej, "Congress and Foreign Policy: The Nixon Years," in *Congress against the President,* edited by Harvey C. Mansfield (New York: Praeger, 1975); I. M. Destler, "Executive-Congressional Conflict in Foreign Policy: Explaining It, Coping with It," in *Congress Reconsidered?* edited by Lawrence C. Dodd and Bruce I. Oppenheimer, 3d ed. (Washington, D.C.: Congressional Quarterly, 1985); and Thomas M. Franck and Edward Weisband, *Foreign Policy by Congress* (New York: Oxford University Press, 1979). The role of Congress in a variety of national security matters is discussed in George C. Edwards III and Wallace Earl Walker, eds., *National Security and the U.S. Constitution: The Impact of the Political System* (Baltimore: Johns Hopkins University Press, 1988).

11. Jack Dennis, "Dimensions of Public Support for the Presidency" (Paper presented at the annual meeting of the Midwest Political Science Association, Chicago, 1975), tables 4, 8; Hazel Erskine, "The Polls: Presidential Power," *Public*

Opinion Quarterly 37 (Fall 1973): 492, 495; News Release, *CBS News/The New York Times Poll,* 14 September 1987, table 12. An exception is Roberta S. Sigel, "Image of the American Presidency: Part II of an Exploration into Popular Views of Presidential Power," *Midwest Journal of Political Science* 10 (February 1966): 125; Sigel found more people favoring the president's leading Congress and the people rather than following what the people and Congress decided. Perhaps this result is due to the survey's taking place in 1966 and the sample's being limited to Detroit, a population highly favorable toward the president at the time.

12. Erskine, "The Polls," 499–500.

13. George H. Gallup, *The Gallup Poll: Public Opinion 1972–1977,* vol. 1 (Wilmington, Del.: Scholarly Resources, 1978), 210–11.

14. News release, *CBS News/The New York Times Poll,* 9 July 1987, table 4.

15. Ibid., 17 July 1987, table 11.

16. Ibid., 23 September 1987, table 14.

17. See, e.g., Samuel P. Huntington's classic article, "Congressional Responses to the 20th Century," in *The Congress and America's Future,* edited by David Truman (Englewood-Cliffs, N.J.: Prentice-Hall, 1965), 5–31.

18. William A. Niskanen, *Reaganomics* (New York: Oxford University Press, 1988), 29, 31–32; Lawrence J. Korb, "Spending without Strategy," *International Security* 12, no. 1 (Summer 1987): 169.

19. Niskanen, *Reaganomics,* 32–33; see also Korb, "Spending without Strategy," 166, 169.

20. Quoted in Nicholas Lemann, "The Peacetime War," *Atlantic Monthly* 254 (October 1984): 72.

21. Korb, "Spending without Strategy," 169.

22. Ibid., 166, 171–74.

23. See *Report of the Congressional Committees Investigating the Iran-Contra Affair* (Washington, D.C.: USGPO, 1987); *The Tower Commission Report* (New York: Bantam, 1987).

24. See, e.g., Donald Regan, *For the Record: From Wall Street to Washington* (San Diego: Harcourt, Brace, Jovanovich, 1988).

25. *Weekly Compilation of Presidential Documents* 23 (4 March 1987): 220.

26. Michael K. Deaver, *Behind the Scenes* (New York: William Morrow, 1987); David Stockman, *The Triumph of Politics: Why the Reagan Revolution Failed* (New York: Harper & Row, 1986).

27. Ronald Reagan, *National Security Strategy of the United States* (Washington, D.C.: USGPO, January 1988).

28. Henry A. Kissinger, in *Department of State Bulletin* 72 (1975): 562.

29. J. William Fulbright, *The Arrogance of Power* (New York: Random House, 1966), 46.

30. For an evaluation of the impact of the American constitutional system on national security policy see Edwards and Walker, *National Security and the U.S. Constitution.*

31. Philip D. Zelikow, "The United States and the Use of Force: A Historical Summary," in *Democracy, Strategy, and Vietnam,* edited by George K. Osborn et al. (Lexington, Mass.: Lexington, 1987), 31–81.

32. The 1986 Defense Reorganization Act is also an exception. This measure was initiated by Congress, but one must consider several points in this regard. First, the executive (in particular the Department of Defense) had resisted early congres-

sional efforts to work on this measure in consort; the president was clearly uninterested, despite the fact that Congress sensed a great deal of mass and elite concern
over the operation of the Department of Defense. Second, retiring Senator Barry
Goldwater attached his personal prestige to the measure. In many respects, the
passage is indicative of the esteem with which Senator Goldwater was held by his
colleagues.

Chapter 6. Discriminate Deterrence

This chapter is excerpted from the Report of the Commission on Integrated Long-
Term Strategy, *Discriminate Deterrence* (Washington, D.C.: USGPO, January 1988).

Chapter 7. U.S. Grand Strategy for the 1990s

1. My thoughts on U.S. grand strategy have been heavily influenced by the writings
of Stephen Van Evera, especially his *American Strategic Interests: Why Europe
Matters, Why the Third World Doesn't,* testimony prepared for Hearings before the
Panel on Defense Burdensharing, U.S. Congress, House, Committee on Armed Ser-
vices, 100th Cong., 2d sess., 2 March 1988; and (with Barry R. Posen) "Reagan
Administration Defense Policy: Departure from Containment," in *Eagle Resurgent?
The Reagan Era in American Foreign Policy,* edited by Kenneth A. Oye, Robert J.
Lieber, and Donald Rothchild (Boston: Little, Brown, 1988), 75–114. He is not
responsible, of course, for the analysis in this article or for the use I have made of
his ideas.

2. In the nuclear age, the importance of avoiding war is hardly debatable. The
goal of preventing Soviet expansion reflects the traditional U.S. interest in preventing
any single power from controlling the combined resources of the Eurasian landmass.
On this point see Walter Lippmann, *American Foreign Policy: Shield of the Republic*
(Boston: Little, Brown, 1943), 108–13 and passim; Hans J. Morgenthau, *In Defense
of the National Interest* (1951; reprint ed., Lanham, Md.: University Press of America, 1982), 5–7 and passim; and Nicholas Spykman, *America's Strategy in World
Politics: The United States and the Balance of Power* (New York: Harcourt, Brace,
1942), pt. 1.

3. Regrettably, no clear and authoritative statement of U.S. grand strategy exists.
On the evolution of postwar U.S. grand strategy and the shifts in ends and means
see John L. Gaddis, *Strategies of Containment* (New York: Oxford University Press,
1982); and idem, "Containment and the Logic of Strategy," *National Interest,* Winter
1987/88, 27–38.

4. This theme has been examined and publicized by Paul M. Kennedy, *The Rise
and Fall of the Great Powers: Economic Change and Military Conflict from 1500
to 2000* (New York: Random House, 1987); Robert Gilpin, *U.S. Power and the
Multinational Corporation* (New York: Basic Books, 1975); and idem, *War and
Change in World Politics* (New York: Cambridge University Press, 1981). For examples of those who question the magnitude of U.S. decline see Bruce Russett, "The
Mysterious Case of Vanishing Hegemony; or, Is Mark Twain Really Dead?" *International Organization* 39, no. 2 (1985): 207–31; and Kenneth N. Waltz, *Theory
of International Politics* (Reading, Mass.: Addison-Wesley, 1979), chaps. 7–9.

5. We should not forget that containment was initially a controversial strategy.
Walter Lippmann attacked George F. Kennan's famous "X article" in a series of
newspaper columns that were later published in the book *The Cold War: A Study*

in U.S. Foreign Policy (New York: Harper & Brothers, 1947)—and the decision to focus on Europe, the U.S. entry into NATO, and the deployment of U.S. troops in Europe were all hotly debated at the time.

6. Leading representatives of this view include Richard A. Falk, *A Study of Future Worlds* (New York: Free Press, 1975); Robert C. Johansen, *The National Interest and the Human Interest: An Analysis of American Foreign Policy* (Princeton: Princeton University Press, 1980); and Randall Forsberg, "Confining the Military to Defense as a Route to Disarmament," *World Policy Journal* 1, no. 2 (1984): 285–318.

7. Although advocates of this strategy often prefer euphemisms such as "strategic independence," my use of this term is not intended to be pejorative.

8. Advocates of this view include: Earl Ravenal, *NATO: The Tides of Discontent* (Berkeley: Institute of International Studies, 1987); "Europe without America: The Erosion of NATO," *Foreign Affairs* 63, no. 5 (1985): 1020–35; and "The Case for a Withdrawal of Our Forces," *New York Times Magazine*, 6 March 1983; Laurence Radway, "Let Europe Be Europe," *World Policy Journal* 1, no. 1 (1983): 23–43; and Christopher Layne, "Ending the Alliance," *Journal of Contemporary Studies* 6, no. 3 (1983): 5–31; and "Atlanticism without NATO," *Foreign Policy*, no. 67, Summer 1987, 22–45. Some supporters of withdrawal also argue for greater efforts to promote international economic coordination, a view that analysts such as Ravenal would undoubtedly reject. See Jerry W. Sanders, "Security and Choice," *World Policy Journal* 1, no. 4 (1984), esp. 698–707; Jerry W. Sanders and Sherle R. Schwenninger, "The Democrats and a New Grand Strategy" (in 2 parts), ibid. 3, no. 3 (1986): 369–418 and 4, no. 1 (1986/87): 1–49; and Richard J. Barnet, "The Four Pillars," *New Yorker*, March 1987, 76–98. Also advocating withdrawal is Melvyn Krauss, *How NATO Weakens the West* (New York: Simon & Schuster, 1986).

9. The best example of this view is David Calleo, *Beyond American Hegemony: The Future of the Atlantic Alliance* (New York: Basic Books, 1987). For a proposal that the United States focus greater attention on the Western Hemisphere and the Pacific see James Chace, "A New Grand Strategy," *Foreign Policy*, no. 70, Spring 1988, 3–25. Strategists advocating a reduction in Europe in order to increase U.S. capabilities in the Third World include Jeffrey Record, *Revising U.S. Military Strategy: Tailoring Means to Ends* (Washington, D.C.: Pergamon-Brassey's, 1984); Eliot A. Cohen, "The Long Term Crisis in the Alliance," *Foreign Affairs* 61, no. 2 (1983/84): 342; and Zbigniew Brzezinski, *Game Plan: How to Conduct the U.S.-Soviet Contest* (Boston: Atlantic Monthly Press, 1986), 181 and passim. Brzezinski's other recommendations—which would involve substantial increases in U.S. defense capabilities—suggest that his views lie closer to "global containment." Similarly, although he is essentially a neo-isolationist, Christopher Layne suggests that after withdrawing from Europe, "America's out-of-area capabilities could be strengthened by reallocating remaining defense resources to stress strategic mobility and naval power projection" ("Atlanticism without NATO," 45).

10. Examples of this view include: Samuel P. Huntington, ed., *The Strategic Imperative: New Policies for American Security* (Cambridge: Ballinger, 1982), especially Huntington's essay "The Renewal of Strategy," 152; Aaron Wildavsky, ed., *Beyond Containment: Alternative American Policies toward the Soviet Union* (San Francisco: Institute for Contemporary Studies, 1983); and Commission on Integrated Long-Term Strategy, *Discriminate Deterrence* (Washington, D.C.: USGPO, 1988). This strategy is essentially the one followed by the Reagan administration (see Posen

and Van Evera, "Reagan Administration Defense Policy," 89–98; and Richard Melanson, *Writing History and Making Policy* [Lanham, Md.: University Press of America, 1983], 200–204).

11. The classic statement of the rollback strategy is James Burnham, *Containment or Liberation? An Inquiry into the Aims of U.S. Foreign Policy* (New York: John Day, 1952). This view is especially prominent in the writings of the "neo-conservative" movement. For recent versions see Irving Kristol, "Foreign Policy in an Age of Ideology," *National Interest,* Spring 1987, 6–15; Charles Krauthammer, "The Poverty of Realism," *New Republic,* 17 February 1986, 14–22; Norman Podhoretz, *The Present Danger* (New York: Simon & Schuster, 1980); and Jeanne J. Kirkpatrick, "American Foreign Policy in a Cold Climate," *Encounter* 61, no. 3 (1988): 9–33.

12. See above, nn. 2 and 3. The prescriptions of Kennan, Morgenthau, and Lippmann were not always consistent, however. For example, Kennan favored U.S. involvement in the Korean War (though it was not a "key center of industrial power") and was clearly ambivalent about intervention in peripheral areas (see Walter L. Hixson, "Containment on the Perimeter: George Kennan and Vietnam," *Diplomatic History* 12, no. 2 [1988]: 149–64).

13. Not only has the United States used military force in a variety of Third World countries (e.g., Vietnam, the Dominican Republic, Lebanon) but it also worked to overthrow a number of leftist or Marxist regimes on several occasions (e.g., Cuba, Iran, and Guatemala, as well as the targets of the Reagan Doctrine).

14. According to Barry Posen, grand strategy is a "political-military means-ends chain, a state's theory about how it can best 'cause' security for itself" (Barry R. Posen, *The Sources of Military Doctrine: France, Britain, and Germany between the World Wars* [Ithaca: Cornell University Press, 1984], 13). For similar conceptions see Edward Mead Earle, "Introduction," in *Makers of Modern Strategy,* edited by Edward Mead Earle (Princeton: Princeton University Press, 1943), vii; Bernard Brodie, "Strategy as a Science," *World Politics* 1, no. 4 (1949): 467–88; Basil H. Liddel Hart, *Strategy,* 2d rev. ed. (New York: Praeger, 1967), 335–36; and Karl von Clausewitz, *On War,* edited by Michael Howard and Peter Paret (Princeton: Princeton University Press, 1976), 142–44.

15. See Alexander George and Richard Smoke, "Theory for Policy in International Relations," in *Deterrence in American Foreign Policy: Theory and Practice* (New York: Columbia University Press, 1974), 617–25.

16. On the importance and measurement of national power see Hans J. Morgenthau, *Politics Among Nations* (New York: Alfred A. Knopf, 1948), pt. 3; E. H. Carr, *The Twenty Years' Crisis, 1919–1939* (New York: Harper Torchbooks, 1964), chap. 8; Waltz, *Theory of International Politics,* chaps. 6–8; Klaus Knorr, *The War Potential of Nations* (Princeton: Princeton University Press, 1955); idem, *Military Power and Potential* (Lexington: D. C. Heath, 1970); idem, *The Power of Nations: The Political Economy of International Relations* (New York: Basic Books, 1975), chaps. 3 and 4; and Harold Sprout and Margaret Sprout, *Foundations of International Politics* (Princeton: Van Nostrand, 1962).

17. As E. H. Carr puts it, "The supreme importance of the military instrument lies in the fact that the *ultima ratio* of power in international relations is war" (*Twenty Years' Crisis,* 109).

18. On this point see Waltz, *Theory of International Politics,* 129–31.

19. Some theorists of international politics argue that the relative importance of economic strength has increased, while the importance of military capability has

declined (see, e.g., Robert O. Keohane and Joseph S. Nye, Jr., *Power and Interdependence: World Politics in Transition* [Boston: Little, Brown, 1978], 8, 16–17, 24–29, 227–29). Echoing this view (albeit in less sophisticated form), some writers on U.S. grand strategy have suggested that the United States should abandon containment and focus on promoting international economic cooperation (see Sanders, "Security and Choice," 698–707; Barnet, "The Four Pillars," 88–89; and Sanders and Schwenninger, "The Democrats and a New Grand Strategy," 375–82 and passim). This view understates the role that containment plays in encouraging economic cooperation among the industrial powers. If the United States were to withdraw from its present alliances, the other industrial powers would worry more about each other and would be more inclined to protect their relative positions through mercantilistic policies (for theoretical background on this point see Joseph Grieco, "Anarchy and Cooperation: A Realist Critique of the Newest Liberal Institutionalism," *International Organization* 42, no. 3 [1988]: 485–507).

20. See Falk, *A Study of Future Worlds,* chap. 5; and Johansen, *National Interest and Human Interest,* 20–37.

21. Thus Norman Podhoretz criticized the U.S. rapprochement with Communist China by lamenting "the loss of political clarity it inevitably entails. Playing one Communist power against another may be sound geopolitics, but it increases the difficulty of explaining to ourselves and our friends what we are fighting for and what we are fighting against" (*The Present Danger,* 98). Similarly, Irving Kristol suggests that America's European allies are of little value because they do not support the "assertive American foreign policy" he favors ("Foreign Policy in an Age of Ideology," 14).

22. The classic expression of this view is Burnham, *Containment or Liberation?* esp. 176–82. See also Kristol, "Foreign Policy in an Age of Ideology"; and Krauthammer, "Poverty of Realism." Sidney Blumenthal's portrait of Kristol and Norman Podhoretz in *The Rise of the Counter-Establishment: From Conservative Ideology to Political Power* (New York: Times Books, 1986) is also illuminating.

23. Although ideals can be exported, their promoters rarely retain control of those they convert. The papacy lost control of Christendom following the Protestant Reformation, the Socialist International collapsed in 1914, the international Communist movement quickly split once Marxist states free from Soviet control emerged, and the efforts to institutionalize liberal democracy in the former colonial areas have failed more often than not.

24. To note a few examples: the Soviet Union quickly subordinated the goal of "world revolution" to its own state interests under the doctrine of "socialism in one country." Despite their hostility to Communist ideology, the United States and Great Britain allied with the Soviet Union in World War II to combat the common threat of Nazi Germany. Similarly, fear of the Soviet Union explains the more recent rapprochement between the United States and Communist China.

25. As Paul Kennedy shows in his *Rise and Fall of the Great Powers,* the ability to shape international events—including the ability to promote particular political ideas—rests first and foremost on the military and economic capabilities of different competitors.

26. See Morgenthau, *In Defense of the National Interest,* 5–7 and passim; and Lippmann, *American Foreign Policy,* 108–13.

27. In the nineteenth century (when the United States was relatively weak), rivalries among the European powers discouraged them from challenging U.S. in-

dependence. When the United States attained the pinnacle of power after World War II, maintaining the division of industrial Eurasia ensured that no single state could amass enough industrial and military capacity to threaten U.S. security directly.

28. For a summary and analysis of Kennan's reasoning see Gaddis, *Strategies of Containment,* chap. 2.

29. This strategic perspective helps explain why Kennan, Lippmann, and Morgenthau came to oppose U.S. intervention in places such as Vietnam. Communist control of Southeast Asia could not affect the global balance of power, because the unity of international Communism was more apparent than real and because this region did not contain any militarily significant assets. As a result, it was foolish for the United States to squander its own capabilities to defend it (see Ronald Steel, *Walter Lippmann and the American Century* [Boston: Atlantic Monthly/Little, Brown, 1980], 565–67 and passim; Hans J. Morgenthau, "We Are Deluding Ourselves in Vietnam," *New York Times Magazine,* 18 April 1965; and idem, *A New Foreign Policy for the United States* [New York: Praeger, 1969], esp. 129–56). Walter Hixson has shown that Kennan's views on Third World intervention were partly contradictory; his concern for U.S. prestige—based in part on a fear that U.S. allies needed reassurance lest they "bandwagon" with the Soviet Union—led him to support actions well beyond the boundaries implied by his early formulations of containment (see Hixson, "Containment on the Perimeter"). Not surprisingly, the preeminent contemporary realist, Kenneth Waltz, opposed the war on essentially the same grounds (see his "The Politics of Peace," *International Studies Quarterly* 11, no. 3 [1967]: 199–211).

30. In the 1950s, for example, the fear of Soviet nuclear superiority was repeatedly invoked to justify increased arms expenditures, a tactic that was successfully repeated by alarmists invoking a theoretical "window of vulnerability" in the late 1970s. Others argued that "geopolitical momentum" increasingly favored the Soviet Union, implying that containment had failed to prevent the Soviet Union from expanding its influence significantly. For examples of these arguments, along with a useful critique, see Robert Johnson, "Periods of Peril: The Window of Vulnerability and Other Myths," *Foreign Affairs* 61, no. 4 (1983): 950–70; and David T. Johnson and Stephen D. Goose, "Soviet Geopolitical Momentum: Myth or Menace? Trends in Soviet Influence around the World from 1945–1986," *Defense Monitor* 15, no. 5 (1986): 1–32.

31. For example, advocates of a U.S. withdrawal from Western Europe usually assert that Europe's economic recovery has left it fully capable of providing for its own defense (see Calleo, *Beyond American Hegemony,* 150–71; Record, *Revising U.S. Military Strategy,* 49, 50, 57–74; Layne, "Atlanticism without NATO," 38; Chace, "A New Grand Strategy," 4, 12; and Radway, "Let Europe Be Europe," 28, 38–43). Others point to the impressive economic growth of Japan and the Association of Southeast Asian Nations (ASEAN), as well as the considerable economic potential of China, to argue that America's economic and security interests are shifting away from Western Europe and toward the Pacific basin (see Chace, "A New Grand Strategy," 16–21). More hardline analysts suggest that the Third World is now the principal arena of global conflict and that the United States should increase its military capabilities or reallocate the forces it already has (see Brzezinski, *Game Plan,* 182–84; and Strategy Commission, *Discriminate Deterrence,* 13–15).

32. For the data on which these figures are based see Stephen M. Walt, *The*

Origins of Alliances (Ithaca: Cornell University Press, 1987), 263–65 and app. 2.

33. While the United States has close ties with West Germany, France, Great Britain, Japan, and China, the Soviet Union "enjoys" the opportunity to prop up states such as Cuba, Angola, Ethiopia, South Yemen, and Vietnam. Much of Eastern Europe is an economic liability as well, and its loyalty to the Soviet Union is questionable. By comparison, NATO is a model of strength and cohesion. On the burdens of the Soviet empire see Valerie Bunce, "The Empire Strikes Back: The Evolution of the Soviet Bloc from a Soviet Asset to a Soviet Liability," *International Organization* 39, no. 1 (1985): 1–46.

34. A contrasting view is Charles Wolf's assertion that "the gains and extension of the Soviet empire have vastly exceeded its losses and retrenchments," although Wolf does not provide any evidence to support this far-reaching claim (see his "Extended Containment," in Wildavsky, *Beyond Containment,* 154). The most systematic examination of this issue reaches the opposite conclusion (see Johnson and Goose, "Soviet Geopolitical Momentum").

35. See Richard Feinberg and Kenneth A. Oye, "After the Fall: U.S. Policy towards Radical Regimes," *World Policy Journal* 1, no. 1 (1983): 199–215.

36. The list would include Angola, Cuba, Ethiopia, Laos, Libya, North Korea, South Yemen, Syria, Vietnam, and India. The Soviets enjoy cordial relations with a number of other regimes, but these cannot be considered close allies.

37. Francis Fukuyama points out that Soviet foreign policy has fluctuated considerably in the past, alternating between periods of adventurism and periods of retrenchment. See his "Patterns of Soviet Third World Policy," *Problems of Communism* 36 (September/October 1987): 1–13.

38. This is a familiar argument among proponents of change, many of whom blame the declining U.S. share of the world economy on "strategic overextension" (see Calleo, *Beyond American Hegemony,* chaps. 6 and 7; Layne, "Atlanticism without NATO," 43; Sanders, "Security and Choice," 700–701; and Chace, "A New Grand Strategy," 3, 12. See also Kennedy, *Rise and Fall of the Great Powers,* 514–35).

39. In particular, writers such as Kennedy and Calleo argue that excessive defense spending and overseas military deployments have caused recurring balance of payments difficulties, persistent budget deficits, reduced investment, and inadequate spending on civilian research and development. Thus, Earl Ravenal has argued that the costs of containment "will wreck our economy and warp our society," and David Calleo suggests that present U.S. military commitments have produced a "fiscal nightmare" (see Ravenal, "The Case for a Withdrawal of Our Forces," 75; and Calleo, *Beyond American Hegemony,* 165 and passim).

40. See Peter G. Peterson, "The Morning After," *Atlantic Monthly* 260 (October 1987): 43–69.

41. On these various points see Aaron Friedberg's chapter in this volume, chapter 4; and Lawrence R. Forest, Jr., *Defense Spending and the Economy* (Washington, D.C.: Congressional Budget Office, 1983), chap. 3.

42. For a good critique of the "relative decline" thesis and its implications for U.S. strategy see Joseph S. Nye, Jr., "Understating U.S. Strengths," *Foreign Policy,* no. 72, Fall 1988, 105–29.

43. With the People's Republic of China included, the percentage reaches 14.7 percent of gross world product, still substantially less than for Western Europe

(calculations based on data in U.S. Arms Control and Disarmament Agency [ACDA], *World Military Expenditures and Arms Transfers* [Washington, D.C.: USGPO, 1986]).

44. See International Institute for Strategic Studies, *The Military Balance, 1987–1988* (London, 1987), 39–45.

45. The United States produced 39 percent of gross world product in 1950, with Western Europe and Japan contributing a total of 17 percent. By 1984 the U.S. share had dropped to 26 percent, while U.S. allies' share had grown to roughly 27 percent (NATO Europe plus Japan). In terms of military spending, the U.S. share of the global total declined from 51 percent in 1960 to 28 percent in 1984, while that of Europe and Japan had grown to more than 13 percent. These trends are evident in other categories as well, such as men under arms. In 1952 the United States mustered more than twice the number of troops provided by France, Great Britain, Japan, and West Germany combined. By 1958 the ratio had fallen to 1.56:1, and to 1.38:1 by 1972. With the rest of NATO included, the present U.S. share is only 38.8 percent of the combined allied total (calculations based on data from International Institute for Strategic Studies, *The Military Balance, 1973–1974* [London, 1974], 79; and ACDA, *World Military Expenditures*).

46. From 1969 to 1979, for example, Western Europe's share of NATO's combined expenditures rose from 22.7 percent to almost 42 percent (see Robert Art, "Fixing Transatlantic Bridges," *Foreign Policy*, no. 46, Spring 1982, 70. See also Gordon Adams and Eric Munz, *Fair Shares: Bearing the Burden of the NATO Alliance* [Washington, D.C.: Center for Budget and Policy Priorities, 1988], 6, 18).

47. On these points see Van Evera, *American Strategic Interests;* Posen and Van Evera, "Reagan Administration Defense Policy," 79; and Keith A. Dunn, "NATO's Enduring Value," *Foreign Policy*, no. 71, Summer 1988, 156–75.

48. See Cohen, "Long Term Crisis," 342; and Brzezinski, *Game Plan*, 182–84. The authors of *Discriminate Deterrence* argue that "nearly all the armed conflicts of the past forty years have occurred . . . in the Third World," and they conclude that "the United States will need to be better prepared to deal with conflict [in these regions]." Yet they offer no evidence (not even an extended discussion) for why events in the Third World should be seen as vital to U.S. interests. The importance of the Third World is simply assumed; the conclusion follows predictably from the unsupported and questionable premise (see Strategy Commission, *Discriminate Deterrence*, 13–22).

49. On these points see Van Evera, *American Strategic Interests;* and Posen and Van Evera, "Reagan Administration Defense Policy," 95–96.

50. Calculated from *The State of the Economy: Report by the President, 1987* (Washington, D.C.: USGPO, 1987); and International Monetary Fund, *Direction of Trade Statistics Yearbook, 1987* (Washington, D.C., 1987), 404–6.

51. In 1986, total U.S. direct foreign investment was $259.89 billion, equivalent to 6.5 percent of U.S. GNP for that year (total new investment for 1986 was only $30.1 billion). Seventy-five percent of the total was invested in the industrialized nations of Europe and Asia, nearly 50 percent in Europe alone (see Russell B. Scholl, "The International Investment Position of the United States in 1986," *Survey of Current Business*, June 1987, 38–45).

52. For pessimistic appraisals of Western raw materials dependence see Uri Ra'anan and Charles M. Perry, *Strategic Minerals and International Security* (Washington, D.C.: Pergamon-Brassey's, 1985); Alan C. Brownfeld, "The Growing United

States' Dependency on Imported Strategic Minerals," *Atlantic Community Quarterly* 20, no. 1 (1982): 62–67; Geoffrey Kemp, "Scarcity and Strategy," *Foreign Affairs* 56, no. 2 (1978): 356–414; Council on Economics and National Security, *Strategic Minerals: A Resource Crisis* (New Brunswick: Transaction Books, 1980); Robert J. Hanks, *Southern Africa and Western Security* (Cambridge, Mass.: Institute for Foreign Policy Analysis, 1983), 10–15, 53; and Daniel Mariaschin, "Soviet Union Is on the Move: It Fights Western Control of Strategic Raw Materials," *Los Angeles Times,* 13 February 1981.

53. On this point see Kenneth N. Waltz, "The Myth of National Interdependence," in *The International Corporation,* edited by Charles Kindleberger (Cambridge: MIT Press, 1970), 205–23; and idem, *Theory of International Politics,* chap. 7.

54. According to the Congressional Budget Office (CBO): "The United States has a considerable range of policy options to reduce its dependence on nonfuel imported minerals and limit the impact of any shortages that might result from such dependence" (see *Strategic and Critical Nonfuel Minerals: Problems and Policy Alternatives* [Washington, D.C.: USGPO, 1983], xi–xii and passim). For other reassuring analysis on this issue see Michael Shafer, "Mineral Myths," *Foreign Policy,* no. 47, Summer 1982, 154–71; Stephen D. Krasner, "Oil Is the Exception," ibid., no. 14, Spring 1974, 68–84; Brian McCartan, "Resource Wars: The Myth of American Mineral Vulnerability," *Defense Monitor* 14, no. 9 (1985): 1–8; Joel P. Clark and Frank R. Field III et al., "How Critical Are Critical Materials?" *Technology Review* 88, no. 6 (1985): 39–46; and Jack A. Finlayson and David G. Haglund, "Whatever Happened to the Resource War?" *Survival* 29, no. 5 (1987): 403–15.

55. Hans Maull argues that Western raw materials dependence is substantial and should be taken seriously, but he also notes that a variety of measures can easily be taken to minimize these risks (see his *Energy, Minerals, and Western Security* [Baltimore: Johns Hopkins University Press, 1984], chap. 4; and idem, "South Africa's Minerals: The Achilles Heel of Western Economic Security?" *International Affairs* 62, no. 4 [1986]: 619–26).

56. Obvious examples are states that border on major international waterways, such as Vietnam, Cuba, South Yemen, or Indonesia (see Robert E. Harkavy, "Soviet Conventional Power Projection and Containment," in *Containment: Concept and Policy,* edited by Terry L. Deibel and John L. Gaddis [Washington, D.C.: National Defense University Press, 1986], 2:311–400; Peter J. Duignan, "Africa between East and West," in *To Promote Peace: U.S. Foreign Policy in the Mid-1980s,* edited by Dennis L. Bark [Stanford: Hoover Institution, 1984], 187; and Michael Gordon, "Reagan's 'Choke Points' Stretch from Sea to Sea," *New York Times,* 13 February 1986, A12).

57. Soviet clients would face an additional worry: if the United States lost a major war in Europe, it would be likely to seek revenge against states such as Cuba or Nicaragua, particularly if they had aided the Soviet Union during the war. By reducing U.S. security significantly, a defeat in Europe would give the United States ample reason to eliminate potential threats from Soviet clients in the Western hemisphere. If the Soviet Union's Third World allies understand this fact (and U.S. leaders should make sure that they do), they will be reluctant to invite either preemptive or retaliatory attack by supporting Moscow.

58. See Robert Johnson, "Exaggerating America's Stakes in Third World Conflicts," *International Security* 10, no. 3 (1985/86): 32–68. On Latin America see Lars Schoultz, *National Security and United States Policy toward Latin America*

(Princeton: Princeton University Press, 1986). For more pessimistic views, focusing on the Caribbean and the Far East respectively, see Michael C. Desch, "Turning the Caribbean Flank," *Survival* 29, no. 6 (1987): 528–51; and Alvin H. Bernstein, "The Soviets in Cam Ranh Bay," *National Interest,* Spring 1986, 17–29.

59. On the general effects of offensive and defensive advantages see Robert Jervis, "Cooperation under the Security Dilemma," *World Politics* 30, no. 2 (1978): 167–214; Stephen Van Evera, "Causes of War" (Ph.D. diss., University of California, Berkeley, 1984); and George Quester, *Offense and Defense in the International System* (New York: John Wiley, 1977). For a sympathetic critique of this literature see Jack S. Levy, "The Offensive/Defensive Balance in Military Technology: A Theoretical and Historical Analysis," *International Studies Quarterly* 28, no. 2 (1984): 219–37.

60. When the offense has the advantage, states are more likely to (1) spend more on military capabilities; (2) adopt offensive military doctrines; (3) seek to acquire territory both because it is easy to do and because territory is more valuable; and (4) engage in more aggressive diplomacy (including preemptive or preventive wars) (see Jervis, "Cooperation under the Security Dilemma"; and Van Evera, "Causes of War").

61. In addition to using direct military action, states can also challenge each other by acts of subversion or propaganda. Such campaigns undermine the legitimacy of the target regime and can be just as dangerous as a military invasion. In general, however, subversive campaigns rarely succeed against stable governments, because the targets usually respond quickly to attempts by foreign powers to mobilize domestic discontent. For evidence and further discussion see Walt, *Origins of Alliances,* 242–51.

62. For example, when seeking congressional support for aid to Greece and Turkey, President Truman declared that the world was choosing between "alternative ways of life" and that the United States must act to aid "free peoples who are resisting attempted subjugation by armed minorities or by outside pressures." Undersecretary of State Dean Acheson reinforced this logic by warning Congress that "a highly possible Soviet breakthrough might open three continents to Soviet penetration. Like apples in a barrel infected by one rotten one, the corruption of Greece would infect Iran and all to the east. It would also carry infection to Africa, . . . and to Europe through Italy and France . . . the Soviet Union was playing one of the greatest gambles in history at minimal cost" (see Dean Acheson, *Present at the Creation: My Years in the State Department* [New York: Norton, 1969], 293).

63. See Burnham, *Containment or Liberation?* chaps. 9–11; Aaron Wildavsky, "Containment Plus Pluralization," in Wildavsky, *Beyond Containment,* 125–45; and Max Singer, "Dynamic Containment," ibid., 169–99. Wildavsky's own views on the offense/defense balance are unclear. He argues that active efforts to promote democracy in the Soviet Union pose little risk of a Soviet response, and he is extremely sanguine about the United States' ability to deal with a Soviet reaction ("Containment Plus Pluralization," 140–41). On the other hand, most of his selections in *Beyond Containment* portray the United States as vulnerable to the Soviet Union.

64. This theme is especially prevalent in Burnham, *Containment or Liberation?* but is echoed by neo-conservative writers such as Irving Kristol (see his "Foreign Policy in an Age of Ideology," 7–9).

65. Analyses stressing the danger of a Soviet offensive in Europe include Gen. Robert Close, *Europe without Defense? 48 Hours That Could Change the Face of*

the World (New York: Pergamon, 1979); U.S. Congress, Senate, Committee on Armed Services, *NATO and the New Soviet Threat,* report by Senators Sam Nunn and Dewey F. Bartlett, 95th Cong., 1st sess., 1977; "Interview with Philip A. Karber," *Armed Forces Journal International,* June 1987, 112–17; John M. Collins, *U.S.-Soviet Military Balance, 1980–1985* (Washington, D.C.: Pergamon-Brassey's, 1985), 127–32; and Huntington, "Renewal of Strategy," 22–23. See also Samuel P. Huntington, "Conventional Deterrence and Conventional Retaliation in Europe," *International Security* 8, no. 3 (1983/84): 32–56. Huntington also writes that "if the Soviets were free to concentrate their forces on Southwest Asia, they clearly could overrun any force that the Western allies and Japan might deploy in a reasonable amount of time" ("Renewal of Strategy," 27).

66. As Huntington puts it: "The great advantage to the offensive is that the attacker chooses the point [of attack] and hence can concentrate his force there." Huntington argues that although NATO's forces are weaker than those of the Warsaw Pact, they can still conduct offensive actions: "History is full of successful offensives by forces that lacked numerical superiority." This view implies that NATO is too weak to defend its own territory but strong enough to conduct a "prompt retaliatory counteroffensive into Eastern Europe." A clearer example of a belief in offense dominance would be hard to find (see Huntington, "Renewal of Strategy," 29–30; and idem, "Conventional Deterrence and Conventional Retaliation," 46–47. For a similar appraisal see Strategy Commission, *Discriminate Deterrence,* 27–28).

67. For optimistic appraisals of the European balance see Barry R. Posen, "Measuring the European Conventional Balance: Coping with Complexity in Threat Assessment," *International Security* 12, no. 4 (1988): 186–202; Joshua M. Epstein, "Dynamic Analysis and the Conventional Balance in Europe," ibid., 154–65; John J. Mearsheimer, "Why the Soviets Can't Win Quickly in Central Europe," ibid. 7, no. 1 (1982): 3–39; and idem, "Numbers, Strategy, and the European Balance," ibid. 12, no. 4 (1988): 174–85. All of these writers assume that defenders have a tactical advantage in a European battle.

68. See Paul H. Nitze, "Deterring Our Deterrent," *Foreign Policy,* no. 25, Winter 1976/77, 195–210; and idem, "Assuring Strategic Stability in an Era of Detente," *Foreign Affairs* 54, no. 2 (1976): 207–32. Other examples of this logic include Victor Utgoff, "In Defense of Counterforce," *International Security* 6, no. 4 (1982): 44–60; and Robert Jastrow, "Why Strategic Superiority Matters," *Commentary* 75, no. 3 (1983): 27–32. For critiques see John Steinbruner and Thomas Garwin, "Strategic Vulnerability: The Balance between Prudence and Paranoia," *International Security* 1, no. 1 (1976): 38–81; Garry D. Brewer and Bruce G. Blair, "War Games and National Security with a Grain of SALT," *Bulletin of the Atomic Scientists* 35, no. 6 (1979): 18–26; and Jan M. Lodal, "Assuring Strategic Stability: An Alternate View," *Foreign Affairs* 54, no. 3 (1976): 462–81.

69. This argument is not new. During the 1950s, critics of "massive retaliation" argued that Soviet parity would render U.S. retaliation incredible, thereby enabling the Soviets to use conventional and subversive forces at will. Accordingly, these analysts—often associated with the U.S. Army—called for the United States to improve its "limited war" capabilities. As Samuel Huntington has observed: "Army espousal of limited war [in the 1950s] was primarily a reaction to the New Look and the threat which it posed to the Army's missions" (See Samuel P. Huntington, *The Common Defense: Strategic Programs in National Politics* [New York: Columbia University Press, 1961], 361).

70. For representative examples see Huntington, "Renewal of Strategy," 32–40; Colin S. Gray, "Nuclear Strategy: The Case for a Theory of Victory," *International Security* 4, no. 1 (1979): 54–87; Strategy Commission, *Discriminate Deterrence,* 35–37; and Brzezinski, *Game Plan,* 159–68. Brzezinski does not explicitly advocate "superiority," but his proposals would lead in this direction.

71. Both superpowers would have substantial nuclear forces left after the best first strike that the other could inflict. For example, the United States would have at least four thousand warheads totaling 1,000 equivalent megatons (EMT) of explosive power left after a Soviet first strike; the Soviets would have at least 500 EMT left if the United States struck first (see Michael Salman, Kevin Sullivan, and Stephen Van Evera, "Analysis or Propaganda? Measuring America's Strategic Nuclear Capability, 1969–1988," in *Nuclear Arguments: The Major Debates in Strategic Nuclear Weapons and Arms Control,* edited by Steven E. Miller and Lynn Eden [Ithaca: Cornell University Press, 1989]; and Joshua M. Epstein, *The 1988 Defense Budget* [Washington, D.C.: Brookings Institution, 1987], 21–27). Another recent study concludes that drastic arms reductions would not confer a first-strike capability on either superpower and would not reduce civilian casualties significantly in a nuclear war (see Michael M. May, George F. Bing, and John D. Steinbruner, *Strategic Arms Reductions* [Washington, D.C.: Brookings Institution, 1988]).

72. See, e.g., Robert Jervis, *The Illogic of American Nuclear Strategy* (Ithaca: Cornell University Press, 1984); and Kenneth N. Waltz, "The Spread of Nuclear Weapons: More May Be Better," Adelphi Paper No. 171 (London: International Institute for Strategic Studies, 1981).

73. See, e.g., Dietrich Fischer, *Preventing War in the Nuclear Age* (Totowa, N.J.: Rowman & Allanheld, 1984); Forsberg, "Confining the Military to Defense," esp. 310; Gene Sharp, *Making Europe Unconquerable* (Cambridge, Mass.: Ballinger, 1985); and the discussion on Non-Offensive Defense, in *Bulletin of the Atomic Scientists* 44, no. 7 (1988): 12–54. For a summary and critique of some of these ideas see David Gates, "Area Defense Concepts: The West German Debate," *Survival* 29, no. 4 (1987): 301–17.

74. See, e.g., Forsberg, "Confining the Military to Defense."

75. As Ho Chi Minh told a French diplomat in 1945: "You will kill ten of our men, but we will kill one of yours and it is you who will finish by wearing yourself out" (quoted in John T. McAlister, Jr., *Viet Nam: The Origins of Revolution* [New York: Alfred A. Knopf, 1969], 296. See also Andrew Mack, "Why Big Nations Lose Small Wars: The Politics of Asymmetric Conflict," *World Politics* 27, no. 2 [1975]: 175–200). Given that the United States can be threatened by one state amassing enormous power but not by many small ones, the growth of modern nationalism is a positive trend for the United States.

76. For further discussion of this point see Walt, *Origins of Alliances,* 244–51.

77. In addition to the major industrial powers, a number of developing countries have become significant arms exporters. According to the U.S. Arms Control and Disarmament Agency, arms exports from the developing world increased by 32 percent annually during 1979–84 (see ACDA, *World Military Expenditures,* 9. For surveys of the global arms market see Anthony Sampson, *The Arms Bazaar: From Lebanon to Lockheed* [New York: Viking Press, 1977]; Stephanie G. Neuman and Robert E. Harkavy, eds., *Arms Transfers in the Modern World* [New York: Praeger, 1979]; and Stockholm International Peace Research Institute, *The Arms Trade with the Third World* [New York: Humanities Press, 1971]).

78. For a discussion of the West's military supremacy in this period see John Ellis, *A Social History of the Machine Gun* (New York: Pantheon, 1975).

79. Among other things, this argument also suggests that the durability of the Soviet empire is due to the fact that the different nationalities within its borders (including Eastern Europe) lack ready access to small arms.

80. A number of scholars have examined the role of nuclear weapons in postwar diplomacy, focusing in particular on superpower crises. These studies suggest that (1) the precise state of the nuclear balance had little if any effect on crisis behavior, and (2) national leaders saw these weapons as placing important constraints on their freedom of action (see Marc Trachtenberg, "The Influence of Nuclear Weapons in the Cuban Missile Crisis," *International Security* 10, no. 1 [1985]: 137–63; Richard Ned Lebow, "The Cuban Missile Crisis: Reading the Lessons Correctly," *Political Science Quarterly* 98, no. 3 [1983]: 431–58; Barry M. Blechman and Douglas M. Hart, "The Political Utility of Nuclear Weapons: The 1973 Middle East Crisis," *International Security* 7, no. 1 [1982]: 132–56; and Richard K. Betts, *Nuclear Blackmail and Nuclear Balance* [Washington, D.C.: Brookings Institution, 1987]). In addition, a comprehensive study of postwar naval diplomacy has confirmed that the side defending the status quo prevailed in virtually all superpower naval confrontations, lending further support to the above arguments (see James M. McConnell, "The Rules of the Game: A Theory of Superpower Naval Diplomacy," in *Soviet Naval Diplomacy,* edited by Bradford Dismukes and James M. McConnell [New York: Pergamon, 1979]). For a provocative argument that nuclear weapons have had relatively little effect on stability see John Mueller, "The Essential Irrelevance of Nuclear Weapons: Stability in the Postwar World," *International Security* 13, no. 2 (1988): 55–79.

81. Attack routes in Central Europe are heavily congested, forcing an attacker into narrow and well-defined attack routes (see Paul Bracken, "Urban Sprawl and NATO Defense," *Survival* 13, no. 6 [1976]: 254–60).

82. On the obstacles facing a Soviet invasion see Joshua M. Epstein, "Soviet Vulnerabilities and the RDF Deterrent," *International Security* 6, no. 2 (1981): 126–58; and Keith A. Dunn, "Constraints on the USSR in Southwest Asia: A Military Analysis," *Orbis* 25, no. 3 (1981): 607–29.

83. Despite his concern over possible Soviet expansion, Samuel Huntington notes that none of the great powers has achieved "an unalloyed string of military successes" since World War II (see Samuel P. Huntington, *American Military Strategy,* Policy Papers in International Affairs, no. 28 [Berkeley: Institute for International Studies, 1986], 7. See also Mueller, "Essential Irrelevance of Nuclear Weapons," 76–79).

84. Examples of successful expansion include Israel's conquest of the Golan Heights and West Bank, India's seizure of Kashmir and Goa, China's seizure of Tibet, North Vietnam's expansion into South Vietnam and Cambodia, Libya's occupation of the Ouzou Strip, Morocco's seizure of Spanish North Africa, and Indonesia's conquest of East Timor. Of these cases, perhaps only Goa, Tibet, and East Timor are not in doubt at present.

85. See Ravenal, *NATO;* Richard J. Barnet, *Real Security* (New York: Simon & Schuster, 1981), 90–98; Layne, "Atlanticism without NATO," 27–28; Sanders and Schwenniger, "The Democrats and a New Grand Strategy"; and Sanders, "Security and Choice," 710. A similar belief in the inherent advantages to the defender is implicit in David Calleo and James Chace's more modest assertions that Europe could mount an effective defense against the Soviet Union either without or with a

greatly reduced U.S. presence (see Calleo, *Beyond American Hegemony,* chap. 9; and Chace, "A New Grand Strategy," 12–16).

86. Among those advocating a "trip-wire" force is Kenneth N. Waltz, in "A Strategy for the Rapid Deployment Force," *International Security* 5, no. 4 (1981): 49–73, and "The Spread of Nuclear Weapons," 7. See also W. S. Bennett, R. R. Sandoval, and R. G. Shreffler, "A Credible Nuclear Emphasis Defense for NATO," *Orbis* 17, no. 2 (1973): 463–79.

87. An obvious example is the Afghan resistance, whose efforts were aided greatly by U.S. provision of Stinger missiles and other military supplies.

88. Many neo-isolationists complain that the U.S. commitment to Europe is an expensive burden directed at a low-probability event (i.e., a Soviet armored invasion). Such analyses ignore the fact that the U.S. commitment is part of the reason why such an event is unlikely.

89. Experts such as former U.S. Secretary of Defense Robert McNamara have admitted that U.S. leaders did not believe nuclear weapons were usable under any circumstances, a position that flatly contradicts NATO's doctrine of "flexible response." If Western experts can question the credibility of the U.S. nuclear guarantee today, it is certainly possible that Soviet decisionmakers might one day conclude that U.S. threats to escalate would not be executed (see Robert McNamara, "The Military Role of Nuclear Weapons: Perceptions and Misperceptions," *Foreign Affairs* 62, no. 1 [1983]: 59–80).

90. It is also in the United States' interest to ensure that it retains the dominant influence in NATO decisions regarding deployment and use of nuclear weapons. Maintaining a large conventional commitment to Europe is the best way to do this.

91. On this general point the classic analysis is Robert Jervis, *Perception and Misperception in International Politics* (Princeton: Princeton University Press, 1976), chap. 3. See also Richard Hermann, *Perceptions and Behavior in Soviet Foreign Policy* (Pittsburgh: University of Pittsburgh Press, 1985), chap. 1; Robert E. Osgood et al., *Containment, Soviet Behavior, and Grand Strategy* (Berkeley: Institute of International Studies, 1981), 8–15; and Barry R. Posen, "Competing Images of the Soviet Union," *World Politics* 39, no. 4 (1987): 579–87.

92. For examples see Burnham, *Containment or Liberation?* Podhoretz, *Present Danger,* 91–95; NSC-68, reprinted in *Containment: Documents on American Policy and Strategy, 1945–1950,* edited by Thomas H. Etzold and John L. Gaddis (New York: Columbia University Press, 1978), esp. 386–89; Wildavsky, "Containment Plus Pluralization"; Committee on the Present Danger, "What Is the Soviet Union Up To?" and "Is America Becoming Number 2?" reprinted in *Alerting America: The Papers of the Committee on the Present Danger,* edited by Charles Tyroler II (Washington, D.C.: Pergamon-Brassey's, 1984), esp. 10–14, 39–40; H. Joachim Maitre, "Soviet Military Power," in Bark, *To Promote Peace,* 215–30; and Strategy Commission, *Discriminate Deterrence,* 63. Harsh assessments of Soviet intentions often portray the Soviet Union as a "paper tiger" that will back down quickly if challenged. This is an ideal argument for those seeking to justify a more assertive U.S. policy; disaster beckons if the United States does not take action, but success is assured if it does. As Richard Hermann points out, such views are difficult to falsify, because "proponents of this theory can interpret evidence inconsistent with the expansionist proposition as evidence of Soviet restraint in the face of U.S. strength; the USSR was simply 'compelled to behave' " (Hermann, *Perceptions and Behavior,* 12).

93. The most extreme version of this line of thinking is the "revisionist" school of cold war historiography, which places primary responsibility for the cold war on the United States. Prominent figures in this school of thought include William Appleman Williams, Joyce and Gabriel Kolko, and Gar Alperowitz. Contemporary writers who take a benign view of Soviet intentions include Radway, "Let Europe Be Europe," 34–38; Richard J. Barnet, "Why Trust the Soviets?" *World Policy Journal* 1, no. 3 (1984): 461–82, and Barnet, "The Four Pillars," 80; Forsberg, "Confining the Military to Defense," 292–93; and Sanders, "Security and Choice," 709–10.

94. Among writers on strategy, this view is reflected in Posen, "Competing Images of the Soviet Union"; Kenneth N. Waltz, "Another Gap?" in Osgood et al., *Containment, Soviet Behavior, and Grand Strategy,* 79–80; John L. Gaddis, "Containment: Its Past and Future," *International Security* 5, no. 4 (1981): 74–102; and Ernst B. Haas, "On Hedging Our Bets: Selective Engagement with the Soviet Union," in Wildavsky, *Beyond Containment,* 93–124.

95. For a summary of these different images, combined with a careful attempt to test their relative validity, see Hermann, *Perceptions and Behavior.* For an earlier assessment of Western views see William Welch, *American Images of Soviet Foreign Policy: An Inquiry into Recent Appraisals from the Academic Community* (New Haven: Yale University Press, 1970).

96. On this point see Hannes Adomeit, *Soviet Risktaking and Crisis Behavior: A Theoretical and Empirical Analysis* (London: Allen & Unwin, 1982).

97. The United States may have been close to a first-strike capability in the early 1960s. The Soviet Union had only a few intercontinental-range bombers, a handful of primitive missile submarines, and less than fifty vulnerable ICBMs, each requiring a lengthy launch period (see Raymond L. Garthoff, "Intelligence Assessment and Policymaking: A Decision Point in the Kennedy Administration," Brookings Institution Staff Paper [Washington, D.C., 1984], 29–31). By contrast, the United States had over one thousand bombers, a growing fleet of Polaris submarines, and was beginning to deploy modern ICBMs. Moreover, satellite reconnaissance had revealed the scope of the U.S. advantage: the United States was way ahead, both sides knew it, and they knew we knew. Thus the Cuban gambit was probably a "quick fix" designed to improve the Soviet Union's delivery capability by placing medium-range missiles on the territory of an ally. (The U.S. deployment of Jupiter missiles in Turkey was an obvious precedent.) Although Soviet tactics were duplicitous and risky (i.e., Soviet officials lied repeatedly to top U.S. officials), under the circumstances, the Cuban crisis is hardly evidence of innate expansive tendencies (see also idem, "The Cuban Missile Crisis: The Soviet Story," *Foreign Policy,* no. 72, Fall 1988, 63–66).

98. See Elizabeth Valkenier, "Revolutionary Change in the Third World: Recent Soviet Assessments," *World Politics* 38, no. 3 (1986): 415–34; Jack L. Snyder, "The Gorbachev Revolution: A Waning of Soviet Expansionism?" *International Security* 12, no. 3 (1987/88): 93–131; and Francis Fukuyama, *Moscow's Post-Brezhnev Reassessment of the Third World,* R-3337-AF (Santa Monica: RAND Corporation, 1986).

99. For a very sophisticated presentation of this view see Snyder, "The Gorbachev Revolution." For a different appraisal see Fukuyama, "Patterns of Soviet Third World Policy"; and Stephen M. Meyer, "The Sources and Prospects of Gorbachev's New Political Thinking on Security," *International Security* 13, no. 2 (1988): 124–63.

100. Perhaps the most significant possibility raised by Gorbachev's ascendancy

is conventional arms reductions in Europe. Mutual reductions might be in the U.S. interest under some circumstances, primarily as a way to save money. For discussions of these issues see Robert D. Blackwill, "Conceptual Problems of Conventional Arms Control," *International Security* 12, no. 4 (1988): 28–47; and Jack L. Snyder, "Limiting Offensive Conventional Forces: Soviet Proposals and Western Options," ibid., 48–77.

101. See Richard Pipes, "Why the Soviet Union Believes It Can Fight and Win a Nuclear War," *Commentary* 64, no. 1 (1977): 21–34; and Seymour Weiss, "Labyrinth under Moscow," *Washington Post,* 25 May 1988, A19.

102. The discussion in this section draws heavily upon Walt, *Origins of Alliances,* chap. 2.

103. Examples of this belief include Strategy Commission, *Discriminate Deterrence,* 13–14; Aaron Wildavsky, "Dilemmas of American Foreign Policy," in Wildavsky, *Beyond Containment,* 13; Podhoretz, *Present Danger,* 40–41, 58–60; Burnham, *Containment or Liberation?* 245–47; and Dimitri K. Simes, "Containment: Choices and Opportunities," in Deibel and Gaddis, *Containment,* 671–72.

104. See Ronald Reagan, "Speech to a Joint Session of Congress on Central America," *New York Times,* 28 April 1983, A12. For other examples of bandwagoning logic see Walt, *Origins of Alliances,* 3–4, 19–20; and Deborah Welch Larson, "The Bandwagon Metaphor and the Role of Institutions," in *Dominos and Bandwagons: Strategic Beliefs and Superpower Competition in the Eurasian Rimland,* edited by Robert Jervis and Jack Snyder (New York: Oxford University Press, forthcoming).

105. For a recent statement of this view, which also attempts to resurrect the "domino theory," see Singer, "Dynamic Containment," 173.

106. Disagreements about the importance of ideology divide those who advocate finite containment (which focuses on containing Soviet power) from those who advocate rollback or global containment (which seeks the containment or elimination of Communist power). Where George Kennan saw the Communist bloc as prone to internal divisions, his opponents in the Truman administration saw the Communist world as a cohesive ideological alliance that could not be divided through positive inducements. Different beliefs about what held the Soviet system together thus gave rise to different policy prescriptions. In retrospect, Kennan's analysis was strikingly prescient (see Kennan's "U.S. Objectives with Respect to Russia," in Etzold and Gaddis, *Containment,* 186–87; and Gaddis, *Strategies of Containment,* 43–45. Similar arguments can be found in Morgenthau, *In Defense of the National Interest,* chap. 3).

107. On balancing behavior in the European great power system see Ludwig Dehio, *The Precarious Balance* (New York: Vintage, 1965); and F. H. Hinsley, *Power and the Pursuit of Peace: Theory and Practice in the History of Relations between States* (Cambridge: Cambridge University Press, 1963). For evidence from several other contexts see Walt, *Origins of Alliances,* esp. chaps. 5 and 6; idem, "Alliance Formation and the Balance of World Power," *International Security* 9, no. 4 (1985): 3–43; and idem, "Testing Theories of Alliance Formation: The Case of Southwest Asia," *International Organization* 42, no. 2 (1988): 275–316.

108. Although the United States has made no serious effort to overthrow the Soviet Union itself, it has tried to overthrow the Marxist regimes in Cuba, Angola, and Nicaragua and the left-wing, non-Marxist governments in Guatemala (1954), Iran (1953), and the Dominican Republic (1965).

109. The fear of bandwagoning explains why some early proponents of con-

tainment (including Kennan himself) supported U.S. intervention in Korea and also why Kennan was initially reluctant to advocate withdrawal from Vietnam (see Hixson, "Containment on the Perimeter," 149, 159).

110. Third World suspicions of the United States are also due to their perception of the United States as the successor to the colonial empires of Britain and France. The Soviet Union seemed a more attractive ally because it was an apparently successful model of development and had never been a colonial power in these regions. U.S. policy reinforced these suspicions; after its initial support for decolonization, the United States repeatedly intervened in several Third World countries using a variety of military, economic, and covert means. Once the Soviet Union began to follow suit in the 1970s, however, its standing within the Third World countries began to decline (see Richard Lowenthal, *Model or Ally? The Communist Powers and the Developing Countries* [London: Oxford University Press, 1977]; Stephen S. Kaplan, *Diplomacy of Power: Soviet Armed Forces as a Political Instrument* [Washington, D.C.: Brookings Institution, 1980]; Richard J. Barnet, *Intervention and Revolution: The United States in the Third World* [New York: New American Library, 1968]; Robert Packenham, *Liberal America and the Third World* [Princeton: Princeton University Press, 1973]; Cole Blasier, *The Hovering Giant: U.S. Response to Revolutionary Change in Latin America* [Pittsburgh: University of Pittsburgh Press, 1976]; Melvin Gurtov, *The United States against the Third World* [New York: Praeger, 1974]; and William Blum, *The CIA: A Forgotten History—U.S. Global Interventions since World War II* [London: Zed Books, 1986]).

111. It is worth noting that most U.S. allies oppose U.S. intervention in places such as Central America and that the Vietnam War was equally unpopular with most U.S. allies.

112. There are important differences among the various advocates of withdrawal. Some favor total withdrawal from NATO; others call for a partial military disengagement. Some writers favor demobilizing the forces to be withdrawn from Europe and/or Asia; others argue for reconfiguring and/or redeploying them into other regions. Still others advocate withdrawal in order to free the United States from the "constraints" of allied opinion. For representative examples of these different views see Chace, "A New Grand Strategy," 12–13; Kristol, "Foreign Policy in an Age of Ideology," 14; Layne, "Atlanticism without NATO," 32, 38–39; Ravenal, *NATO,* 86–88; Calleo, *Beyond American Hegemony,* 165–71; Brzezinski, *Game Plan,* 180; Record, *Revising U.S. Military Strategy,* chap. 6; and Sanders and Schwenninger, "The Democrats and a New Grand Strategy," 369–418.

113. At first glance, the distribution of burdens within the Alliance appears extremely skewed. Western Europe's combined GNP now exceeds that of the United States, but the U.S. defense expenditures are still over 50 percent of NATO's combined total. Similarly, although Japan may now be the world's second largest economy, it ranks only tenth in annual defense spending, at 1–2 percent of GNP. Thus the accusation that the United States is bearing a disproportionate burden is partly true.

114. Allied contributions include the territory upon which NATO forces are stationed (along with the various social costs involved), the provision of "host-nation support" for U.S. troops, and the economic aid they supply to NATO members such as Turkey. On this general question see Adams and Munz, *Fair Shares;* Congressional Budget Office, *Alliance Burdensharing: A Review of the Data* (Washington, D.C.: USGPO, June 1987); James B. Steinberg, "Rethinking the Debate on Burdensharing," *Survival* 29, no. 1 (1987): 56–78; Dunn, "NATO's Enduring Value," 164–

65; and Michael Legge and Richard Perle, "Burdensharing Debated," *National Interest*, Summer 1988, 34–46.

115. If European military manpower were priced according to U.S. pay scales, the annual defense expenditures for Europe would increase by roughly 20 percent. This does not tell us which manpower system is better, but it does help explain why European defense expenditures are less than those of the United States (see Ruth Sivard, *World Military and Social Expenditures, 1981* [Leesburg, Va.: World Priorities, 1981], 37; and CBO, *Alliance Burdensharing*, 12).

116. It follows that if U.S. allies' assessment of the threat is more accurate, then the United States could do less in certain areas (such as the Third World) provided that its allies maintained their present level of effort elsewhere. A more equitable division of costs within the Alliance would result.

117. According to Keith Dunn, if the United States were to remove one hundred thousand troops, the allies would have to increase their defense spending by 18–30 percent over two years to offset the removal (see Dunn, "NATO's Enduring Value," 170). Nor would these U.S. troops be available for reinforcement in a crisis. Removing troops from Europe would save money only if they were demobilized; otherwise, expensive lift capacity would be needed to move them to Europe in the event of war.

118. For example, the number of West German males between the ages of seventeen and thirty will decline by more than 30 percent in the next decade. Similar trends exist in France and Britain as well (see International Institute for Strategic Studies, *The Military Balance, 1983–1984* [London, 1983], 145–47).

119. The best recent attempt is Calleo, *Beyond American Hegemony*, chap. 9. Calleo argues that Europe can easily match the Warsaw Pact through greater reliance on reserves, but even he does not provide an adequate description of the force he envisions or its effectiveness against the Warsaw Pact.

120. See Krauss, *How NATO Weakens the West*, 237; and Layne, "Atlanticism without NATO," 33.

121. The classic analysis of the collective goods problem in alliances is Mancur Olson and Richard Zeckhauser, "An Economic Theory of Alliances," *Review of Economics and Statistics* 48, no. 3 (1966): 266–79.

122. See Joseph Joffe, "Europe's American Pacifier," *Foreign Policy*, no. 54, Spring 1984, 64–82; and Dunn, "NATO's Enduring Value," 171–72.

123. This point is nicely made in Henry A. Kissinger, "The Rearming of Japan— and the Rest of Asia," *Washington Post*, 29 January 1987, A25.

124. On the conditions for successful conventional deterrence see John J. Mearsheimer, *Conventional Deterrence* (Ithaca: Cornell University Press, 1982).

125. Because Britain did not make its commitment to France clear in 1914, Germany's leaders convinced themselves that Britain would not fight. Because Hitler doubted the Allied commitment to Poland in 1939, he chose to ignore British and French warnings. Had Germany's leaders known that they would eventually face the power of the United States, both of these wars might have been avoided entirely.

126. This view is most apparent in the writings of Earl Ravenal; see his *NATO*, 60–63, 72–75.

127. See Van Evera, *American Strategic Interests*, 20.

128. Idealist approaches downplay the continued role of power in international politics and offer no plausible defense of existing U.S. interests. At best, such ap-

proaches are premature; at worst, they are simply utopian. Isolationist strategies exaggerate Soviet and U.S. weakness, are too optimistic about Soviet intentions, overstate the allies' ability to balance, and ignore the positive role played by U.S. military commitments. Proposals that the United States "revise containment" either make similar errors on a smaller scale or favor removing U.S. forces from key areas in order to protect less important regions. By contrast, global containment rests on excessively gloomy views: it overstates the importance of the Third World, exaggerates the ease of offense, assumes that Soviet intentions are extremely bellicose, and erroneously predicts that allies will flock to the Soviet Union if the United States is not ceaselessly vigilant. Finally, rollback rests upon even more extreme errors, especially in its exaggerated belief in the role of ideology as a motivating force in international politics.

129. For summaries of recent work in this field see Joseph S. Nye, Jr., and Sean M. Lynn-Jones, "International Security Studies: A Report of a Conference on the State of the Field," *International Security* 12, no. 4 (1988): 5–27; and John L. Gaddis, "Expanding the Data Base: Historians, Political Scientists, and the Enrichment of Security Studies," ibid. 12, no. 1 (1987): 3–21.

130. The static comparisons (bean counts) often invoked to show Warsaw Pact superiority are largely meaningless, because they ignore the areas in which NATO is superior (e.g., logistics, aircraft quality, command and control, training). NATO spends roughly 20 percent more each year on defense than the Pact does, and it has about the same number of troops under arms. Moreover, roughly 15 percent of Soviet forces are directed against China, which makes NATO's task even easier. As one scholar has noted, "If we are militarily weaker than they are, we must be doing something very wrong" (see Kenneth N. Waltz, "Faltering Giant," *Inquiry*, 23 February 1981, 27). For optimistic appraisals of the conventional balance see Posen, "Measuring the European Conventional Balance"; Epstein, "Dynamic Analysis and the Conventional Balance in Europe"; Mearsheimer, "Why the Soviets Can't Win Quickly in Central Europe"; and idem, "Numbers, Strategy, and the European Balance." More pessimistic views can be found in Kim R. Holmes, "Measuring the Conventional Balance in Europe," *International Security* 12, no. 4 (1988): 166–73; Andrew Hamilton, "Redressing the Conventional Balance: NATO's Reserve Military Manpower," ibid. 10, no. 1 (1985): 111–36; and Eliot A. Cohen, "Towards Better Net Assessment: Rethinking the European Conventional Balance," ibid. 13, no. 1 (1988): 50–89.

131. For example, close support aircraft such as the A-10 are a better choice than high-priced items such as the F-15 or Tornado aircraft, because the deep interdiction mission is both more difficult and less important to a successful defense. Greater attention to terrain preparation and various types of prepared defenses would slow a Pact advance and improve exchange ratios as well.

132. The United States would still possess an adequate intervention capability after these reductions (e.g., the 82d Airborne and 101st Air Assault divisions, as well as the marines). Because these troops are assigned missions in the Persian Gulf, the United States' ability to intervene in the Third World would be limited in the early stages of a major war. But in the event of a major war in Europe or the Gulf, intervention elsewhere in the Third World would be the least of the United States' concerns.

133. See Epstein, "Soviet Vulnerabilities"; and Dunn, "Constraints on the USSR."

For a pessimistic assessment see Jeffrey Record, *The Rapid Deployment Force and U.S. Military Intervention in the Persian Gulf* (Cambridge, Mass.: Institute for Foreign Policy Analysis, 1981).

134. The U.S. Central Command is assigned four and one-third army divisions, one and one-third marine divisions, three carrier battle groups, seven tactical fighter wings, and a variety of special forces and support units (see John D. Mayer, Jr., "Rapid Deployment Forces: Policy and Budgetary Implications" [Washington, D.C.: Congressional Budget Office, 1983], xv; and Caspar W. Weinberger, *Annual Report to the Congress: Fiscal Year 1984* [Washington, D.C.: USGPO, 1983], 195).

135. The rationale for and primacy of this mission is explained in John J. Mearsheimer, "A Strategic Misstep: The Maritime Strategy and Deterrence in Europe," *International Security* 11, no. 2 (1986): 3–57.

136. A defensive sea control strategy would establish barriers to Soviet attack across "choke points" such as the Sea of Japan and the Greenland–Iceland–United Kingdom (GIUK) gap. The Soviet navy is unlikely to challenge these barriers, because its main mission is to defend Soviet ballistic missile–carrying submarines in the Arctic Sea. If it did attack the SLOCs, however, these barriers would pose a highly effective defense (see William W. Kaufmann, *A Thoroughly Efficient Navy* [Washington, D.C.: Brookings Institution, 1987], chap. 7, esp. 79–81).

137. Although aircraft carriers have their own antisubmarine and antiaircraft capabilities, the United States can, according to Kaufmann, operate patrol aircraft and fighters from land bases more efficiently than from the more costly and vulnerable carrier battle groups (see ibid., 83).

138. Assuming that two carriers are in overhaul at any time, a force of eight carriers would ensure wartime deployment of three carriers in the Persian Gulf (as currently assigned to Central Command), two in the Atlantic, and one in the Pacific. Because carriers are relatively ineffective in projecting power against the Soviet Union and play a minor role in SLOC defense, this force would be more than enough in a global war. And such a force would still provide ample naval muscle for lesser contingencies (on the minor importance of aircraft carriers for SLOC defense see Epstein, *1988 Defense Budget,* 49–50; and Mearsheimer, "A Strategic Misstep," 55). Using extremely conservative assumptions, William Kaufmann suggests that twelve carrier battle groups would satisfy U.S. naval requirements in a major war with the Soviet Union. He assumes that SLOC defense might require prompt amphibious and air attacks on a Soviet base in each ocean, each assault requiring three carriers. Assuming that one carrier out of four is in port and that three are assigned to the Persian Gulf, a total requirement of twelve carriers is produced. However, it is not clear exactly where these Soviet bases might be (especially in the Atlantic); nor is it clear why land-based aircraft could not deal with them more efficiently (see Kaufmann, *A Thoroughly Efficient Navy,* 84–99). In any case, all three authors agree that a fifteen-carrier fleet is unjustified and extravagant.

139. The Maritime Strategy is infeasible because carrier battle groups are an inefficient means of projecting power (i.e., much of the battle group's capability is devoted to defending itself), yet the strategy calls for the surface navy to attack heavily defend Soviet bases (e.g., the Kola Peninsula). By one estimate, this mission would require more than twenty carrier battle groups. The strategy is destabilizing because it also calls for deliberate attacks on Soviet ballistic missile submarines, thereby threatening the Soviets' second-strike capability and tempting them to escalate. Finally, the strategy is unnecessary because neither of these actions would

have much effect on the critical ground war in Europe. Maintaining the SLOCs is essential, but a naval offensive against the Soviet fleet or against Soviet territory is not. On these points see Epstein, *1988 Defense Budget*, 45–55; Kaufmann, *A Thoroughly Efficient Navy*, 12–21 and passim; Mearsheimer, "A Strategic Misstep"; and Barry R. Posen, "Inadvertent Nuclear War: Escalation and NATO's Northern Flank," *International Security* 7, no. 2 (1982): 28–54. For arguments in favor of the Maritime Strategy see Adm. James D. Watkins, *The Maritime Strategy* (Annapolis: U.S. Naval Institute Press, 1986); Linton F. Brooks, "Naval Power and National Security: The Case for the Maritime Strategy," *International Security* 11, no. 2 (1986): 58–88; and Bradford Dismukes, "Strategic ASW and the Conventional Defense of Europe," Professional Paper No. 453 (Alexandria, Va.: Center for Naval Analyses, April 1987).

140. See Salman, Sullivan, and Van Evera, "Analysis or Propaganda?"; and Epstein, *1988 Defense Budget*, 21–27.

141. One recent estimate shows that 100 one-megaton airbursts would kill 45–77 million Soviet citizens and cause a total of 73–93 million lethal and nonlethal injuries (see Barbara G. Levi, Frank N. von Hippel, and William H. Daugherty, "Civilian Casualties from 'Limited' Nuclear Attacks on the USSR," *International Security* 12, no. 3 [1987/88]: 168–69).

142. The search for superiority has been utterly futile: although both superpowers have devoted considerable effort and expense to enhancing their ability to attack each other's forces, both have far more survivable warheads now than they did twenty years ago.

143. On U.S. retaliatory capabilities after these reductions see Epstein, *1988 Defense Budget*, 21–32.

144. Despite its name, the SDI program would create an offensive weapon that would give its possessor a first-strike capability by negating the opponent's ability to retaliate. Assuming that it did work, deploying a defense would create an especially unstable world. Both sides would be forced to search for a way to overcome such defenses, driven by the fear that the other side might achieve a breakthrough first. Intense arms races and yawning "windows of opportunity" would be the likely result. For studies challenging the feasibility of SDI see Kurt Gottfried, "The Physicists Size Up SDI," *Arms Control Today* 17 (July/August 1987): 28–32; John Tirman, *Empty Promise: The Growing Case Against Star Wars* (New York: Vintage Books, 1986); and Sidney Drell, David Holloway, and Philip Farley, "Preserving the ABM Treaty: A Critique of the Reagan Strategic Defense Initiative," *International Security* 9, no. 2 (Fall 1984): 51–91. For analyses suggesting that SDI would be undesirable even if it were possible see Charles Glaser, "Why Even Good Defenses May Be Bad," ibid. 9, no. 2 (1984): 92–123; and idem, "Do We Want the Missile Defenses We Can Build?" ibid. 10, no. 1 (1985): 25–57.

145. To note the most recent example, in its campaign to "promote democracy" in Central America, the Reagan administration supported a war against Nicaragua that claimed over twenty-five thousand civilian lives. This campaign involved violating international law (for which the United States was condemned by the World Court), a series of illegal arms shipments (including the famous Iran-contra scandal), and a carefully orchestrated misinformation campaign designed to deceive the American people about the true nature of the conflict in Central America (see Robert Parry and Peter Kornbluh, "Iran-Contra's Untold Story," *Foreign Policy*, no. 72, Fall 1988, 3–30).

146. Even some of the most fervent advocates of the Reagan Doctrine have

admitted that U.S. security interests are not at stake in the Third World. For example, Charles Krauthammer has written that "if the security of the United States is the only goal of American foreign policy, all that is needed is a minimal deterrent arsenal, a small navy, a border patrol, and hardly any foreign policy at all" ("Poverty of Realism," 16). This view implies that the United States should spend over $200 billion each year on defense and promote civil war against Marxist regimes solely in order to get other peoples to adopt the U.S. view of the ideal political order.

147. On these points see Van Evera, *American Strategic Interests.*

148. By contrast, the acquisition of nuclear weapons or a major increase in Japanese ground forces or intervention capabilities would be especially alarming to other countries in the region.

149. Rather than eliminate elements of the U.S. force structure, the normal approach is to reduce the rate of weapons procurement (without eliminating major programs) and to cut operations and maintenance expenditures. Force size remains fixed, but readiness declines.

150. On the political forces that distort the development of strategy see Stephen M. Walt, "The Search for a Science of Strategy: A Review Essay on *Makers of Modern Strategy,*" *International Security* 12, no. 1 (1987), esp. 146–60.

151. A classic example is the exaggerated attention paid to international terrorism. Although terrorism attracts widespread media attention (and helped lead to the establishment of a separate Special Operations Command), it is at most a very minor threat. For example, in 1987, 7 U.S. citizens were killed and 47 were wounded in terrorist incidents. (The worldwide totals were 633 and 2,272, respectively.) By contrast, over 50,000 Americans died in car accidents in the same period (See U.S. Department of State, *Patterns of Global Terrorism: 1987* [Washington, D.C.: USGPO, August 1988], 1).

Chapter 8. Realism Redux

1. Realist thinking on this point was influenced by Nicholas J. Spykman's seminal geopolitical study, *America's Strategy in World Politics: The United States and the Balance of Power* (New York: Harcourt, Brace, 1942).

2. For critiques of cold war internationalism see Christopher Layne, "The Real Conservative Agenda," *Foreign Policy,* no. 61, Winter 1985/86, 73–93; and Alan Tonelson, "The Real National Interest," ibid., 49–72.

3. Robert Gilpin, *War and Change in World Politics* (New York: Cambridge University Press, 1981), 7.

4. See Stephen M. Walt, "Alliance Formation and the Balance of World Power," *International Security* 9, no. 4 (1985): 3–43.

5. Henry A. Kissinger, *White House Years* (Boston: Little, Brown, 1979), 55.

6. Robert W. Tucker, "The American Outlook," in *America and the World,* edited by Robert E. Osgood (Baltimore: Johns Hopkins Press, 1970), 32.

7. Charles Krauthammer, "The Poverty of Realism," *New Republic,* 17 February 1986.

8. David Calleo, *Beyond American Hegemony: The Future of the Atlantic Alliance* (New York: Basic Books, 1987); Paul Kennedy, *The Rise and Fall of the Great Powers: Economic Change and Military Conflict from 1500 to 2000* (New York: Random House, 1997). For an overview of the so-called school of decline see Peter Schmeisser, "Taking Stock: Is America in Decline?" *New York Times Magazine,* 17 April 1988, 24.

9. Joseph S. Nye, Jr., "America's Decline: A Myth," *New York Times,* 10 April 1988, 31. For a more detailed presentation of this argument see idem, *Bound to Lead* (New York: Basic Books, 1990).

10. A good example is Samuel P. Huntington, "The U.S.—Decline or Renewal?" *Foreign Affairs* 67, no. 2 (1988/89): 76–96.

11. Ibid.; Daniel P. Moynihan, "What Was Done in the 1980s Can Be Undone," *New York Times Magazine,* 19 June 1988, 34.

12. Huntington, "The U.S.—Decline or Renewal?" 85.

13. Ibid.; James R. Schlesinger, "We Sometimes Forget . . . How Powerful This Nation Is," *New York Times Magazine,* 19 June 1988, 35; Paul Seabury, "The Solvency Boys," *National Interest,* Fall 1988.

14. Gilpin, *War and Change in World Politics;* Kennedy, *Rise and Fall of the Great Powers.*

15. Gilpin, *War and Change in World Politics,* 158–59.

16. The case for reform is set out in Calleo, *Beyond American Hegemony;* James Chace, "A New Grand Strategy," *Foreign Policy,* no. 70, Spring 1988, 3–25; William G. Hyland, "Setting Global Priorities," ibid., no. 73, Winter 1988/89, 22–40; and Stephen Walt, "Two Cheers For Containment" (Paper presented at the Cato Institute conference "Collective Security or Strategic Independence? Alternative Strategies for the Future," Washington, D.C., 2–3 December 1987).

17. Hyland, "Setting Global Priorities," 25.

18. Thomas Hughes, "The Twilight of Internationalism," *Foreign Policy,* no. 61, Winter 1985/86, 25–48.

19. See Charles Krauthammer, "Isolationism, Left and Right," *New Republic,* 4 March 1985; and idem, "Poverty of Realism."

20. Walter Lippmann, *American Foreign Policy: Shield of the Republic* (Boston: Little, Brown, 1943), 9.

21. The American people seem to share this assessment. A 1987 World Policy Institute survey indicated that Americans now believe that economic strength is more important than military power in assuring U.S. world influence (E. J. Dionne, "U.S. Poll Stresses Economic Strength," *New York Times,* 11 November 1987, 13). A March 1988 poll showed that Americans now perceive Japan, because of its economic power, to be a greater threat to U.S. security than is the Soviet Union. In this same survey, Americans also favored reducing American commitments abroad (Richard Moran, "Maybe We're Chasing After the Wrong 'Evil Empire,' " *Washington Post,* 16–22 May 1988, National Weekly Edition, 34).

22. See Christopher Layne, "Continental Divide—Time to Disengage in Europe," *National Interest,* Fall 1988, 13.

23. For an interesting discussion of the emerging multipolar system see Kennedy, *Rise and Fall of the Great Powers,* chap. 8.

24. For an analysis of these trends and their impact on U.S. Third World policy, see Ted Galen Carpenter, "Benign Realism: A New U.S. Security Policy in the Third World," and Terry L. Deibel, "Neither With Us nor Against Us—Revisiting an 'Immoral and Shortsighted Conception,' " (Papers presented at the Cato Institute conference "Collective Security or Strategic Independence? Alternative Strategies for the Future," Washington, D.C., 2–3 December 1987). Both Carpenter and Deibel argue that the United States should cease viewing Third World countries as mere pawns in the superpower struggle. The United States need not be obsessed with Third World countries' internal political systems, only with their external policies

insofar as they threaten American strategic interests. Accordingly, the wisest course American foreign policy could take in the Third World is to capitalize on pluralist trends and encourage Third World states to be truly nonaligned in the superpower competition.

25. Arnold Wolfers, "The Pole of Power and the Pole of Indifference," in *Discord and Collaboration* (Baltimore: Johns Hopkins Press, 1962), 91.

26. E. H. Carr, *The Twenty Years' Crisis, 1919–1939* (New York: Harper & Row, 1951), 117.

27. Pat Choate and Juyne Linger, "Tailored Trade: Dealing with the World As It Is," *Harvard Business Review* 88, no. 1 (1988): 89.

28. Ibid., 86.

29. See Martin Tolchin and Susan Tolchin, *Buying Into America* (New York: Times Books, 1988).

30. Clyde Prestowitz, *Trading Places* (New York: Basic Books, 1988), 13.

31. Stephen S. Cohen and John Zysman, *Manufacturing Matters: The Myth of the Post-Industrial Economy* (New York: Basic Books, 1987).

32. Daniel Burstein, *Yen!* (New York: Simon & Schuster, 1988), 259.

33. Robert Gilpin, *The Political Economy of International Relations* (Princeton: Princeton University Press, 1987), 209–15; Cohen and Zysman, *Manufacturing Matters,* 221–32.

34. Corelli Barnett, *The Pride and the Fall: The Dream and Illusion of Britain as a Great Nation* (New York: Free Press, 1987), 205.

35. Gilpin, *Political Economy of International Relations,* 337.

36. In the fall of 1987 a *Los Angeles Times* poll found that 64 percent of the American people oppose a tax increase for the purpose of reducing the deficit (George Skelton, "64% Oppose Raising Taxes to Cut Deficit," *Los Angeles Times,* 5 November 1987, 1).

37. See Leonard Sullivan, "A New Approach to Burden Sharing," *Foreign Policy,* no. 60, Fall 1985, 91; Richard Halloran, "Two Studies Say Defense of Western Europe Is Biggest Military Cost," *New York Times,* 20 July 1984; Earl Ravenal, *NATO: The Tides of Discontent* (Berkeley: Institute of International Studies, 1987).

38. Fred Hiatt and Rick Atkinson, "The Hidden Costs of the Defense Buildup," *Washington Post,* 16 December 1985, National Weekly Edition, 10.

39. George F. Kennan, "Resume of World Situation," in *Containment: Documents on American Policy and Strategy, 1945–1950,* edited by Thomas H. Etzold and John L. Gaddis (New York: Columbia University Press, 1978), 91.

40. George F. Kennan, quoted in John L. Gaddis, *The Long Peace* (New York: Oxford University Press, 1987), 57–58.

41. See Christopher Layne, "Atlanticism without NATO," *Foreign Policy,* no. 67, Summer 1987, 22–45.

42. For an extended discussion of the risks of extended deterrence see Layne, "Continental Divide"; and idem, "Atlanticism without NATO."

43. For a fuller discussion see Layne, "Atlanticism without NATO."

44. "X" [George F. Kennan], "The Sources of Soviet Conduct," *Foreign Affairs* 25, no. 4 (1947): 566–82.

45. See, e.g., Andrey V. Kozyrev, "Why Soviet Foreign Policy Went Sour," *New York Times,* 7 January 1989, 17.

46. Kenneth N. Waltz, *Theory of International Politics* (Reading, Mass.: Addison-Wesley, 1979), 209.

47. Graham Fuller, quoted in David Ignatius and Michael Getler, "The Great Non-Debate in American Foreign Policy," *Washington Post,* 23 October 1988, Cl.

48. Karl Deutsch and J. David Singer, "Multipolar Power Systems and International Stability," in *International Politics and Foreign Policy,* edited by James N. Rosenau (New York: Free Press, 1969), 318.

49. Walter Lippmann, quoted in Simon Serfaty, *American Foreign Policy in a Hostile World* (New York: Praeger, 1985), 55.

50. Ibid.

51. See William G. Hyland, *Mortal Rivals: Superpower Relations from Nixon to Reagan* (New York: Random House, 1987), 25–27; and Kissinger, *White House Years,* 183–86.

52. See Christopher Layne, "Bush Can Turn The Tables on Gorbachev," *Wall Street Journal,* 9 December 1988; and idem, "Europe between the Superpowers: New Trends in East-West Relations," in *Collective Defense or Strategic Independence?* edited by Ted Galen Carpenter (New York: Lexington, 1989), 49–68.

53. Michael Hunt, *Ideology and American Foreign Policy* (New Haven: Yale University Press, 1987), chap. 2.

54. James R. Schlesinger, "Excerpts from Schlesinger's Senate Testimony," *New York Times,* 7 February 1985.

55. See Christopher Layne, "Requiem for the Reagan Doctrine," *SAIS Review* 8, no. 1 (1987/88): 1–17; and idem, "The Overreaching Reagan Doctrine," *Wall Street Journal,* 15 April 1987.

56. Huntington, "The U.S.—Decline or Renewal?" 87–88.

57. Quoted in John L. Gaddis, *Strategies of Containment* (New York: Oxford University Press, 1982), 134–36.

Chapter 9. Liberalism and the Formulation of U.S. Strategy

1. The sources of classic, laissez-faire liberalism can be found in Locke, Kant, and today in Robert Nozick, *Anarchy, State and Utopia* (New York: Basic Books, 1974). Expositions of welfare liberalism are in the work of the Fabians and John Rawls, *A Theory of Justice* (Cambridge: Harvard University Press, 1971). Amy Gutmann, *Liberal Equality* (New York: Cambridge University Press, 1980), discusses variants of liberal thought. Uncomfortably paralleling each of the high roads are "low roads" that, while achieving certain liberal values, fail to reconcile freedom and order. An overwhelming terror of anarchy and a speculation on preserving property can drive laissez-faire liberals to support a law-and-order authoritarian rule that sacrifices democracy. This shapes the argument of right-wing liberals who seek to draw a distinction between "authoritarian" and "totalitarian" dictatorships. The justification sometimes advanced by liberals for the former is that they can be temporary and educate the population into an acceptance of property, individual rights, and, eventually, representative government (see Jeanne J. Kirkpatrick, "Dictatorships and Double Standards," *Commentary* 68, no. 5 [1979]: 34–45). Complementarily, when social inequalities are judged to be extreme, the welfare liberal can argue that establishing (or reestablishing) the foundations of liberal society requires a nonliberal method of reform, a second low road of redistributing authoritarianism. Aristide Zolberg reports a "liberal left" sensibility among U.S. scholars of African politics that was sympathetic to progressive autocracies (*One Party Government in the Ivory Coast* [Princeton: Princeton University Press, 1969], vii).

2. Clarence Streit seems to have been the first to point out (in contemporary

foreign relations) the empirical tendency of democracies to maintain peace among themselves, and he made this the foundation of his proposal for a (non-Kantian) federal union of the fifteen leading democracies of the 1930s (see *Union Now: A Proposal for a Federal Union of the Leading Democracies* [New York: Harper's, 1938], 88, 90–92). D. V. Babst performed a quantitative study of this phenomenon of "democratic peace" (see "A Force for Peace," *Industrial Research,* April 1972, 55–58). And R. J. Rummel did a similar study of "libertarianism" (in the sense of laissez faire) focusing on the postwar period ("Libertarianism and International Violence," *Journal of Conflict Resolution* 27, no. 1 [1983]: 27–71). I use the term *liberal* in a wider (Kantian) sense in my discussion of this issue in "Kant, Liberal Legacies, and Foreign Affairs, Part 1," *Philosophy and Public Affairs* 12 (1983): 205–35. In that essay, I survey the period from 1790 to the present and find no war among liberal states.

3. Kant argued that perpetual peace will be guaranteed by the widening acceptance of "three definitive articles" of peace. The First Definitive Article requires that the civil constitution of the state be republican. These liberal republics will progressively establish peace among themselves by means of the *foedus pacificum* (a treaty or union) described in his Second Definitive Article. The pacific union establishes peace among free states and securely maintains the rights of each state. The world will not have achieved the "perpetual peace" that provides the ultimate guarantor of republican freedom until "a late stage and after many unsuccessful attempts" (noted in "The Idea for a Universal History with a Cosmopolitan Purpose," in *Kant's Political Writings,* edited by Hans Reiss, translated by H. B. Nisbet [New York: Cambridge University Press, 1970], 47). Not until then will individuals enjoy perfect republican rights or the full guarantee of a global and just peace. But in the meantime, the "pacific federation" of liberal republics — "an enduring and gradually expanding federation likely to prevent war" — brings within it more and more republics, creating an expanding separate peace. See "Perpetual Peace," in ibid., 105. The pacific union is neither a single peace treaty ending one war nor a world state or state of nations. Kant appears to have had in mind a mutual nonaggression pact, perhaps a collective security agreement, and the cosmopolitan law of unfettered exchange described in the Third Definitive Article.

4. Woodrow Wilson, *The Messages and Papers of Woodrow Wilson,* edited by Albert Shaw (New York: Review of Reviews, 1924), 378.

5. Babst did make a preliminary test of the significance of the distribution of alliance partners in World War I. He found that the possibility that the actual distribution of alliance partners could have occurred by chance was less than 1 percent ("A Force for Peace," 56). But this possibility assumes an equal possibility that any two nations could have gone to war with each other, and this is a strong assumption. Rummel, "Libertarianism and International Violence," contains a further discussion of significance as it applies to his libertarian thesis.

6. There is a rich contemporary literature devoted to explaining international cooperation and integration. Karl Deutsch's *Political Community and the North Atlantic Area* (Princeton: Princeton University Press, 1957) develops the idea of a "pluralistic security community" that bears a resemblance to the "pacific union," but Deutsch limits it geographically and finds compatibility of values, mutual responsiveness, and predictability of behavior among decisionmakers to be its essential foundations. These are important, but their particular content, liberalism, appears to be more telling. Joseph S. Nye, Jr., in *Peace in Parts* (Boston: Little, Brown, 1971)

steps away from the geographic limits Deutsch sets and focuses on levels of development, but his analysis is directed toward explaining integration, a more intensive form of cooperation than the pacific union.

7. The new historical classic making these arguments is Paul Kennedy's *Rise and Fall of the Great Powers* (New York: Random House, 1987). Robert Gilpin in *War and Change in World Politics* (New York: Cambridge University Press, 1981) developed a model of hegemonic transitions.

8. David Hume, "Of the Balance of Power," in *Essays: Moral, Political, and Literary (1741–1742)* (New York: Oxford University Press, 1963), 346–47. With "imprudent vehemence," Hume referred to the English reluctance to negotiate an early peace with France and the total scale of the effort devoted to prosecuting war, which together were responsible for over half the length of the fighting and an enormous war debt. Hume, of course, was not describing fully liberal republics as defined here; but the characteristics he describes do seem to reflect some of the liberal republican features of the English eighteenth-century constitution (i.e., the influence of both popular opinion and a representative, if severely limited, legislature). He contrasts these effects with the "prudent politics" that should govern the balance of power and to the special but different failings characteristic of "enormous monarchies," which are prone to strategic overextension, bureaucratic, and ministerial decay in court intrigue, praetorian rebellion (347–48).

9. There are, however, serious studies showing that Marxist regimes have higher military spending per capita than do non-Marxist regimes (James Payne, "Marxism and Militarism," *Polity* 19, no. 2 [1986]: 270–89). But this should not be interpreted as a sign of the inherent aggressiveness of authoritarian or totalitarian governments or—with even greater enthusiasm—of the inherent and global peacefulness of liberal regimes. Marxist regimes in particular represent a minority in the current international system; they are strategically encircled, and due to their lack of domestic legitimacy, they might be said to "suffer" the dual burden of needing defenses against both external and internal enemies. Stanislav Andreski, moreover, argues in "On the Peaceful Disposition of Military Dictatorships," *Journal of Strategic Studies* 3 (1980): 3–10, that (purely) military dictatorships, due to their domestic fragility, have little incentive to engage in foreign military adventures.

10. The following paragraphs build on arguments I presented in "Kant, Liberal Legacies, and Foreign Affairs: Part 2," *Philosophy and Public Affairs* 12 (1983): 323–53.

11. U.S. Congress, Senate, Committee on Foreign Relations, *Hearings before the Committee on Foreign Relations on the Nomination of John Foster Dulles, Secretary of State Designate, 15 January 1953*, 83d Cong., 1st sess. (Washington D.C.: USGPO, 1953), 5–6. John L. Gaddis noted logistical differences between laissez-faire and social-welfare liberals in policy toward the Soviet Union. In U.S. policy, until the advent of the Reagan administration the fiscal conservatism of Republicans led them to favor a narrow strategy; the fiscal liberality of Democrats led to a broader strategy (*Strategies of Containment* [New York: Oxford University Press, 1982]).

12. Thirty-three divisions, the withdrawal of the Soviet bloc from the Mediterranean, political disarray in the Communist movement—these advantages called out for a quick and friendly response. An effective U.S. ambassador in place to present Tito's position to Washington, the public character of the expulsion from the Cominform (June 1948), and a presidential administration in the full flush of creative statesmanship (and an electoral victory) also contributed to Truman's decision to

rescue Yugoslavia from the Soviet embargo by providing trade and loans (1949). Nonetheless (according to Yugoslav sources), this crisis was also judged to be an appropriate moment to put pressure on Yugoslavia to resolve the questions of Trieste and Carinthia, to cut its support for the guerrillas in Greece, and to repay prewar (prerevolutionary) debts compensating the property owners of nationalized land and mines. Nor did Yugoslavia's strategic significance exempt it from inclusion among the countries condemned as "captive nations" (1959) or secure most-favored-nation trade status in the 1962 Trade Expansion Act. Ideological anticommunism and the porousness of the American political system to lobbies combined (according to Kennan, ambassador to Yugoslavia at that time) to add these inconvenient burdens to a crucial strategic relationship (John C. Campbell, *Tito's Separate Road* [New York: Council on Foreign Relations/Harper & Row, 1967], 18–27; Suctozar Vukmanovic- Tempo, in Vladimir Dedijer, *The Battle Stalin Lost* [New York: Viking, 1970], 268; George F. Kennan, *Memoirs, 1950–1963* [Boston: Little, Brown, 1972], chap. 12).

13. Kirkpatrick, "Dictatorships and Double Standards." In 1851 the liberal French historian Guizot made a similar argument in a letter to Gladstone urging that Gladstone appreciate that the despotic government of Naples was the best guarantor of liberal law and order then available. Reform, in Guizot's view, meant the unleashing of revolutionary violence (Philip Magnus, *Gladstone* [New York: Dutton, 1964], 100.)

14. Richard J. Barnet, *Intervention and Revolution: The United States in the Third World* (New York: New American Library, 1968), chap. 10; and on Nicaragua, see *New York Times,* 11 March 1982, for a description of the training direction and funding ($20 million) of anti-Sandinista guerrillas by the United States.

15. Arthur Schlesinger, *A Thousand Days* (Boston: Houghton Mifflin, 1965), 769; and quoted in Barnet, *Intervention and Revolution,* 158.

16. During the Alliance for Progress era in Latin America, the Kennedy administration supported Juan Bosch in the Dominican Republic in 1962. See also William P. Bundy, "Dictatorships and American Foreign Policy," *Foreign Affairs* 54, no. 1 (1975): 51–60.

17. For examples of the successful export of liberal institutions in the postwar period see Samuel P. Huntington, "Human Rights and American Power," *Commentary* 72, no. 3 (1981): 37–43; and George Quester, "Consensus Lost," *Foreign Policy,* no. 40, Fall 1980, 18–32.

18. Charles Kindleberger, *The World in Depression* (Berkeley: University of California Press, 1973); Robert Gilpin, *U.S. Power and the Multinational Corporation* (New York: Basic Books, 1975); Fred Hirsch and Michael Doyle, "Politicization in the World Economy," in *Alternatives to Monetary Disorder,* by Fred Hirsch, Michael Doyle, and Edward Morse (New York: Council on Foreign Relations/McGraw Hill, 1977).

19. Kirkpatrick points out U.S. neglect of the needs of the authoritarians (see Kirkpatrick, "Dictatorships and Double Standards"). Theodore Lowi argues that Democratic and Republican policies toward the acquisition of bases in Spain reflected this dichotomy ("Bases in Spain," in *American Civil-Military Decisions,* edited by Harold Stein [University: University of Alabama Press, 1963], 699). In other cases where both the geopolitical and the domestic orientation of a potential neutral might be influenced by U.S. aid, liberal institutions (representative legislatures) impose delay or public constraints and conditions on diplomacy that allow the Soviet Union

to steal a march. Warren Christopher has suggested that this occurred in U.S. relations with Nicaragua in 1979 ("Ceasefire between the Branches," *Foreign Affairs* 60, no. 5 [1982]: 998).

20. Ideological formulations often accompany these policies. Fear of bolshevism was used to excuse not forming an alliance with the Soviet Union in 1938 against Nazi imperialism. And Nazi and fascist regimes were portrayed as defenders of private property and social order. But the connection liberals draw between domestic tyranny and foreign aggression may also operate in reverse. When the Nazi threat to the survival of liberal states did require a liberal alliance with the Soviet Union, Stalin became for a short period the liberal press's "Uncle Joe."

21. See, e.g., Graham Allison, "Testing Gorbachev," *Foreign Affairs* 67, no. 1 (1988): 18–32.

22. These and similar policies are developed by C. Fred Bergsten et al., "The Reform of International Institutions," and Richard N. Cooper et al., "Towards a Renovated International System," both in *Trilateral Commission Task Force Reports: 9–14* (New York: New York University Press, 1978).

23. Louis Hartz, *The Liberal Tradition in America* (New York: Harcourt, Brace, & World, 1953). The United States is one of the few liberal nations both of whose leading political parties are liberal. Others have shared or competitive parties or factions: aristocratic or statist-bureaucratic or communist factions contesting more centrally liberal factions.

Contributors

David S. Clark, Major, U.S. Army, is currently serving with the 4th Infantry Division (Mechanized), at Fort Carson, Colorado. Formerly assistant professor of international relations and national security studies at the U.S. Military Academy, his military service includes tours with armored cavalry units in Germany and the United States.

Michael W. Doyle is associate professor of politics and international affairs at Princeton University. The recipient of a MacArthur Fellowship, his books include *Empires* and *Escalation and Intervention*. His articles on international politics, political economy, and political philosophy have appeared in numerous journals, including the *American Political Science Review, Philosophy and Public Affairs,* and *World Politics.*

George C. Edwards III is professor of political science at Texas A&M University. He is the author or editor of a dozen books and numerous articles on the presidency and the public policy–making process, including *At the Margins, The Public Presidency, Implementing Public Policy, Presidential Leadership, Presidential Influence in Congress,* and *The Policy Predicament.* He also has served as president of the presidency research section of the American Political Science Association.

Aaron L. Friedberg is assistant professor of politics and international affairs at Princeton University, where he holds a joint appointment in the Department of Politics and the Woodrow Wilson School. He has served as a consultant for the National Security Council and the Office of Net Assessment in the Office of the Secretary of Defense. He also served as a member of the Presidential Commission on Integrated Long-Term Strategy. His articles have appeared in a number of journals, including *Foreign Policy, International Security,* the *Journal of Strategic*

Studies, and *The National Interest.* He is the author of *The Weary Titan: Britain and the Experience of Relative Decline, 1895–1905.*

Samuel P. Huntington is Eaton Professor of the Science of Government and Director of the Olin Institute for Strategic Studies at Harvard University. He has served as associate director of the Institute of War and Peace Studies at Columbia University and chairman of the Department of Government and director of the Center for International Studies at Harvard. He also served as coordinator of security planning on the National Security Council staff in 1977–78 and as a member of the Presidential Commission on Integrated Long-Term Strategy. A past president of the American Political Science Association, he is the author of over a dozen books and seventy scholarly articles. His most recent books include *The Strategic Imperative* and *American Politics: The Promise of Disharmony.*

Daniel J. Kaufman, Colonel, U.S. Army, is professor of international relations and deputy head of the Department of Social Sciences at the U.S. Military Academy at West Point. His military service includes tours with armor and cavalry units in Vietnam and the United States. He has also served as a member of the National Security Council staff and in the Office of the Secretary of Defense. His books include *U.S. National Security: A Framework for Analysis* (with Jeffrey S. McKitrick and Thomas J. Leney); *Democracy, Strategy, and Vietnam* (with George K. Osborn, Asa A. Clark, and Douglas E. Lute); and *NATO at Forty* (with James R. Golden, Asa A. Clark, and David H. Petraeus).

Christopher Layne is an attorney in Los Angeles and an adjunct scholar at the Cato Institute, in Washington, D.C. He has also served as an analyst of NATO and Western European affairs at the U.S. Army's Arroyo Center. His articles on foreign policy and strategy have appeared in a number of journals, including *Foreign Policy, Orbis, SAIS Review,* and the *Journal of Contemporary Studies.* He also contributes frequently to the *Los Angeles Times, New Republic,* and the *Chicago Tribune.*

Augustus Richard Norton, Colonel, U.S. Army, is professor of comparative politics in the Department of Social Sciences at the U.S. Military Academy at West Point. His military service includes tours with infantry units in the United States, Vietnam, and Germany. He also has served as a member of the United Nations Peacekeeping Force in the Middle East. He has published widely on Middle Eastern affairs and peacekeeping operations. His books include *Amal and the Shi'a, The International Relations of the PLO,* and *Studies in Nuclear Terrorism.*

Kevin P. Sheehan, Major, U.S. Army, is currently serving as a special assistant to the Under Secretary of State for Security Assistance. Formerly an assistant professor of political science in the Department of Social Sciences at the U.S. Military Academy at West Point, his military service includes tours with infantry units in the United States and Germany. He is the author of *The Limits to Intervention: U.S. Army Doctrinal Change, 1951–1986.*

Notra Trulock III is a strategic planner at the National Defense University. He is a former director of Soviet military studies at the Pacific-Sierra Research Corporation. He has served as a consultant to the Under Secretary of Defense for Policy and as a member of the Presidential Commission on Integrated Long-Term Strategy. He has authored several studies on the potential impact of new technologies on future warfare and on Soviet strategic military planning.

Stansfield Turner was selected as the first John M. Olin Distinguished Professor of National Security Studies at the United States Military Academy at West Point. During his naval career he attained the rank of admiral and served as commander of the U.S. Second Fleet and as commander in chief of NATO's Southern Flank. In 1977 he was named director of Central Intelligence, a position he held throughout the Carter administration. He is the author of *Secrecy and Democracy.*

Stephen M. Walt is associate professor of politics and international affairs at the University of Chicago. He has served as a staff member at the Center for Naval Analyses, in Washington, D.C., and has been a resident associate at the Carnegie Endowment for International Peace and a research fellow at the Center for Science and International Affairs at Harvard University. He is the author of *The Origins of Alliances* and of a number of articles on international politics and national security policy.

Index

U.S. National Security Strategy for the 1990s

Designed by Ann Walston

Composed by Capitol Communication Systems, Inc.
in Sabon with Sabon Bold display

Printed by R. R. Donnelly & Sons Company
on 50-lb. S.D. Warren's Cream White Sebago